THE WORLD'S GREATEST HUNTING STORIES

The World's Greatest Hunting Stories

Edited by Lamar Underwood

Essex, Connecticut

An imprint of The Globe Pequot Publishing Group, Inc.
64 South Main Street
Essex, CT 06426
www.globepequot.com

Distributed by NATIONAL BOOK NETWORK

British Library Cataloguing in Publication Information available

Library of Congress Cataloging-in-Publication Data
Names: Underwood, Lamar, editor.
Title: The world's greatest hunting stories / edited by Lamar Underwood.
Description: Essex, Connecticut : Lyons Press, [2024] | Includes bibliographical references.
Identifiers: LCCN 2024012754 (print) | LCCN 2024012755 (ebook) | ISBN 9781493085224 (trade paperback) | ISBN 9781493085231 (epub)
Subjects: LCSH: Hunting stories.
Classification: LCC SK35 .W8927 2024 (print) | LCC SK35 (ebook) | DDC 799.2–dc23/eng/20240708
LC record available at https://lccn.loc.gov/2024012754
LC ebook record available at https://lccn.loc.gov/2024012755

Contents

Introduction

by the editor, Lamar Underwood

After years of editing that have included *Sports Afield* and *Outdoor Life* magazines and many books, I can honestly say the stories about the great outdoors I remember most are about the simple pleasures of camps and gatherings—the comradeship of kindred spirits, the pre-hunt hours when time seems to stand still and success in the field seems assured, the preparation comings and goings that evoke visions of exciting days to come.

Sometimes, just as in real life, the hunts on the printed pages go wrong, are doomed to failure, or result in life-threatening events. Those tales make such good reading that they are heavily promoted in cover blurbs that shout out to the reader: "Danger Ahead!"

In this story collection my intention has been to present both kinds of hunting stories—the fireside, whiskey-time tales that stir your deep love of hunting or fishing, and the sometimes-desperate accounts of moments when both luck and time seem to have run out.

There are many writers whose experiences in the field have been exhilarating, but whose prose skills make their stories read like "Dick and Jane ran up the hill."

That's not good enough. The job of the writer is to create prose that has "a felt life," as novelist E. M. Forster describes it. Achieving this "felt life" goal makes the writer's job a lot more difficult than putting commas in the right places. The storyteller's role from caveman time to today has been to create mental pictures of moments afield, made interesting by the drama of locations, weather, and the strange habits of the wild creatures we seek.

When this exalted state of storytelling is reached, the tale becomes a permanent fixture in the memory of the audience, or even saved on bookshelves to be enjoyed repeatedly.

Allow me to show you what I've been talking about.

Onward now!

CHAPTER I

The Heart of the Hunter

by Theodore Roosevelt

THE STRENUOUS OUTDOOR LIFE . . . THE INQUIRING MIND OF A scholar. Mix these with potent measures of creativity and talent, and in Theodore Roosevelt you have a writer whose books about his experiences form a true literary treasure from which we all may "profit," as he used the word. And if you are a hunter, passionately committed to the spirit of the chase as TR himself, then Roosevelt's books can represent a true mother lode of reading pleasure. Never mind the stereotyped images (we've all seem them) of TR that come to mind: the flashing teeth, the political bully pulpit, the big stick, the wire-rimmed glasses, the Rough Riders, and San Juan Hill. All these are but temporary masks for Theodore Roosevelt, the dedicated outdoorsman, the man who savored every moment afield and then wrote about them in some of the most engaging prose ever put onto paper. Roosevelt's overall literary output was prodigious, a staggering forty-two volumes plus countless articles. His chosen subjects ranged from such expected areas as politics to history, biography, philosophy, and what clearly was his favorite—the outdoors and hunting.

* * *

The man should have youth and strength who seeks adventure in the wide, waste spaces of the earth, in the marshes, and among the vast mountain masses, in the northern forests, amid the steaming jungles of the tropics, or on the deserts of sand or of snow. He must long greatly for the lonely winds that blow across the wilderness, and for sunrise and sunset over the rim of the empty world. His heart must thrill for the saddle and not for the hearthstone. He must be helmsman and chief, the cragsman, the rifleman, the boat steerer. He must be the wielder of axe and of paddle, the rider of fiery horses, the master of the craft that leaps through white water. His eye must be true and quick, his hand steady and strong. His heart must never fail nor his head grow bewildered, whether he face brute and human foes, or the frowning strength of hostile nature, or the awful fear that grips those who are lost in trackless lands. Wearing toil and hardship shall be his; thirst and famine he shall face, and burning fever. Death shall come to greet him with poison-fang or poison-arrow, in shape of charging beast or of scaly things that lurk in lake and river; it shall lie in wait for him among untrodden forests, in the swirl of wild waters, and in the blast of snow blizzard or thunder-shattered hurricane. Not many men can with wisdom make such a life their permanent and serious occupation. Those whose tasks lie along other lines can lead it for but a few years. For them it must normally come in the hardy vigor of their youth, before the beat of the blood has grown sluggish in their veins.

Nevertheless, older men also can find joy in such a life, although in their case it must be led only on the outskirts of adventure, and although the part they play therein must be that of the onlooker rather than that of the doer. The feats of prowess are for others. It is for other men to face the peril of unknown lands, to master unbroken horses, and to hold their own among their fellows with bodies of supple strength. But much, very much, remains for the man who has "warmed both hands before the fire of life," and who, although he loves the great cities, loves even more the fenceless grass-land, and the forest-clad hills.

The grandest scenery of the world is his to look at if he chooses; and he can witness the strange ways of tribes who have survived into an alien age from an immemorial past, tribes whose priests dance in honor of the serpent and worship the spirits of the wolf and the bear. Far and wide, all the continents are open to him as they never were to any of his forefathers; the Nile and the Paraguay are easy of access, and the borderland between savagery and civilization; and the veil of the past has been lifted so that he can dimly see how, in time immeasurably remote, his ancestors—no less remote—led furtive lives among uncouth and terrible beasts, whose kind has perished utterly from the face of the earth. He will take books with him as he journeys; for the keenest enjoyment of the wilderness is reserved for him who enjoys also the garnered wisdom of the present and the past. He will take pleasure in the companionship of the men of the open; in South America, the daring and reckless horsemen who guard the herds of the grazing country, and the paddlers who guide their clumsy dugouts down the dangerous equatorial rivers; the hunters of the Rockies, and of the Canadian woodland; and in Africa the faithful gun-bearers who have stood steadily at his elbow when the lion came on with coughing grunts, or when the huge mass of the charging elephant burst asunder the vine-tangled branches.

The beauty and charm of the wilderness are his for the asking, for the edges of the wilderness lie close beside the beaten roads of present travel. He can see the red splendor of desert sunsets, and the unearthly glory of the afterglow on the battlements of desolate mountains. In sapphire gulfs of ocean he can visit islets, above which the wings of myriads of sea-fowl make a kind of shifting cuneiform script in the air. He can ride along the brink of the stupendous cliff-walled canyon, where eagles soar below him, and cougars make their lairs on the ledges and harry the big-horned sheep. He can journey through the northern forests, the home of the giant moose, the forests of fragrant and murmuring life in summer, the iron-bound and melancholy forests of winter.

The joy of living is his who has the heart to demand it.

THEODORE ROOSEVELT.
SAGAMORE HILL, January 1, 1916.

CHAPTER 2

Hunting in "Brightest Africa"

by Carl Akeley

WHEN CARL AKELEY WROTE HIS MEMORIES OF HIS PIONEERING years of African hunting, he chose the title "In Brightest Africa." The common expression of his time (1864–1926) was "Darkest Africa." For Akeley, the "Darkest Africa" fears of hunting unexplored lands ruled by wild beasts and native tribes never materialized. Instead, he found hunting adventures bristling with dangers and narrow escapes. He wrote of these in *In Brightest Africa*, his stirring book, first published in 1920. In this excerpted chapter he reveals his fascination with the biggest and most dangerous big game of all—the African elephant.

* * *

I have sat in the top of a tree in the middle of a herd a quarter of a mile from a native village in Uganda in a last desperate effort to inspect the two hundred and fifty elephants which had been chevying me about so fast that I had not had a chance to see whether there were any desirable specimens among them or not. I have spent a day and a night in the Budongo Forest in the middle of a herd of seven hundred elephants. I have stood on an ant-hill awaiting the rush of eleven elephants which had got my wind and were determined to get me. I have spent a day following and fighting an old bull which took twenty-five shots of our elephant rifles before he succumbed. And once also I had such close contact with an old bull up on the slopes of Mt. Kenia that I had to save myself from being gored by grabbing his tusks with my hands and swinging in between them.

I have spent many months studying elephants in Africa—on the plains, in the forests, in the bamboo, up on the mountains. I have watched them in herds and singly, studied their paths, their feeding grounds, everything about them I could, and I have come to the conclusion that of all the wild animals on this earth now, the African elephant is the most fascinating, and that man, for all the thousands of years he has known of elephants, knows mighty little about him. I am speaking only of the African elephant. He has not been domesticated as his Indian cousin has. The two are different in size and different in shape and different in habits. The low point of an African elephant's back line is the highest point of that of the Indian elephant. The African elephant's ears and tusks are larger, and his tusks usually spread wider at the points instead of coming together. Unless one studies him in his native haunts, one cannot get to know him. His disposition is held to be wilder than that of the Indian elephant, but the infrequency of his appearance in circuses and in zoölogical parks may be attributed to the ease with which tamed elephants may be obtained from India rather than to a difference of temper in the two beasts. An African elephant at Washington and one in the Bronx zoölogical park are the only ones I know of in this country, and no animal in captivity can give one more than a slight idea of his natural habits in his jungle home.

Very few people have studied African elephants in the field. Ninety-five percent of those who have followed them have been purely hunters and their desire has been, not to study, but to shoot—to see the elephant in the shortest possible time. Time to judge the ivories and get a bead on the brain was all that they wanted. Of other elephant knowledge all that they needed was the simple facts of how to follow and find them. The comparatively few men who have tried to study the elephant have not gained as much knowledge as one would imagine, because without trying it one cannot realize how extremely difficult it is to study the live African elephant.

For example, as I said before, I spent a day with seven hundred elephants in the Budongo Forest, but although I heard them all the time and was very acutely conscious that they were near me, I do not believe that I actually had my eyes on an elephant more than half an hour, all told, during the day. It happened this way.

One night about dark, after a week or two of hunting, we heard the squeal of an elephant while we were sitting at dinner. A little later there were more squeals and occasional trumpeting—more and more, clearer and clearer—and by the time we had finished dinner the noise was only a mile or so away. It was a continuous row which suggested a tremendous herd. We went to bed early with elephants getting closer to camp all of the time. There is little danger of elephants attacking a camp, and, as there is no way to study them at night, about the only thing left to do was to go to bed and get in good shape for the next day. Along about midnight Mrs. Akeley came over to my tent and said that she had loaded my guns and that they were all ready. She could not sleep; so she went out to sit by the fire. The elephants were then within a hundred yards of our tents and there was a continuous roar made up of trumpetings, squealing, and the crashing of bushes and trees.

I got up in the morning and had breakfast before daybreak. The elephants had moved on down the edge of the forest. What had been a jungle of high grass and bush the day before was trampled flat. There were at least seven hundred elephants in the herd—government officials had counted them on the previous day as they came down. I followed the trails to the edge of the forest but saw none. I started back to cross a little *nullah* (a dry water course), but felt suspicious and decided to look the situation over a little more closely. I ran up on a sloping rock and, almost under me on the other side, I saw the back of a large elephant. Over to one side there was another one, beyond that another, and then I realized that the little *nullah* through which I had planned to pass was very well sprinkled with them. I backed off and went up to a higher rock to one side. Elephants were drifting into the forest from all directions. The sun was just coming up over the hills and was shining upon the forest, which sparkled in the sunlight—morning greetings to the forest people. The monkeys greeted one another with barks and coughs. Everything was waking up—it was a busy day. There was not a breath of air. I had gone back a million years; the birds were calling back and forth, the monkeys were calling to one another, a troop of chimpanzees in the open screamed, and their shouts were answered from another group inside the forest. All the forest life was awake and moving about as that huge herd of elephants, singly and in groups, flowed into the forest from the plain. There was one continuous roar of noise, all the wildlife joining, but above it all were the crashing of trees and the squealing of the elephants as they moved into the forest on a front at least a mile wide. It was the biggest show I ever saw in Africa.

Then an old cow just at the edge of the forest suddenly got my wind, and wheeling about, she let out a scream. Instantly every sound ceased, everything was quiet. The monkeys, the birds—all the wildlife—stopped their racket; the elephants stood still, listening and waiting. For a moment I was dazed. The thought came through my mind—"What does it all mean? Have I been dreaming?" But soon I heard the rustling of the trees as though a great storm were coming. There was no movement of the air, but there was the sound of a windstorm going through a forest. It gradually died away, and I realized that the elephants had made it as they moved off. It was the rustling of the dry leaves on the ground under their feet and the rubbing of their bodies through the dried foliage of the forest. I never heard a noise like that made by elephants—before or since. The conditions were unique, for everything was thoroughly parched, and there had not even been a dew. Ordinarily, if there is any moisture, elephants when warned can travel through a forest without the slightest noise. In spite of their great bulk they are as silent and sometimes as hard to see in their country as a jack rabbit is in his. I remember on one occasion being so close to an old cow in the jungle that I could hear the rumbling of her stomach, and yet when she realized my presence the rumbling ceased, as it always does when they are suspicious, and she left the clump of growth she was in without my hearing a sound.

But going back to the big herd. From the time I had seen the first elephant until the last of them disappeared in the forest it had been perhaps fifteen minutes—fifteen minutes in which to see the sight of a lifetime, a thing to go to Africa a dozen times to get one glimpse of. But what did I learn about the habits of the elephant in that fifteen minutes? A little perhaps but not much. It takes a long time and much patience to get at all intimate with old Tembo, as the Swahilis call him, on his native soil.

After the herd disappeared in the forest I watched for ten or fifteen minutes and heard the squeal of the elephants and the noise of the monkeys again. Their suspicions were over. I followed into the forest where the trails showed me that they had broken up into small bands. I followed along on the trail of one of these bands until I got a glimpse of an elephant about fifty yards ahead of me in the trail. You don't see a whole elephant in the forest. What you do see is just a glimpse of hide or tusk or trunk through the trees. And if you want to get this glimpse without disturbing him you must do your glimpsing from down the wind.

There was a little open space ahead of the group I was following. I worked around until I got to a place where I could see them as they passed through this open space. They were moving along slowly, feeding. Two or three came out into the opening, then they became suspicious and wheeled into the forest again. I followed cautiously. I had gone only a short distance when I saw a very young calf about twenty yards ahead of me. As I halted, the mother came trotting back down the trail looking for the baby. I froze to the side of a tree with my gun ready. She came to the baby and turning, boosted it along with her trunk after the rest of the herd. I followed along after them into an opening where I found them rounded up in a patch of burned-over ground. They were milling around in a rather compact mass seemingly preparing for defence. I could not see very plainly, for a cloud of dust rose from the burned ground as they shuffled about. I stood watching them a little time and suddenly caught sight of a fine tusk—an old bull and just what I wanted for the group I was working on for the Museum of Natural History. I ran up behind a bush at the edge of the clearing and peeked through it. There, not more than twenty yards from me, was my bull, partially exposed and partially covered by the other animals. I could not get a shot at his brain as he was standing, but the foreleg on my side was forward exposing his side so that I had a good shot at his heart—a shot I had never made before. The heart is eighteen or twenty inches long and perhaps a foot up and down—a good mark in size if one's guess at its location is accurate. If you can hit an elephant's vertebrae and break his back you can kill him. You can kill him by hitting his heart, or by hitting his brain. If you hit him anywhere else you are not likely to hurt him much and the brain and heart shots are the only safe bets. I fired at his heart with both barrels and then grabbed my other gun from the gun boy, ready for their rush, but the whole herd, including the old bull, made off in the other direction, raising a cloud of dust. I ran around and climbed an ant-hill four or five feet high to keep them in sight.

When I caught sight of them they had gone about fifty yards and had stopped. And then I *did* learn something about elephants. My old bull was down on the ground on his side. Around him were ten or twelve other elephants trying desperately with their trunks and tusks to get him on his feet again. They were doing their best to rescue their wounded comrade. They moved his great bulk fifteen or twenty feet in their efforts, but were unable to get him up. I don't know of any other big animals that will do this. I had heard stories that elephants had the chivalry to stick by their wounded and help them, but I was never sure myself until I had actually seen this instance. Sometime later Major Harrison, a very experienced elephant hunter and a keen observer, told me of an even more remarkable instance that he had seen. He was shooting in the Congo and came upon four big bulls. One he killed and another he wounded. The wounded one went down but the two survivors helped him regain his feet, and with one on each side helping him the three moved off. Although Major Harrison followed the rest of the day he was not able to catch up with them.

I did not see the end of their efforts to raise the bull I had shot, for those that were not helping him began to circle about with their ears out to hear anything of their enemy and with their trunks up feeling for my wind. They were moving in ever-increasing circles which threatened to envelop my ant-hill, and I beat a hasty retreat. Not long after they evidently were convinced that the bull was dead and all together they moved away. I then went to the body. He was dead, but as we approached there was a reflex action which twitched his trunk from time to time. This frightened the gun boys so that I went up and slapped the elephant's eye, the customary test, and as there was no reaction the boys were convinced. When I looked the carcass over I was disappointed to find that only one of his tusks was big and well developed. The other was smaller, and out of shape from an injury; consequently I decided not to take him for the museum group. He was, however, a good deal of a temptation, for he was one of the largest elephants I had ever seen, measuring eleven feet four inches to the top of his shoulders, and the circumference of his front foot was sixty-seven and a half inches. To the best of my knowledge this is a record size by about four inches. I did not even skin him but contented myself with taking his tusks, which I sold for nearly $500 without even going down to Nairobi.

The phenomenon of elephants helping each other when wounded is not general by any means. Only a few days after shooting the big bull I had an instance of elephants abandoning one of their number that was wounded and not very badly wounded, either.

I had gone into the forest again, and had come upon another bunch in very thick country. I could only get little glimpses of a patch of hide or ivory once in a while. After working along with them for a while in the hope of getting into more open ground I tried the experiment of beating on the tree trunks with sticks. This was as new to them as it was to me. I felt sure it would make them run but I wasn't sure whether they would go toward it or away from it. Happily they bolted from the forest into the high grass, grumbling all the while. I followed as closely as I dared until finally, in hope of getting a view over the top of the high grass, I started to climb a tree. Just then they rushed back into the forest, fortunately to one side of me. I thought it was time to quit, so we started back to camp. At that moment I heard another group of elephants. They were coming out of the forest into the grass. I climbed up an ant-hill where I could see them as they passed over a ridge. There were eleven of them and not a specimen that I wanted among them. I stood watching to see what would happen next. They were about three hundred yards away when they got my wind. Back they came, rumbling, trumpeting, and squealing. I knew that I had trouble on my hands. The only thing for me to do was to stick, for if I got down in the tall grass I couldn't see anything at all. They came up over a hill, but they were not coming straight toward me and it looked as if they would pass me at forty or fifty yards; but, unfortunately, the cow in front saw me standing in full view on my ant-hill pedestal. They turned straight at me. When the leading cow was as close as I wanted her to get—about twenty-five yards—I fired. She hesitated but again surged on with the others. A second shot knocked her down. The rest surged past her, turned, smelled of her, and ran off into the forest. After a few minutes she got upon her feet and rather groggily went off after them.

Elephants have the reputation of having very bad eyesight. I personally am of the opinion that their sight is pretty good, but on this subject, as on most others about elephants, information is neither complete nor accurate. But my experience makes me think that they can see pretty well. In this case the cow that saw me was only about fifty yards away, but at another time on the Uasin Gishu Plateau an elephant herd charged me from 250 yards with the wind from them to me. The behaviour of this particular herd gave me a clue to their reputation for bad eyesight. The elephant is not afraid of any animal except man, and consequently he is not on the alert for moving objects as are animals that are hunted. Neither does he eat other animals, so he is not interested in their movements as a hunter. In fact, he isn't normally particularly interested in moving objects at all. He pays no attention. When we first came up with this herd on the Uasin Gishu Plateau we could move around within fifty yards of them without attracting their attention. However, after they got our wind and recognized us as enemies, they were able to see us at a distance of 250 yards, and charge us.

But however good the elephant's sight, it is nothing in comparison with his smelling ability. An elephant's trunk is probably the best smelling apparatus in the world, and he depends on his sense of smell more than on any other sense. When he is at all suspicious he moves his trunk around in every direction so that he catches the slightest taint in the air, from whichever way it comes. I have often seen elephants, when disturbed, with their trunks high in air reaching all around for my wind. I likewise, on one occasion, had an intimate view of a very quiet smelling operation by which an old cow escaped me. I was on an elephant path one day on Mt. Kenia looking for an elephant I had heard, when my gun-bearer gripped my shoulder and pointed into the forest. I looked and looked but could see nothing but the trees. Finally I noticed that one of the trees diminished in size toward the ground and I recognized an elephant's trunk. My eyes followed it down. At the very tip it was curled back, and this curled-back part, with the nostrils distended, was moving slowly from side to side quietly fishing for my wind. She was waiting concealed beside the trail to pick me up as I came along. She was no more than forty feet away, but when she decided to give up and moved away, I could not hear her going although it was a dense forest and she was accompanied by two youngsters. Very often in the forest where there is very little air stirring it is hard to tell the direction of the wind. I used to light wax taper matches as tests, for they could be struck without any noise and the flame would show the direction of the slightest breath of air.

In many other ways besides its smelling ability the elephant's trunk is the most extraordinary part of this most extraordinary animal. A man's arm has a more or less universal joint at the shoulder. The elephant's trunk is absolutely flexible at every point. It can turn in any direction and in whatever position it is, and has tremendous strength. There is no bone in it, of course, but it is constructed of interwoven muscle and sinew so tough that one can hardly cut it with a knife. An elephant can shoot a stream of water out of it that would put out a fire; lift a tree trunk weighing a ton and throw it easily; or it is delicate enough to pull a blade of grass with. He drinks with it, feeds himself with it, smells with it, works with it, and at times fights with it. Incidentally, a mouse that endeavoured to frighten an elephant by the traditional nursery rhyme method of running up his trunk would be blown into the next county. There is nothing else like an elephant's trunk on earth. And for that matter, there is nothing else like the elephant. He has come down to us through the ages, surviving the conditions which killed off his earlier contemporaries, and he now adapts himself perfectly to more different conditions than any other animal in Africa.

He can eat anything that is green or ever has been green, just so long as there is enough of it. He can get his water from the aloe plants on the arid plains, or dig a well in the sand of a dry river bed with his trunk and fore feet, and drink there, or he is equally at home living half in the swamps of better-watered regions. He is at home on the low, hot plains of the seacoast at the equator or on the cool slopes of Kenia and Elgon. So far as I know, he suffers from no contagious diseases and has no enemies except man. There are elephants on Kenia that have never lain down for a hundred years. Some of the plains elephants do rest lying down, but no one ever saw a Kenia elephant lying down or any evidence that he does lie down to rest. The elephant is a good traveller. On good ground a good horse can outrun him, but on bad ground the horse would have no chance, and there are few animals that can cover more ground in a day than an elephant. And in spite of his appearance, he can turn with surprising agility and move through the forest as quietly as a rabbit.

An elephant's foot is almost as remarkable as his trunk. In the first place, his foot is encased in a baglike skin with a heavy padded bottom, with some of the characteristics of an anti-skid tire. An elephant walks on his toes. His toes form the front part of his foot and the bones of his foot run not only back but up. Underneath these bones at the back of his foot is a gelatine-like substance, which is a much more effective shock absorber than rubber heels or any other device. One of the curious things about this kind of a foot is that it swells out when the weight is on it and contracts when the weight is removed. As a consequence an elephant may sink four feet into a swamp but the minute he begins to lift his legs, his feet will contract and come out of the hole they have made without suction. The elephant's leg, being practically a perpendicular shaft, requires less muscular effort for him to stand than it does for ordinary animals. This is one of the reasons why he can go for a century without lying down.

A country that elephants have long inhabited takes on some of the particular interest of the animals themselves. I believe that before the white man came to East Africa the elephant was nearly as much a plains animal as a forest animal, but he now tends to stay in the forests where the risk is not so great. On the plains there are no elephant paths now, if there ever were, for in open country elephants do not go in single file. But in the forests there are elephant paths everywhere. In fact, if it were not for the elephant paths travel in the forest would be almost impossible, and above the forests in the bamboo country this is equally true. One travels practically all the time on their trails and they go everywhere except in the tree ferns. Tree fern patches are not very extensive, but I have never seen an elephant track or an elephant in them. The elephants are constantly changing the paths for various reasons; among others, because the natives are in the habit of digging elephant pits in the trails. But there are some trails that have evidently been used for centuries. One time we had followed a band of elephants on the Aberdare Plateau and had devilled them until they began to travel away. We followed until the trail led through a pass in the mountains and we realized that they were going into a different region altogether. That trail in the pass was a little wider than an elephant's foot and worn six inches deep in the solid rock. It must have taken hundreds of years for the shuffling of elephants to wear that rock away.

At another place on Kenia I found an elephant passage of a stream where the trail was twenty feet wide. Single paths came in from many directions on one side of the stream and joined in this great boulevard, which crossed the stream and broke up again on the other side into the single paths radiating again in every direction. In many places where the topography of the ground is such that there is only one place for a trail there will be unmistakable evidence that the trails have stayed in the same place many years—such as trees rubbed half in two by the constant passing of the animals or damp rocks polished by the caress of their trunks.

And along all the trails, old and new, are elephant signs, footprints, dung, and gobs of chewed wood and bark from which they have extracted the juices before spitting them out.

But finding the elephants is not so frequent or easy as the multiplicity of the signs would indicate. One reason is that the signs of elephants—tracks, rubbed trees, and so forth—are more or less enduring, many of them being very plain in places where the elephants have not been for months or even years. If, however, you come on fresh elephant tracks, not more than a day old, you can usually catch up with the elephants, for as they feed along through the country they do not go fast. Only if they are making a *trek* from one region to another it may take much longer to catch them.

Once up with an elephant, if you are shooting, you are pretty sure that, even if he is charging you, a bullet from an elephant gun, hitting him in the head, will stop him even if it does not hit him in a vital spot. Moreover, if you stop the leader of a bunch that is charging you, the bunch will stop. I never heard of a case in which the leader of an elephant charge was stopped and the others kept on, and I doubt if we ever will hear of such a thing, for if it does happen there won't be any one to tell about it. It is unusual for an elephant to keep on after being hit even if the hit does not knock him down. The old cow that charged me at the head of ten others was rather the exception to this rule, for after my first shot stopped her she came on again until my second shot knocked her down. But I had one experience that was entirely at variance with this rule. One old bull took thirteen shots from my rifle and about as many from Mrs. Akeley's before he was content either to die or run away.

In Uganda, after six months in the up-country after elephants, we decided to go down to the Uasin Gishu Plateau for lion spearing, for the rainy season was beginning and the vegetation growing so thick that elephant hunting was getting very difficult. On the way down we came one morning upon the fresh trail of a herd of elephants. We followed for about two hours in a high bush country over which were scattered clumps of trees. Finally we came upon the elephants at the time of their mid-day siesta. The middle of the day is the quietest time of the twenty-four hours with elephants. If they are in a herd, they will bunch together in the shade. They do not stand absolutely still, but mill about very slowly, changing positions in the bunch but not leaving. They are neither feeding nor travelling but, as nearly as they ever do, resting. I even saw a young bull once rest his tusks in the crotch of a tree during this resting period. We got up to within twenty-five yards of them behind some bushes down the wind. We finally decided upon one of the bulls as the target. Mrs. Akeley studied carefully and shot. The bull went down, apparently dead. Ordinarily, we should rush in for a finishing shot, but in this case the rest of the herd did not make off promptly, so we stood still. When they did go off we started toward the apparently dead animal. As we did so, he got upon his feet and, in spite of a volley from us, kept on after the herd. We followed, and after half an hour's travel we caught sight of him again. We kept along behind him, looking for a place where we could swing out to one side and get abreast to fire a finishing shot at him. He was moving slowly and groggily. It was hard to move anywhere except in his trail without making a noise, and I suddenly discovered that the trail was turning so that the wind was from us to him.

Immediately we swung off to one side, but it was too late. I didn't see him when he got our wind but I knew perfectly he had it for there was the sudden crash of his wheel in the bushes and a scream. An elephant's scream is loud and shrill and piercing. And it is terrifying, too—at least to anyone who knows elephants—for it means an angry animal and usually a charge. Then came a series of grunts and rumblings. A second or two later he came in sight, his ears spread out twelve feet from tip to tip, his trunk up and jerking fiercely from side to side. There is no way of describing how big an elephant looks under these conditions, or the speed at which he comes. At about thirty yards I shot, but he took it. He stopped, seemingly puzzled but unhurt. I shot the second barrel and looked for my other gun which was thirty feet behind me. The boy ran up with it and I emptied both barrels into the elephant's head, and still he took it like a sand hill. In the meanwhile, Mrs. Akeley had been firing, too. And then he turned and went off again. I went back to Mrs. Akeley. Everything that I knew about elephant shooting had failed to apply in this case. I had stopped him with one shot. That was normal enough. But then I had put three carefully aimed shots into his head at short range, any one of which should have killed him. And he had taken them with only a slight flinch and then had gone off. I felt completely helpless. Turning to Mrs. Akeley, I said: "This elephant is pretty well shot up, and perhaps we had better wait for developments." She said: "No, we started it; so let's finish it."

I agreed as we reloaded, and we were about to start following when his screaming, grunting, roaring attack began again. Exactly the same thing happened as the first time except that this time Mrs. Akeley, the boy, and I were all together. We fired as we had before. He stopped with the first shot and took all the others standing, finally turning and retreating again. Apparently our shots had no effect except to make him stop and think. I was sick of it, for maybe next time he wouldn't stop and evidently we couldn't knock him down. We had about finished reloading when we heard him once more. There was nothing to do but stand the charge, for to run was fatal. So we waited. There was an appreciable time when I could hear his onrush but couldn't see him. Then I caught sight of him. He wasn't coming straight for us, but was charging at a point thirty yards to one side of us and thrashing back and forth a great branch of tree in his trunk. Why his charge was so misdirected I didn't know, but I was profoundly grateful. As he ran I had a good brain shot from the side. I fired, and he fell stone dead. With the greatest sense of relief in the world I went over to him. As I stood by the carcass I felt very small indeed. Mrs. Akeley sat down and drew a long breath before she spoke.

"I want to go home," she said at last, "and keep house for the rest of my life."

Then I heard a commotion in the bush in front of the dead elephant and as I looked up a boy carrying a cringing monkey appeared. He was scared to an ashen colour and he was still trembling, and the monkey was as frightened as the boy. It was J. T. Jr., Mrs. Akeley's pet monkey, and Alli, the monkey's nurse. They had followed to see the sport without our knowledge, and they had drawn the elephant's last charge.

This experience with an animal that continued to make charge after charge was new to me. It has never happened again and I hope never will, but it shows that with elephants it isn't safe to depend on any fixed rule, for elephants vary as much as people do. This one was the heaviest-skulled elephant I ever saw, and the shots that I had fired would have killed any ordinary animal. But in his case all but the last shot had been stopped by bone.

I couldn't measure his height, but I measured his ear as one indication of his size. It was the biggest I ever heard of. And his tusks were good sized—80 pounds. He was a very big animal, but his foot measurement was not so large as the big bull of the Budongo Forest. Later I made a dining table of his ear, supporting it on three tusks for legs. With the wooden border it was eight feet long and seated eight people very comfortably.

Most wild animals, if they smell man and have an opportunity to get away, make the most of it. Even a mother with young will usually try to escape trouble rather than bring it on, although, of course, they are quickest to fight. But elephants are not always in this category. In the open it has been my experience that they would rather leave than provoke a fight; if you hunt elephants in the forest, you are quite likely to find that two can play the hunting game, and find yourself pretty actively hunted by the elephants. If the elephants after you are making a noise, it gives you a good chance. When they silently wait for you, the game is much more dangerous.

The old bull, who is in the centre of the elephant group in the Museum of Natural History now, tried to get me by this silent method. I was out on a trail and I saw that a big bunch of animals were near. I wasn't following any particular trail for they had moved about so that signs were everywhere and much confused. Finally I came to a gully. It wasn't very broad or very deep, but the trail I was on turned up it to where a crossing could be made on the level. The forest here was high and very thick, and consequently it was quite dark. As I looked up the trail I saw a group of big shapes through the branches. I thought they were elephants and peered carefully at them, but they turned out to be boulders. A minute later I saw across the gully another similar group of boulders, but as I peered at them I saw through a little opening in the leaves, plain and unmistakable, an elephant's tusk. I watched it carefully. It moved a little, and behind it I caught a glimpse of the other tusk. They were big, and I decided that he would do for my group. I couldn't get a glimpse of his eye or anything to sight by, so I carefully calculated where his brain ought to be from the place where his tusk entered his head, and fired. Then there was the riot of an elephant herd suddenly starting. A few seconds later there was a crash. "He's down," I thought, and Bill, the gun boy, and I ran over to the place where the animals had been. We followed their tracks a little way and found where one of the elephants had been down, but he had recovered and gone on. However, he had evidently gone off by himself when he got up, for while the others had gone down an old trail he had gone straight through the jungle, breaking a new way as he went. With Bill in the lead, we pushed along behind him. It was a curious trail, for it went straight ahead without deviation as if it had been laid by compass. One hour went by and then another. We had settled down for a long *trek*. The going wasn't very good and the forest was so thick that we could not see in any direction. We were pushing along in this fashion when, with a crash and a squeal, an elephant burst across our path within fifteen feet of us. It was absolutely without warning, and had the charge been straight on us we could hardly have escaped. As it was, I fired two hurried shots as he disappeared in the growth on the opposite side of the trail. The old devil had grown tired of being hunted and had doubled back on his own trail to wait for us. He had been absolutely silent. We hadn't heard a thing, and his plan failed, I think, only because the growth was so thick that he charged us on scent or sound without being able to see us. I heard him go through the forest a way and then stop. I followed until I found a place a little more open than the rest, and with this between me and the trees he was in I waited. I could hear him grumbling in there from time to time. I didn't expect him to last much longer so I got my lunch and ate it while I listened and watched. I had just finished and had a puff or two on my pipe when he let out another squeal and charged. He evidently had moved around until he had wind of me. I didn't see him but I heard him, and grabbing the gun I stood ready. But he didn't come. Instead I heard the breaking of the bushes as he collapsed. His last effort had been too much for him.

The efforts of the next elephant who tried the quiet waiting game on me were almost too much for me.

We had just come down from the ice fields seventeen thousand feet up on the summit of Mt. Kenia, overlord of the game regions of British East Africa, and had come out of the forest directly south of the pinnacle and within two or three miles of an old camping ground in the temperate climate, five or six thousand feet above sea level, where we had camped five years before and again one year before. Instead of going on around toward the west to the base camp we decided to stop here and have the base camp brought up to us. Mrs. Akeley was tired, so she said she would stay at the camp and rest; and I decided to take advantage of the time it would take to bring up the base camp to go back into the bamboo and get some forest photographs.

There was perfectly good elephant country around our camp but I wanted to go back up where the forests stop and the bamboo flourishes, because it was a bamboo setting that I had selected for the group of elephants I was then working on for the African Hall in the American Museum of Natural History. I started out with four days' rations, gun boys, porters, camera men, and so forth— fifteen men in all. The second day out brought me to about nine thousand feet above sea level where the bamboo began. Following a well-worn elephant trail in search of this photographic material, I ran on to a trail of three old bulls. The tracks were old—probably as much as four days—but the size was so unusual that I decided to postpone the photography and follow them. I did not expect to have to catch up their four days' travel, for I hoped that they would be feeding in the neighbourhood and that the trail I was on would cross a fresher trail made in their wanderings around for food. I had run upon their tracks first about noon. I followed until dark without finding any fresher signs. The next morning we started out at daybreak and finally entered an opening such as elephants use as a feeding ground. It is their custom to mill around in these openings, eating the vegetation and trampling it down until it offers little more, and then move on. In six months or so it will be grown up again eight or ten feet high and they are very apt to revisit it and go through the same process again. Soon after we entered this opening I came suddenly upon fresh tracks of the elephants I had been following. Not only were the tracks fresh but the droppings were still steaming and I knew that the animals were not far away; certainly they had been there not more than an hour before. I followed the trail amongst the low bush in the opening but it merely wandered about repeatedly bringing me back to the place where I had first seen the fresh tracks, and I realized that I might do this indefinitely without getting closer to the elephants. I decided to go outside the opening and circle around it to see if I could find the trail of my bulls as they entered the forest. This opening was at the point on the mountain where the forest proper and the bamboos merged. I followed an elephant path out of the opening on the bamboo side and had gone but a little way when I discovered fresh signs of my three bulls, who had evidently left the opening by the same path that I was following, and at about the same time I heard the crackling of bamboo ahead, probably about two hundred yards away. This was the signal for preparation for the final stalk.

I stood for a moment watching one of the trackers going up the trail to a point where it turned at right angles in the direction of the sounds I had heard. There he stopped at rest, having indicated to me by signs that they had gone in that direction. I turned my back to the trail, watching the porters select a place to lay down their loads amidst a clump of large trees that would afford some protection in case of a stampede in their direction. The gun boys came forward presenting the guns for inspection. I took the gun from the second boy, sending him back with the porters. After examining this gun I gave it to the first boy and took his. When I had examined this I leaned it against my body while I chafed my hands which were numb from the cold mists of the morning, knowing that I might soon need a supple trigger finger. During this time the first gun boy was taking the cartridges, one by one, from his bandoleer and holding them up for my inspection—the ordinary precaution to insure that all the ammunition was the right kind, and an important insurance, because only a full steel-jacketed bullet will penetrate an elephant's head. While still warming my hands, inspecting the cartridges, and standing with the gun leaning against my stomach, I was suddenly conscious that an elephant was almost on top of me. I have no knowledge of how the warning came. I have no mental record of hearing him, seeing him, or of any warning from the gun boy who faced me and who must have seen the elephant as he came down on me from behind. There must have been some definite signal, but it was not recorded in my mind. I only know that as I picked up my gun and wheeled about I tried to shove the safety catch forward. It refused to budge, and I remember the thought that perhaps I had left the catch forward when I inspected the gun and that if not I must pull the triggers hard enough to fire the gun anyway. This is an impossibility, but I remember distinctly the determination to do it, for the all-powerful impulse in my mind was that I must shoot instantly. Then something happened that dazed me. I don't know whether I shot or not. My next mental record is of a tusk right at my chest. I grabbed it with my left hand, the other one with my right hand, and swinging in between them went to the ground on my back. This swinging in between the tusks was purely automatic. It was the result of many a time on the trails imagining myself caught by an elephant's rush and planning what I would do, and a very profitable planning, too; for I am convinced that if a man imagines such a crisis and plans what he would do, he will, when the occasion occurs, automatically do what he planned. Anyway, I firmly believe that my imaginings along the trail saved my life.

He drove his tusks into the ground on either side of me, his curled-up trunk against my chest. I had a realization that I was being crushed, and as I looked into one wicked little eye above me I knew I could expect no mercy from it. This thought was perfectly clear and definite in my mind. I heard a wheezy grunt as he plunged down and then—oblivion.

The thing that dazed me was a blow from the elephant's trunk as he swung it down to curl it back out of harm's way. It broke my nose and tore my cheek open to the teeth. Had it been an intentional blow it would have killed me instantly. The part of the trunk that scraped off most of my face was the heavy bristles on the knuckle-like corrugations of the skin of the underside.

When he surged down on me, his big tusks evidently struck something in the ground that stopped them. Of course my body offered practically no resistance to his weight, and I should have been crushed as thin as a wafer if his tusks hadn't met that resistance—stone, root, or something—underground. He seems to have thought me dead for he left me—by some good fortune not stepping on me—and charged off after the boys. I never got much information out of the boys as to what did happen, for they were not proud of their part in the adventure. However, there were plenty of signs that the elephant had run out into the open space again and charged all over it; so it is reasonable to assume that they had scattered through it like a covey of quail and that he had trampled it down trying to find the men whose tracks and wind filled the neighbourhood.

Usually, when an elephant kills a man, it will return to its victim and gore him again, or trample him, or pull his legs or arms off with its trunk. I knew of one case where a man's porters brought in his arm which the elephant that had killed him had pulled off his body and left lying on the ground. In my case, happily, the elephant for some reason did not come back. I lay unconscious for four or five hours. In the meanwhile, when they found the coast was clear, the porters and gun boys returned and made camp, intending, no doubt, to keep guard over my body until Mrs. Akeley, to whom they had sent word, could reach me. They did not, however, touch me, for they believed that I was dead, and neither the Swahili Mohammedans nor the Kikuyus will touch a dead man. So they built a fire and huddled around it and I lay unconscious in the cold mountain rain at a little distance, with my body crushed and my face torn open. About five o'clock I came to in a dazed way and was vaguely conscious of seeing a fire. I shouted, and a little later I felt myself being carried by the shoulders and legs. Later again I had a lucid spell and realized that I was lying in one of the porter's tents, and I got clarity of mind enough to ask where my wife was. The boys answered that she was back in camp. That brought the events back to me, how I had left her at camp, found the trail of the three old bulls, followed them and, finally, how I was knocked out. I was entirely helpless. I could move neither my arms nor legs and I reached the conclusion that my back was broken. I could not move, but I felt no pain whatever. However, my coldness and numbness brought to my mind a bottle of cocktails, and I ordered one of the boys to bring it to me. My powers of resistance must have been very low, for he poured all there was in the bottle down my throat. In the intervals of consciousness, also, I got them to give me hot bovril—a British beef tea—and quinine. The result of all this was that the cold and numbness left me. I moved my arms. The movement brought pain, but I evidently wasn't entirely paralyzed. I moved my toes, then my feet, then my legs. "Why," I thought in some surprise, "my back isn't broken at all!" So before I dropped off again for the night I knew that I had some chance of recovery. The first time I regained consciousness in the morning, I felt that Mrs. Akeley was around. I asked the boys if she had come. They said no, and I told them to fire my gun every fifteen minutes. Then I dropped off into unconsciousness again and awoke to see her sitting by me on the ground.

When the elephant got me, the boys had sent two runners to tell Mrs. Akeley. They arrived about six in the evening. It was our custom when separated to send notes to each other, or at least messages. When these boys came on to say that an elephant had got me, and when she found that there was no word from me, it looked bad. Mrs. Akeley sent word to the nearest government post for a doctor and started her preparations to come to me that night. She had to go after her guides, even into the huts of a native village, for they did not want to start at night. Finally, about midnight, she got under way. She pushed along with all speed until about daybreak, when the guides confessed that they were lost. At this juncture she was sitting on a log, trying to think what to do next. And then she heard my gun. She answered, but it was more than an hour before the sounds of her smaller rifle reached our camp. And about an hour after the boys heard her gun she arrived.

She asked me how I was, and I said that I was all right. I noticed a peculiar expression on her face. If I had had a looking glass, I should probably have understood it better. One eye was closed and the forehead over it skinned. My nose was broken and my cheek cut so that it hung down, exposing my teeth. I was dirty all over, and from time to time spit blood from the hemorrhages inside. Altogether, I was an unlovely subject and looked hardly worth saving. But I did get entirely over it all, although it took me three months in bed. The thing that was serious was that the elephant had crushed several of my ribs into my lungs, and these internal injuries took a long time to heal. As a matter of fact, I don't suppose I would have pulled through even with Mrs. Akeley's care if it hadn't been for a Scotch medical missionary who nearly ran himself to death coming to my rescue. He had been in the country only a little while and perhaps this explains his coming so fast when news reached him of a man who had been mauled by an elephant. The chief medical officer at Fort Hall, knowing better what elephant mauling usually meant, came, but he didn't hurry. I saw him later and he apologized, but I felt no grievance. I understood the situation. Usually when an elephant gets a man a doctor can't do anything for him.

But this isn't always so. Some months later I sat down in the hotel at Nairobi with three other men, who like myself had been caught by elephants and had lived to tell the tale. An elephant caught Black in his trunk, and threw him into a bush that broke his fall. The elephant followed him and stepped on him, the bush this time forming a cushion that saved him, and although the elephant returned two or three times to give him a final punch, he was not killed. However, he was badly broken up.

Outram and a companion approached an elephant that was shot and down, when the animal suddenly rose, grabbed Outram in his trunk and threw him. The elephant followed him, but Outram scrambled into the grass while the elephant trampled his pith helmet into the ground, whereupon Outram got right under the elephant's tail and stuck to this position while the elephant turned circles trying to find him, until, becoming faint from his injuries, Outram dived into the grass at one side. Outram's companion by this time got back into the game and killed the elephant.

Hutchinson's story I have forgotten a little now, but I remember that he said the elephant caught him, brushed the ground with him, and then threw him. The elephant followed him and Hutchinson put off fate a few seconds by somehow getting amongst the elephant's legs. The respite was enough, for the gun boy, by this time, began firing and drove the elephant off.

In all of these cases, unlike mine, the elephants had used their trunks to pick up their victims and to throw them, and they had intended finishing them by trampling on them. This use of the trunk seems more common than the charge with the tusks that had so nearly finished me. Up in Somaliland Dudo Muhammud, my gun boy, showed me the spot where he had seen an elephant kill an Italian prince. The elephant picked the prince up in his trunk and beat him against his tusks, the prince, meanwhile, futilely beating the elephant's head with his fists. Then the elephant threw him upon the ground, walked on him, and then squatted on him, rubbing back and forth until he had rubbed his body into the ground.

But elephants do use their tusks and use them with terrible effect. About the time we were in the Budongo Forest, Mr. and Mrs. Longdon were across Lake Albert in the Belgian Congo. One day Longdon shot a bull elephant and stood watching the herd disappear, when a cow came down from behind, unheard and unseen, ran her tusk clear through him and, with a toss of her head, threw him into the bush and went on. Longdon lived four days.

But although the elephant is a terrible fighter in his own defence when attacked by man, that is not his chief characteristic. The things that stick in my mind are his sagacity, his versatility, and a certain comradeship which I have never noticed to the same degree in other animals. I like to think of the picture of the two old bulls helping along their comrade wounded by Major Harrison's gun; to think of several instances I have seen of a phenomenon, which I am sure is not accidental, when the young and husky elephants formed the outer ring of a group protecting the older ones from the scented danger. I like to think back to the day I saw the group of baby elephants playing with a great ball of baked dirt two and a half feet in diameter which, in their playing, they rolled for more than half a mile, and the playfulness with which this same group teased the babies of a herd of buffalo until the cow buffaloes chased them off. I think, too, of the extraordinary fact that I have never heard or seen African elephants fighting each other. They have no enemy but man and are at peace amongst themselves.

It is my friend the elephant that I hope to perpetuate in the central group in the Roosevelt African Hall as it is now planned for the American Museum of Natural History—a hall with groups of African animal skins mounted on sculptured bodies, with backgrounds painted from the country itself. In this, which we hope will be an everlasting monument to the Africa that was, the Africa that is now fast disappearing, I hope to place the elephant group on a pedestal in the centre of the hall—the rightful place for the first animal of them all.

And it may not be many years before such museum exhibits are the only remaining records of my jungle friends. As civilization advances in Africa, the extinction of the elephant is being accomplished slowly but quite as surely as that of the American buffalo two generations ago. It is probably not true that the African elephant cannot be domesticated. In fact, somewhere in the Congo is a farm where fifty tame elephants, just as amenable as those in India, are at work. But taming elephants is not a sound proposition economically. Elephant farming is a prince's game, and Africa has no princes to play it. An elephant requires hundreds of acres of land, infinitely more than cattle and sheep and the other domesticated animals. So it is that as man moves on the land, the elephant must move off.

Moreover, African settlers are making every effort to hasten the process. Wherever the elephants refuse to be confined to their bailiwicks and annoy the natives by raiding their farms, the Government has appointed official elephant killers. The South African elephant in the Addoo bush was condemned to be exterminated several years ago. Here, however, the hunters sent into the bush to kill them off found the elephant too much for them and finally gave up the attempt. Now they are being shot only as they come out to molest the natives, with the result that they are able to persist in the bush in limited numbers. Uganda also has official elephant killers wherever the elephants make trouble in the natives' gardens. In British East Africa and in Tanganyika a similar situation exists. The game must eventually disappear as the country is settled, and with it will be wiped out the charm of Africa.

We had heard much of Ruindi Plains in the Belgian Congo as the wonderful game country that it no doubt used to be. To me it seems a vast graveyard. There, too, commercialism has played its part in exterminating the animals and, while we found two or three species of antelope and many lions, other large game is very rare. I suppose that the Ruindi Valley was discovered among the last of the great game pockets and that ivory poachers are responsible for the disappearance of much of the other game as well as of the elephant. The forested valley, which I went through for perhaps ten miles, carried every evidence of having been a wonderful game country in the past, but only a pitiful remnant of the splendid animals who once made it their home remains. Along great elephant boulevards, all overgrown, weaving through the forest, one may occasionally track a single elephant or a small band. A small herd of buffalo grazes where a few years ago there were great numbers.

In our journey north from Cape Town by rail we saw not a single head of game until we reached the Lualaba River, and during the five days that we spent going down that river we saw only a few antelope, perhaps a half dozen elephants and, as I remember it, two or three hippopotami. On the entire journey to within fifty miles of Lake Edward and in all our hunting we found signs of only a few small bands of elephants. Men have spoken of darkest Africa, but the dark chapters of African history are only now being written by the inroads of civilization.

CHAPTER 3

A Dangerous Moose

by Theodore Roosevelt

IN THIS HUNTING ENCOUNTER FROM HIS BOOK *A BOOK-LOVER'S Holidays in the Open*, Theodore Roosevelt describes a hunt for a moose with behavior so unreal that he asked his companions to sign sworn affidavits that the details were true.

* * *

In 1915 I spent a little over a fortnight on a private game reserve in the province of Quebec. I had expected to enjoy the great northern woods, and the sight of beaver, moose, and caribou; but I had not expected any hunting experience worth mentioning. Nevertheless, toward the end of my trip, there befell me one of the most curious and interesting adventures with big game that have ever befallen me during the forty years since I first began to know the life of the wilderness.

In both Canada and the United States the theory and indeed the practise of preserving wildlife on protected areas of land have made astonishing headway since the closing years of the nineteenth century. These protected areas, some of very large size, come in two classes. First, there are those which are public property, where the protection is given by the State. Secondly, there are those where the ownership and the protection are private.

By far the most important, of course, are the public preserves. These by their very existence afford a certain measure of the extent to which democratic government can justify itself. If in a given community unchecked popular rule means unlimited waste and destruction of the natural resources—soil, fertility, water-power, forests, game, wildlife generally—which by right belong as much to subsequent generations as to the present generation, then it is sure proof that the present generation is not yet really fit for self-control, that it is not yet really fit to exercise the high and responsible privilege of a rule which shall be both by the people and for the people. The term "for the people" must always include the people unborn as well as the people now alive, or the democratic ideal is not realized. The only way to secure the chance for hunting, for the enjoyment of vigorous field-sports, to the average man of small means, is to secure such enforced game laws as will prevent anybody and everybody from killing game to a point which means its diminution and therefore ultimate extinction. Only in this way will the average man be able to secure for himself and his children the opportunity of occasionally spending his yearly holiday in that school of hardihood and self-reliance—the chase. New Brunswick, Maine, and Vermont during the last generation have waked up to this fact. Moose and deer in New Brunswick and Maine, deer in Vermont, are so much more plentiful than they were a generation ago that young men of sufficient address and skill can at small cost spend a holiday in the woods, or on the edge of the rough backwoods farm land, and be reasonably sure of a moose or a deer. To all three commonwealths the game is now a real asset because each moose or deer alive in the woods brings in, from the outside, men who spend among the inhabitants much more than the money value of the dead animal; and to the lover of nature the presence of these embodiments of the wild vigor of life adds immensely to the vast majesty of the forests.

In Canada there are many great national reserves; and much—by no means all—of the wilderness wherein shooting is allowed, is intelligently and faithfully protected, so that the game does not diminish. In the summer of 1915 we caught a glimpse of one of these great reserves, that including the wonderful mountains on the line of the Canadian Pacific, from Banff to Lake Louise, and for many leagues around them. The naked or snow-clad peaks, the lakes, the glaciers, the evergreen forest shrouding the mountainsides and valleys, the clear brooks, the wealth of wild flowers, make up a landscape as lovely as it is varied. Here the game—big-horn and white goat-antelope, moose, wapiti, and black-tail deer and white-tail deer—flourish unmolested. The flora and fauna are boreal, but boreal in the sense that the Rocky Mountains are boreal as far south as Arizona; the crimson paint-brush that colors the hillsides, the water-ousel in the rapid torrents—these and most of the trees and flowers and birds suggest those of the mountains which are riven asunder by the profound gorges of the Colorado rather than those which dwell among the lower and more rounded Eastern hill-masses from which the springs find their way into the rivers that flow down to the North Atlantic. Around these and similar great nurseries of game, the hunting is still good in places; although there has been a mistaken lenity shown in permitting the Indians to butcher mountain-sheep and deer to the point of local extermination, and although, as is probably inevitable in all new communities, the game laws are enforced chiefly at the expense of visiting sportsmen, rather than at the expense of the real enemies of the game, the professional meat and hide hunters who slaughter for the profit.

In Eastern Canada, as in the Eastern United States, there has been far less chance than in the West to create huge governmental game reserves. But there has been a positive increase of the big game during the last two or three decades. This is partly due to the creation and enforcement of wise game laws—although here also it must be admitted that in some of the Provinces, as in some of the States, the alien sportsman is judged with Rhadamanthine severity, while the home offenders, and even the home Indians, are but little interfered with. It would be well if in this matter other communities copied the excellent example of Maine and New Brunswick. In addition to the game laws, a large part is played in Canadian game preservation by the hunting and fishing clubs. These clubs have policed, and now police many thousands of square miles of wooded wilderness, worthless for agriculture; and in consequence of this policing the wild creatures of the wilderness have thriven, and in some cases have multiplied to an extraordinary degree, on these club lands.

In September, 1915, I visited the Tourilli Club, as the guest of an old friend, Doctor Alexander Lambert, a companion of previous hunting trips in the Louisiana cane-brakes, in the Rockies, on the plains bordering the Red River of the south, and among the Bad Lands through which the Little Missouri flows. The Tourilli Club is an association of Canadian and American sportsmen and lovers of the wilderness. The land, leased from the government by the club, lies northwest of the attractive Old World city of Quebec—the most distinctive city north of the Mexican border, now that the Creole element in New Orleans has been almost swamped. The club holds about two hundred and fifty square miles along the main branches and the small tributaries of the Saint Anne River, just north of the line that separates the last bleak farming land from the forest. It is a hilly, almost mountainous region, studded with numerous lakes, threaded by rapid, brawling brooks, and covered with an unbroken forest growth of spruce, balsam, birch and maple.

On the evening of the day I left Quebec I camped in a neat log cabin by the edge of a little lake. I had come in on foot over a rough forest trail with my two guides or porters. They were strapping, good-humored French Canadians, self-respecting and courteous, whose attitude toward their employer was so much like that of Old World guides as to be rather interesting to a man accustomed to the absolute and unconscious democracy of the Western cow camps and hunting trails. One vital fact impressed me in connection with them as in connection with my Spanish-speaking and Portuguese-speaking friends in South America. They were always fathers of big families as well as sons of parents with big families; the big family was normal to their kind, just as it was normal among the men and women I met in Brazil, Argentina, Chile, Uruguay, and Paraguay, to a degree far surpassing what is true of native Americans, Australians, and English-speaking Canadians. If the tendencies thus made evident continue to work unchanged, the end of the twentieth century will witness a reversal in the present positions of relative dominance, in the new and newest worlds, held respectively by the people who speak English, and the people who speak the three Latin tongues. Darwin, in the account of his famous voyage, in speaking of the backwardness of the countries bordering the Plate River, dwells on the way they lag behind, in population and material development, compared to the English settlers in Australia and North America. Were he alive now, the development of the countries around Buenos Ayres and Montevideo would make him revise his judgment. And, whatever may be the case in the future, so far this material development has not, as in the English-speaking world and in old France, been accompanied by a moral change which threatens complete loss of race supremacy because of sheer dwindling in the birth-rate. The men and women of Quebec, Brazil, and Argentina are still primarily fathers and mothers; and unless this is true of a race it neither can nor ought to permanently prosper. The atrophy of the healthy sexual instinct is in its effects equally destructive whether it be due to licentiousness, asceticism, coldness, or timidity; whether it be due to calculated self-indulgence, love of ease and comfort, or absorption in worldly success on the part of the man, or, on the part of the woman, to that kind of shrieking "feminism," the antithesis of all worth calling womanly, which gives fine names to shirking of duty, and to the fear of danger and discomfort, and actually exalts as praiseworthy the abandonment or subordination by women of the most sacred and vitally important of the functions of womanhood. It is not enough that a race shall be composed of good fighters, good workers, and good breeders; but, unless the qualities thus indicated are present in the race foundation, then the superstructure, however seemingly imposing, will topple. As I watched my French guides prepare supper I felt that they offered fine stuff out of which to make a nation.

Beside the lake an eagle-owl was hooting from the depths of the spruce forest; hoohoo—h-o-o-o—hoohoo. From the lake itself a loon, floating high on the water, greeted me with eerie laughter. A sweetheart-sparrow sang a few plaintive bars among the alders. I felt as if again among old friends.

Next day we tramped to the comfortable camp of the president of the club, Mr. Glen Ford McKinney. Half-way there Lambert met me; and for most of the distance he, or one of the guides, carried a canoe, as the route consisted of lakes connected by portages, sometimes a couple of miles long. When we reached the roomy comfortable log houses on Lake McKinney, at nightfall, we were quite ready for our supper of delicious moose venison. Lambert, while fishing in his canoe, a couple of days previously, had killed a young bull as it stood feeding in a lake, and for some days moose meat was our staple food. After that it was replaced by messes of freshly caught trout, and once or twice by a birch-partridge. Mrs. Lambert was at the camp, and Mr. and Mrs. McKinney joined us there. A club reserve such as this, with weather-proof cabins scattered here and there beside the lakes, offers the chance for women of the outdoors type, no less than for men no longer in their first youth, to enjoy the life of the wonderful northern wilderness, and yet to enjoy also such substantial comforts as warmth, dry clothes, and good food at night, after a hard day in the open.

Such a reserve offers a fine field for observation of the life histories of the more shy and rare wild creatures practically unaffected by man. Many persons do not realize how completely on these reserves the wildlife is led under natural conditions, wholly unlike those on small artificial reserves. Most wild beasts in the true wilderness lead lives that are artificial in so far as they are primarily conditioned by fear of man. In wilderness reserves like this, on the contrary, there is so much less dread of human persecution that the lives led by such beasts as the moose, caribou, and beaver more closely resemble life in the woods before the appearance of man. As an example, on the Tourilli game reserve wolves, which did not appear until within a decade, have been much more destructive since then than men, and have more profoundly influenced for evil the lives of the other wild creatures.

The beavers are among the most interesting of all woodland beasts. They had been so trapped out that fifteen years ago there were probably not a dozen individuals left on the reserve. Then they were rigidly protected. After ten years they had increased literally a hundredfold. At the end of that time trapping was permitted for a year; hundreds of skins were taken, and then trapping was again prohibited.

The beaver on the reserve at present number between one and two thousand. We saw their houses and dams everywhere. One dam was six feet high; another dam was built to the height of about a foot and a half, near one of our camping places, in a week's time. The architects were a family of beavers; some of the branches bore the big marks of the teeth of the parent beavers, some the marks of the small teeth of the young ones. It was interesting to see the dams grow, stones being heaped on the up-current side to keep the branches in place. Frequently we came across the animals themselves, swimming a stream or lake, and not much bothered by our presence. When left unmolested they are quite as much diurnal as nocturnal. Again and again, as I sat hidden on the lake banks, beaver swam to and fro close beside me, even at high noon. One, which was swimming across a lake at sunset, would not dive until we paddled the canoe straight for it as hard as we could; whereupon it finally disappeared with a slap of its tail. Once at evening Lambert pulled his canoe across the approach to a house, barring the way to the owner—a very big beaver. It did not like to dive under the canoe, and swam close up on the surface, literally gritting its teeth, and now and then it would slap the water with its tail, whereupon the heads of other beaver would pop up above the waters of the lake.

By damming the outlets of some of the lakes and killing the trees and young stuff around the edges, the beaver on this reserve had destroyed some of the favorite haunts of the moose. We saw the old and new houses on the shores of the lakes and beside the streams; some of them were very large, taller than a man, and twice as much across. Some of the old dams, at the pond outlets and across the streams, had become firm causeways, grown-up with trees. The beaver is a fecund animal, its habits are such that few of the beasts of ravin can kill it more than occasionally, and when not too murderously persecuted by man it increases with extraordinary rapidity.

This is primarily due to the character of its food. The forest trees themselves furnish what it eats. This means that its food supply is practically limitless. It has very few food rivals. The trunks of full grown trees offer what is edible to a most narrowly limited number of vertebrates, and therefore—a fact often lost sight of—until man appears on the scene forests do not support anything like the same number and variety of large beasts as open, grassy plains. There are tree-browsing creatures, but these can only get at the young growth; the great majority of beasts prefer prairies or open scrub to thick forest. The open plains of central North America were thronged with big game to a degree that was never true of the vast American forests, whether subarctic, temperate, or tropical. The great game regions of Africa were the endless dry plains of South and East Africa, and not the steaming West African forests. There are, of course, some big mammals that live exclusively on low plants and bushes that only grow in the forest, and some trees at certain seasons yield fruits and nuts which fall to the ground; but, speaking generally, an ordinary full-grown tree of average size yields food only to beasts of exceptional type, of which the most conspicuous in North America are the tree-porcupine and the beaver. Even these eat only the bark; no vertebrate, so far as I know, eats the actual wood of the trunk.

These bark-eaters, therefore, have almost no food rivals, and the forest furnishes them food in limitless quantities. The beaver has developed habits more interesting and extraordinary than those of any other rodent—indeed as interesting as those of any other beast—and its ways of life are such as to enable it to protect itself from its enemies, and to insure itself against failure of food, to a degree very unusual among animals. It is no wonder that, when protected against man, it literally swarms in its native forests. Its dams, houses, and canals are all wonderful, and on the Tourilli they were easily studied. The height at which many of the tree trunks had been severed showed that the cutting must have been done in winter when the snow was deep and crusted. One tree which had not fallen showed a deep spiral groove going twice round the trunk. Evidently the snow had melted faster than the beavers worked; they were never able to make a complete ring, although they had gnawed twice around the tree, and finally the rising temperature beat the teeth, and the task was perforce abandoned.

I was surprised at the complete absence from the Tourilli of the other northern tree-eater—bark-eater—the porcupine. Inquiry developed the fact that porcupines had been exceedingly numerous until within a score of years or less. Then a mysterious disease smote the slow, clumsy, sluggish creatures, and in the course of two or three years they were absolutely exterminated. In similar fashion from some mysterious disease (or aggregation of diseases, which sometimes all work with virulence when animals become too crowded) almost all the rabbits in the reserve died off some six years ago. In each case it was a universally, or well-nigh universally, fatal epidemic, following a period during which the smitten animals had possessed good health and had flourished and increased greatly in spite of the flesh-eaters that preyed on them. In some vital details the cases differed. Hares, compared to porcupines, are far more prolific, far more active, and with far more numerous foes; and they also seem to be much more liable to these epidemics, although this may be merely because they so much more quickly increase to the point that seems to invite the disease. The porcupines are rather unsocial, and are so lethargic in their movements that the infection took longer to do its full work. But this work was done so thoroughly that evidently the entire race of porcupines over a large tract of country was exterminated. Porcupines have few foes that habitually prey on them, although it is said that there is an exception in the shape of the pekan—the big, savage sable, inappropriately called fisher by the English-speaking woodsmen. But they breed so slowly (for rodents) and move about so little that when exterminated from a district many years elapse before they again begin to spread throughout it. The rabbits, on the contrary, move about so much that infectious diseases spread with extraordinary rapidity and they are the habitual food of every fair-sized bird and beast of prey, but their extraordinary fecundity enables them rapidly to recover lost ground. As regards these northern wood-rabbits, and doubtless other species of hares, it is evident that their beast and bird foes, who prey so freely on their helplessness, nevertheless are incompetent to restrain the overdevelopment of the species. Their real foes, their only real foes, are the minute organisms that produce the diseases which at intervals sweep off their swarming numbers. The devastation of these diseases, whether the agents spreading them are insects or still smaller, microscopic creatures, is clearly proved in the case of these North American rabbits and porcupines; probably it explains the temporary and local extermination of the Labrador meadow-mice after they have risen to the culminating crest of one of those "waves of life" described by Doctor Cabot. It has ravaged among big African ruminants on an even more extensive scale than among these North American rodents. Doubtless such disease-devastation has been responsible for the extinction of many, many species in the past; and where for any cause species and individuals became crowded together, or there was an increase in moisture and change in temperature, so that the insect carriers of disease became more numerous, the extinction might easily befall more than one species.

Of course, such epidemic disease is only one of many causes that may produce such extermination or reduction in numbers. More efficient food rivals may be a factor; just as sheep drive out cattle from the same pasturage, and as, in Australia, rabbits drive out sheep. Or animal foes may be a cause. Fifteen years ago, in the Tourilli, caribou were far more plentiful than moose. Moose have steadily increased in numbers. But some seven years ago wolves, of which none had been seen in these woods for half a century, made their appearance. They did not seriously molest the full-grown moose (nor the black bears), although they occasionally killed moose calves, and very rarely, when in a pack, an adult, but they warred on all the other animals, including the lucivees when they could catch them on the ice in winter. They followed the caribou unceasingly, killing many, and in consequence the caribou are now far less common. Barthelmy Lirette, the most experienced hunter and best observer among the guides—even better than his brother Arthur—told me that the wolves usually made no effort to assail the moose, and that never but once had he heard of their killing a grown moose. But they followed any caribou they came across, big or little. Once on snowshoes he had tracked such a chase all day long. A single wolf had followed a caribou for twenty-five miles before killing it. Evidently the wolf deliberately set about tiring his victim so that it could not resist. In the snow the caribou sank deep. The wolf ran lightly. His tracks showed that he had galloped whenever the caribou had galloped, and walked behind it when it became too tired to run, and then galloped again when under the terror of his approach the hunted thing once more flailed its fading strength into flight. Its strength was utterly gone when its grim follower at last sprang on it and tore out its life.

An arctic explorer once told me that on a part of the eastern coast of Greenland he found on one visit plenty of caribou and arctic foxes. A few years later he returned. Muskoxen had just come into the district, and wolves followed them. The muskox is helpless in the presence of human hunters, much more helpless than caribou, and can exist only in the appalling solitudes where even arctic man cannot live; but against wolves, its only other foes, its habits of gregarious and truculent self-defense enable it to hold its own as the caribou cannot. The wolves which were hangers-on of the muskox herds speedily killed or drove out both the foxes and the caribou on this stretch of Greenland coast, and as a result two once plentiful species were completely replaced by two other species, which change also doubtless resulted in other changes in the smaller wildlife.

Here we can explain the reason for the change as regards three of the animals, inasmuch as this change was ultimately conditioned by the movements of the fourth, the muskox. But we know nothing of the cause which produced the muskox migration, which migration resulted in such unsettling of life conditions for the wolves, caribous, and foxes of this one locality. Neither can we with our present knowledge explain the causes which in Maine and New Brunswick during the last thirty or forty years have brought about a diminution of the caribou, although there has been an increase in the number of moose and deer; wolves cannot have produced this change, for they kill the deer easier than the caribou. Field naturalists have in such questions an ample opportunity for work of the utmost interest. Doubtless they can in the future give us complete or partial explanations of many of these problems which are at present insoluble. In any event these continuous shiftings of faunas at the present day enable us to form some idea of the changes which must have occurred on innumerable occasions during man's history on this planet. Beyond question many of the faunas which seem to us contemporary when their remains are found associated with those of prehistoric man were really successive and may have alternated again and again before one or both finally disappeared. Life is rarely static, rarely in a state of stable equilibrium. Often it is in a condition of unstable equilibrium, with continual oscillations one way and the other. More often still, while there are many shifts to and fro, the general tendency of change is with slow steadiness in one direction.

After a few days the Lamberts and I shifted to Lambert's home camp; an easy two days' journey, tramping along the portage trails and paddling across the many lakes. It was a very comfortable camp, by a beautiful lake. There were four log cabins, each water-tight and with a stove; and the largest was in effect a sitting-room, with comfortable chairs and shelves of books. They stood in a sunny clearing. The wet, dense forest was all around, the deep mossy ground spangled with bright-red partridgeberries. Behind the cabins was a small potato patch. Wild raspberries were always encroaching on this patch, and attracted the birds of the neighborhood, including hermit and olive-back thrushes, both now silent. Chickadees were in the woods, and woodpeckers—the arctic, the hairy, and the big log-cock—drummed on the dead trees. One mid-afternoon a great gray owl called repeatedly, uttering a short loud sound like that of some big wild beast. In front of the main cabin were four graceful mountain ashes, brilliant with scarlet berry clusters. On a neighboring lake Coleman Drayton had a camp; the view from it across the lake was very beautiful. He killed a moose on the lake next to his and came over to dinner with us the same evening.

On the way to Lambert's camp I went off by myself for twenty-four hours, with my two guides, Arthur Lirette, one of the game wardens of the club, and Odilon Genest. Arthur was an experienced woodsman, intelligent and responsible, and with the really charming manners that are so much more common among men of French or Spanish blood than among ourselves. Odilon was a strong young fellow, a good paddler and willing worker. I wished to visit a lake which moose were said to frequent. We carried our canoe thither.

After circling the lake in the canoe without seeing anything, we drew it ashore among some bushes and sat down under a clump of big spruces to watch. Although only partially concealed, we were quiet; and it is movement that attracts the eyes of wild things. A beaver house was near by and the inmates swam about not thirty feet from us; and scaup-ducks and once a grown brood of dusky mallard drifted and swam by only a little farther off. The beaver kept slapping the water with their broad trowel-tails, evidently in play; where they are wary they often dive without slapping the water. No bull appeared, but a cow moose with two calves came down to the lake, directly opposite us, at one in the afternoon and spent two hours in the water. Near where the three of them entered the lake was a bed of tall, coarse reed-grass standing well above the water. Earlier in the season this had been grazed by moose, but these three did not touch it. The cow, having entered the water, did not leave. She fed exclusively with her head under water. Wading out until only the ridge of her back was above the surface, and at times finding that the mud bothered even her long legs, she plunged her huge homely head to the bottom, coming up with between her jaws big tufts of dripping bottom-grass— the moose grass—or the roots and stems of other plants. After a time she decided to change her station, and, striking off into deep water, she swam half a mile farther down the lake. She swam well and powerfully, but sunk rather deep in the water, only her head and the ridge of her withers above it. She continued to feed, usually broadside to me, some three hundred and fifty yards off; her big ears flopped forward and back, and her long snout, with the protuberant nostrils, was thrust out as she turned from time to time to look or smell for her calves. The latter had separated at once from the mother, and spent only a little time in the water, appearing and disappearing among the alders, and among the berry-bushes on a yielding bog of pink and gray moss. Once they played together for a moment, and then one of them cantered off for a few rods.

When moose calves go at speed they usually canter. By the time they are yearlings, however, they have adopted the trot as their usual gait. When grown they walk, trot when at speed, and sometimes pace; but they gallop so rarely that many good observers say that they never gallop or canter. This is too sweeping, however. I have myself, as will be related, seen a heavy old bull gallop for fifty yards when excited, and I have seen the tracks where a full-grown cow or young bull galloped for a longer distance. Lambert came on one close up in a shallow lake, and in its fright it galloped ashore, churning through the mud and water. In very deep snow one will sometimes gallop or bound for a dozen leaps, and under sudden fright from an enemy nearby even the biggest moose will sometimes break into a gallop which may last for several rods. More often, even under such circumstances, the animal trots off; and the trot is its habitual, and, save in exceptional circumstances, its only, rapid gait, even when charging.

As the cow and her young ones stood in the water or on the bank it was impossible not to be struck by the conspicuously advertising character of the coloration. The moose is one of the few animals of which the body is inversely countershaded, being black save for the brownish or grayish of the back. The huge black mass at once attracts the eye, and the whitish or grayish legs are also strikingly visible. The bright-red summer coat of the white-tail deer is, if anything, of even more advertising quality; but the huge bulk of a moose, added to its blackness, makes it the most conspicuous of all our beasts.

Moose are naturally just as much diurnal as nocturnal. We found them visiting the lakes at every hour of the day. They are so fond of water as to be almost amphibious. In the winter they feed on the buds and twig tips of young spruce and birch and swamp-maple; and when there is no snow they feed freely on various ground plants in the forest; but for over half the year they prefer to eat the grasses and other plants which grow either above or under the water in the lakes. They easily wade through mud not more than four feet deep, and take delight in swimming. But until this trip I did not know that moose, while swimming, dived to get grass from the bottom. Mr. McKinney told me of having seen this feat himself. The moose was swimming to and fro in a small lake. He plunged his head beneath water, and then at once raised it, looking around, evidently to see if any enemy were taking advantage of his head being concealed to approach him. Then he plunged his head down again, threw his rump above water, and dived completely below the surface, coming up with tufts of bottom-grass in his mouth. He repeated this several times, once staying down and out of sight for nearly half a minute.

After the cow moose left the water she spent an hour close to the bank, near the inlet. We came quite near to her in the canoe before she fled; her calves were farther in the woods. It was late when we started to make our last portage; a heavy rain-storm beat on us, speedily drenching us, and the darkness and the driving downpour made our walk over the rough forest trail one of no small difficulty. Next day we went to Lambert's camp.

Some ten miles northeast of Lambert's camp lies a stretch of wild and mountainous country, containing many lakes, which has been but seldom visited. A good cabin has been built on one of the lakes. A couple of years ago Lambert went thither, but saw nothing, and Coleman Drayton was there the same summer; Arthur, my guide, visited the cabin last spring to see if it was in repair; otherwise the country had been wholly undisturbed. I determined to make a three days' trip to it, with Arthur and Odilon. We were out of meat and I desired to shoot something for the table. My license permitted me to kill one bull moose. It also permitted me to kill two caribou, of either sex; but Lambert felt, and I heartily agreed with him, that no cow ought to be shot.

We left after breakfast one morning. Before we had been gone twenty-five minutes I was able to obtain the wished-for fresh meat. Our course, as usual, lay along a succession of lakes connected by carries, or portages. We were almost at the end of the first portage when we caught a glimpse of a caribou feeding in the thick woods some fifty yards to the right of our trail. It was eating the streamers of gray-green moss which hung from the dead lower branches of the spruces. It was a yearling bull. At first I could merely make out a small patch of its flank between two tree trunks, and I missed it—fortunately, for, if wounded, it would probably have escaped. At the report, instead of running, the foolish young bull shifted his position to look at us; and with the next shot I killed him. While Arthur dressed him Odilon returned to camp and brought out a couple of men. We took a shoulder with us for our provision and sent the rest back to camp. Hour after hour we went forward. We paddled across the lakes. Between them the trails sometimes led up to and down from high divides; at other times they followed the courses of rapid brooks which brawled over smooth stones under the swaying, bending branches of the alders. Off the trail fallen logs and bowlders covered the ground, and the moss covered everything ankle-deep or knee-deep.

Early in the afternoon we reached the cabin. The lake, like most of the lakes thereabouts, was surrounded by low, steep mountains, shrouded in unbroken forest. The light green domes of the birches rose among the sombre spruce spires; on the mountain crests the pointed spruces made a serrated line against the sky. Arthur and I paddled off across the lake in the light canoe we had been carrying. We had hardly shoved off from shore before we saw a caribou swimming in the middle of the lake. It was a young cow, and doubtless had never before seen a man. The canoe much excited its curiosity. A caribou, thanks probably to its peculiar pelage, is a very buoyant swimmer. Unlike the moose, this caribou had its whole back, and especially its rump, well out of water;

49

the short tail was held erect, and the white under-surface glinted whenever the swimmer turned away from us. At first, however, it did not swim away, being too much absorbed in the spectacle of the canoe. It kept gazing toward us with its ears thrown forward, wheeling to look at us as lightly and readily as a duck. We passed it at a distance of some seventy-five yards, whereupon it took fright and made off, leaving a wake like a paddle-wheel steamer and, when it landed, bouncing up the bank with a great splashing of water and cracking of bushes. A caribou swims even better than a moose, but whereas a moose not only feeds by preference in the water, but half the time has its head under water, the caribou feeds on land, although occasionally cropping water-grass that stands above the surface.

We portaged beside a swampy little stream to the next lake and circled it in the canoe. Silently we went round every point, alert to find what the bay beyond might hold. But we saw nothing; it was night when we returned. As we paddled across the lake the stars were glorious overhead and the mysterious landscape shimmered in the white radiance of the moonlight. Loons called to one another, not only uttering their goblin laughter, but also those long-drawn, wailing cries, which seem to hold all the fierce and mournful loneliness of the northern wastes. Then we reached camp, and feasted on caribou venison, and slept soundly on our beds of fragrant balsam boughs.

Next morning, on September 19, we started eastward, across a short portage, perhaps a quarter of a mile long, beside which ran a stream, a little shallow river. At the farther end of the portage we launched the canoe in a large lake hemmed in by mountains. The lake twisted and turned, and was indented by many bays. A strong breeze was blowing. Arthur was steersman, Odilon bowsman, while I sat in the middle with my Springfield rifle. We skirted the shores, examining each bay.

Half an hour after starting, as we rounded a point, we saw the huge black body and white shovel antlers of a bull moose. He was close to the alders, wading in the shallow water and deep mud and grazing on a patch of fairly tall water-grass. So absorbed was he that he did not notice us until Arthur had skilfully brought the canoe to within eighty yards of him. Then he saw us, tossed his great antlered head aloft, and for a moment stared at us, a picture of burly majesty. He stood broadside on, and a splendid creature he was, of towering stature, the lord of all the deer tribe, as stately a beast of the chase as walks the round world.

The waves were high, and the canoe danced so on the ripple that my first bullet went wild, but with the second I slew the mighty bull.

We had our work cut out to get the bull out of the mud and on the edge of the dry land. The antlers spread fifty-two inches. Some hours were spent in fixing the head, taking off the hide, and cutting up the carcass. Our canoe was loaded to its full capacity with moose meat when we started toward the beginning of the portage leading from the southeastern corner of the lake toward the Lamberts' camp. Here we landed the meat, putting cool moss over it, and left it to be called for on our way back, on the morrow.

It was shortly after three when we again pushed off in the canoe, and headed for the western end of the lake, for the landing from which the portage led to our cabin. It had been a red-letter day, of the ordinary hunting red-letter type. I had no conception that the real adventure still lay in front of us.

When half a mile from the landing we saw another big bull moose on the edge of the shore ahead of us. It looked and was—if anything—even bigger-bodied than the one I had shot in the morning, with antlers almost as large and rather more palmated. We paddled up to within a hundred yards of it, laughing and talking, and remarking how eager we would have been if we had not already got our moose. At first it did not seem to notice us. Then it looked at us but paid us no further heed. We were rather surprised at this but paddled on past it, and it then walked along the shore after us. We still supposed that it did not realize what we were. But another hundred yards put us to windward of it. Instead of turning into the forest when it got our wind, it merely bristled up the hair on its withers, shook its head, and continued to walk after the canoe, along the shore. I had heard of bull moose, during the rut, attacking men unprovoked, if the men were close up, but never of anything as wanton and deliberate as this action, and I could hardly believe the moose meant mischief, but Arthur said it did; and obviously we could not land with the big, evil-looking beast coming for us—and, of course, I was most anxious not to have to shoot it. So we turned the canoe round and paddled on our back track. But the moose promptly turned and followed us along the shore. We yelled at him, and Odilon struck the canoe with his paddle, but with no effect. After going a few hundred yards we again turned and resumed our former course; and as promptly the moose turned and followed us, shaking his head and threatening us. He seemed to be getting more angry, and evidently meant mischief. We now continued our course until we were opposite the portage landing, and about a hundred yards away from it; the water was shallow and we did not wish to venture closer, lest the moose might catch us if he charged. When he came to the portage trail he turned up it, sniffing at our footsteps of the morning, and walked along it into the woods; and we hoped that now he would become uneasy and go off. After waiting a few minutes we paddled slowly toward the landing, but before reaching it we caught his loom in the shadow, as he stood facing us some distance down the trail. As soon as we stopped he rushed down the trail toward us, coming in to the lake; and we backed hastily into deep water. He vented his rage on a small tree, which he wrecked with his antlers. We continued to paddle round the head of the bay, and he followed us; we still hoped we might get him away from the portage, and that he would go into the woods. But when we turned he followed us back, and thus went to and fro with us. Where the water was deep near shore we pushed the canoe close in to him, and he promptly rushed down to the water's edge, shaking his head, and striking the earth with his fore hoofs. We shouted at him, but with no effect. As he paraded along the shore he opened his mouth, lolling out his tongue; and now and then when he faced us he ran out his tongue and licked the end of his muzzle with it. Once, with head down, he bounded or galloped round in a half circle; and from time to time he grunted or uttered a low, menacing roar. Altogether the huge black beast looked like a formidable customer, and was evidently in a most evil rage and bent on man-killing.

For over an hour he thus kept us from the shore, running to meet us wherever we tried to go. The afternoon was waning, a cold wind began to blow, shifting as it blew. He was not a pleasant-looking beast to meet in the woods in the dusk. We were at our wits' ends what to do. At last he turned, shook his head, and with a flourish of his heels galloped—not trotted—for fifty yards up beside the little river which paralleled the portage trail. I called Arthur's attention to this, as he had been telling me that a big bull never galloped. Then the moose disappeared at a trot round the bend. We waited a few minutes, cautiously landed, and started along the trail, watching to see if the bull was lying in wait for us; Arthur telling me that if he now attacked us I must shoot him at once or he would kill somebody.

A couple of hundred yards on the trail led within a few yards of the little river. As we reached this point a smashing in the brush beyond the opposite bank caused us to wheel; and the great bull came headlong for us, while Arthur called to me to shoot. With a last hope of frightening him I fired over his head, without the slightest effect. At a slashing trot he crossed the river, shaking his head, his ears back, the hair on his withers bristling. "Tirez, m'sieu, tirez; vite, vite!" called Arthur, and when the bull was not thirty feet off I put a bullet into his chest, in the sticking point. It was a mortal wound, and stopped him short; I fired into his chest again, and this wound, too, would by itself have been fatal. He turned and recrossed the stream, falling to a third shot, but as we approached he struggled to his feet, grunting savagely, and I killed him as he came toward us.

I was sorry to have to kill him, but there was no alternative. As it was, I only stopped him in the nick of time, and had I not shot straight at least one of us would have paid forfeit with his life in another second. Even in Africa I have never known anything but a rogue elephant or buffalo, or an occasional rhinoceros, to attack so viciously or with such premeditation when itself neither wounded nor threatened.

Gentle-voiced Arthur, in his delightful habitant's French, said that the incident was "pas mal curieux." He used "pas mal" as a superlative. The first time he used it I was completely bewildered. It was hot and sultry, and Arthur remarked that the day was "pas mal mort." How the day could be "not badly dead" I could not imagine, but the proper translation turned out to be "a very lifeless day," which was true.

On reaching Lambert's camp, Arthur and Odilon made affidavit to the facts as above set forth, and this affidavit I submitted to the secretary of mines and fisheries of Quebec, who approved what I had done.

On the day following that on which we killed the two bulls we went back to Lambert's home camp. While crossing one lake, about the middle of the forenoon, a bull moose challenged twice from the forest-clad mountain on our right. We found a pawing-place, a pit where one—possibly more than one—bull had pawed up the earth and thrashed the saplings roundabout with its antlers. The place smelled strongly of urine. The whole of the next day was spent in getting in the meat, skins, and antlers.

I do not believe that this vicious bull moose had ever seen a man. I have never heard of another moose acting with the same determination and perseverance in ferocious malice; it behaved, as I have said, like some of the rare vicious rogues among African elephants, buffaloes, and rhinoceroses. Bull moose during the rut are fierce animals, however, and, although there is ordinarily no danger whatever in shooting them, several of my friends have been resolutely charged by wounded moose, and I know of, and have elsewhere described, one authentic case where the hunter was killed. A boy carrying mail through the woods to the camp of a friend of mine was forced to climb a tree by a bull which threatened him. My friend Pride, of Island Falls, Maine, was charged while in a canoe at night, by a bull moose which he had incautiously approached too near, and the canoe was upset. If followed on snowshoes in the deep snow, or too closely approached in its winter yard, it is not uncommon for a moose to charge when its pursuer is within a few yards. Once Arthur was charged by a bull which was in company with a cow. He was in a canoe, at dusk, in a stream, and the bull rushed into the water after him, while he paddled hard to get away; but the cow left, and the bull promptly followed her. In none of these cases, however, did the bull act with the malice and cold-blooded purposefulness shown by the bull I was forced to kill.

Two or three days later I left the woods. The weather had grown colder. The loons had begun to gather on the larger lakes in preparation for their southward flight. The nights were frosty. Fall was in the air. Once there was a flurry of snow. Birch and maple were donning the bravery with which they greet the oncoming north; crimson and gold their banners flaunted in the eyes of the dying year.

CHAPTER 4

More Tsavo Man-Eaters

by Lt. Col. J. H. Patterson, D.S.O.

WHEN ASSIGNED TO HELP SUPERVISE THE BUILDING OF A Uganda Railroad bridge over the Tsavo River in east Africa in March 1898, Lt. Col. J. H. Patterson, D.S.O., had little idea of the magnitude of the adventure upon which he was embarking. The site of the bridge, which is today a part of Kenya, became the scene of savage attacks by man-eating lions preying on the workers. Col. Patterson's stirring book, *The Man-Eaters of Tsavo*, remains in print to this day. The drama was also captured quite well in the film *The Ghost and the Darkness*, starring Val Kilmer and Michael Douglas. However, Col. Patterson's book does not end with the death of the two most-prominent Tsavo man-eaters; there was more lion-hunting drama to come. Here, we have further lion-hunting adventures with Col. Patterson that happened after the "Tsavo Man-eaters" had been killed.

* * *

When the Athi river had been bridged, the section of the line to Nairobi was pushed forward as rapidly as possible, and from dawn to dark we all exerted ourselves to the very utmost. One day (May 28) the weather was exceptionally hot, and I had been out in the broiling sun ever since daylight superintending the construction of banks and cuttings and the erection of temporary bridges. On returning to my hut, therefore, at about three o'clock in the afternoon, I threw myself into a long deck chair, too tired for anything beyond a long cool drink. Here I rested for an hour or so, amused by the bustle at the small wayside station we had just built, and idly watching our tiny construction engine forging its way, with a great deal of clanking and puffing, up a steep gradient just across the river. It was touch-and-go whether it would manage to get its heavy load of rails and sleepers to the top of the incline or not, and I became so interested in the contest between steam and friction and gravity, that I did not notice that a visitor had approached and was standing quietly beside me.

On hearing the usual salutation, however, I turned round and saw a lean and withered Masai, clothed in a very inadequate piece of wildebeeste hide which was merely slipped under the left arm and looped up in a knot over the right shoulder. He stood for a moment with the right hand held out on a level with his shoulder, the fingers extended and the palm turned towards me—all indicating that he came on a friendly visit. I returned his salutation, and asked him what he wanted. Before answering, he dropped down on his heels, his old bones cracking as he did so. "I want to lead the Great Master to two lions," he said; "they have just killed a zebra and are now devouring it." On hearing this I straightway forgot that I had already done a hard day's work in the full blaze of an equatorial sun; I forgot that I was tired and hungry; in fact, I forgot everything that was not directly connected with the excitement of lion-hunting. Even the old man at my feet grinned when he saw how keen I was about it. I plied him with questions—were they both lions or lionesses? had they manes? how far away were they? and so on. Naturally, to the last question he was bound to answer "M'bali kidogo." Of course they were not far away; nothing ever is to a native of East Africa. However, the upshot was that in a very few minutes I had a mule saddled, and with the old Masai as guide, started off accompanied by my faithful Mahina and another coolie to help to bring home the skin if I should prove successful. I also left word for my friend Spooner, the District Engineer, who happened to be absent from camp just at the moment, that I had gone after two lions, but hoped to be back by nightfall.

We travelled at a good pace, and within an hour had covered fully six miles; still there was no sign of lions. On the way we were joined by some Wa Kamba, even more scantily attired than our guide, and soon a dispute arose between these hangers-on and the old Masai, who refused to allow them to accompany us, as he was afraid that they would seize all the zebra-meat that the lions had not already eaten. However, I told him not to bother, but to hurry up and show me the lions, and that I would look after him all right. Eventually, on getting to the low crest of one of the long swells in the ground, our guide extended a long skinny finger and said proudly, "Tazama, Bwana" ("See, Master"). I looked in the direction in which he pointed, and sure enough, about six hundred yards off were a lion and a lioness busily engaged on the carcase of a zebra. On using my field-glasses, I was amused to observe a jackal in attendance on the pair. Every now and then he would come too close to the zebra, when the lion would make a short rush at him and scare him away. The little jackal looked most ridiculous, scampering off before the huge beast with his tail well down; but no sooner did the lion stop and return to his meal than he crept nearer again. The natives say, by the way, that a lion will eat every kind of animal—including even other lions—except a jackal or a hyena. I was also interested to notice the way in which the lion got at the flesh of the zebra; he took a short run at the body, and putting his claws well into the skin, in this manner tore off great strips of the hide.

While I was thus studying the picture, my followers became impatient at my inactivity, and coming up to the top of the rise, showed themselves on the sky-line. The lions saw them at once, turning round and standing erect to stare at them. There was not an atom of cover to be seen, nor any chance of taking advantage of the rolling ground, for it did not slope in the required direction; so I started to walk in the open in a sidelong direction towards the formidable-looking pair. They allowed me to come a hundred yards or so nearer them, and then the lioness bolted, the lion following her at a more leisurely trot. As soon as they left the body of the zebra, my African following made a rush for it, and began a fierce fight over the remains, so that I had to restore order and leave a coolie to see that our guide got the large share, as he deserved. In the meantime the lion, hearing the noise of the squabble, halted on the crest of the hill to take a deliberate look at me, and then disappeared over the brow. I jumped on to my mule and galloped as hard as I could after him, and luckily found the pair still in sight when I reached the top of the rise. As soon as they saw me following them up, the lioness took covert in some long grass that almost concealed her when she lay down, but the lion continued to move steadily away. Accordingly I made for a point which would bring me about two hundred yards to the right of the lioness, and which would leave a deep natural hollow between us, so as to give me a better chance, in the event of a charge, of bowling her over as she came up the rise towards me. I could plainly make out her light-coloured form in the grass, and took careful aim and fired. In an instant she was kicking on her back and tossing about, evidently hard hit; in a few seconds more she lay perfectly still, and I saw that she was dead.

I now turned my attention to the lion, who meanwhile had disappeared over another rise. By this time Mahina and the other Indian, with three or four of the disappointed Wa Kamba, had come up, so we started off in a body in pursuit of him. I felt sure that he was lurking somewhere in the grass not far off, and I knew that I could depend upon the native eye to find him if he showed so much as the tip of his ear. Nor was I disappointed, for we had scarcely topped the next rise when one of the Wa Kamba spotted the dark brown head of the brute as he raised it for an instant above the grass in order to watch us. We pretended not to have seen him, however, and advanced to within two hundred yards or so, when, as he seemed to be getting uneasy, I thought it best to risk a shot even at this range. I put up the 200-yards sight and the bullet fell short; but the lion never moved. Raising the sight another fifty yards, I rested the rifle on Mahina's back for the next shot, and again missed; fortunately, however, the lion still remained quiet. I then decided to put into practice the scheme I had thought out the day I sat astride the lion I had killed on the Kapiti Plain: so I told all my followers to move off to the right, taking the mule with them, and to make a half-circle round the animal, while I lay motionless in the grass and waited. The ruse succeeded admirably, for as the men moved round so did the lion, offering me at last a splendid shoulder shot. I took very careful, steady aim and fired, with the result that he rolled over and over, and then made one or two attempts to get up but failed. I then ran up to within a few yards of him, and—helpless as he was with a bullet through both shoulders—he was still game, and twist round so as to face me, giving vent all the time to savage growls. A final shot laid him out, however, and we at once proceeded to skin him. While we were busy doing this, one of the Wa Kamba suddenly drew my attention to the fact that we were actually being stalked at that very moment by two other lions, who eventually approached to within five hundred yards' distance and then lay down to watch us skinning their dead brother, their big shaggy heads rising every now and again above the grass to give us a prolonged stare. At the time I little knew what a stirring adventure was in store for me next day while in pursuit of these same brutes.

It was almost dark when the skinning process was finished, so without delay we started on our way back to camp, which was about seven miles off. The lioness I thought I should leave to be skinned the next day; but the men I sent out to do the job on the morrow were unable to find any trace of her—they probably missed the place where she lay, for I am sure that I killed her.

It was a good two hours after night had fallen before we got anywhere near the railway, and the last few miles I was obliged to do by the guidance of the stars. Tramping over the plain on a pitch-dark night, with lions and rhino all about, was by no means pleasant work and I heartily wished myself and my men safely back in camp. Indeed, I was beginning to think that I must have lost my bearings and was getting anxious about it, when to my relief I heard a rifle shot about half a mile ahead of us. I guessed at once that it was fired by my good friend Spooner in order to guide me, so I gave a reply signal; and on getting to the top of the next rise, I saw the plain in front of me all twinkling with lights. When he found that I had not returned by nightfall, Spooner had become nervous about me, and fearing that I had met with some mishap, had come out with a number of the workmen in camp to search for me in the direction I had taken in the afternoon. He was delighted to find me safe and sound and with a lion's skin as a trophy, while I was equally glad to have his escort and company back to camp, which was still over a mile away.

When we had settled down comfortably to dinner that night, I fired Spooner's sporting ardour by telling him of the fine pair of lions who had watched us skinning their companion, and we agreed at once to go out next day and try to bag them both. Spooner and I had often had many friendly arguments in regard to the comparative courage of the lion and the tiger, he holding the view that "Stripes" was the more formidable foe, while I, though admitting to the full the courage of the tiger, maintained from lively personal experience that the lion when once roused was unequalled for pluck and daring, and was in fact the most dangerous enemy one could meet with. He may at times slink off and not show fight; but get him in the mood, or wound him, and only his death or yours will end the fray—that, at least, was my experience of East African lions. I think that Spooner has now come round to my opinion, his conversion taking place the next day in a very melancholy manner.

Long after I had retired to rest that night I lay awake listening to roar answering roar in every direction round our camp, and realised that we were indeed in the midst of a favourite haunt of the king of beasts. It is one thing to hear a lion in captivity, when one knows he is safe behind iron bars; but quite another to listen to him when he is ramping around in the vicinity of one's fragile tent, which with a single blow he could tear to pieces. Still, all this roaring was of good omen for the next day's sport.

According to our over-night arrangement, we were up betimes in the morning, but as there was a great deal of work to be done before we could get away, it was quite midday before we made ready to start. I ought to mention before going further that as a rule Spooner declined my company on shooting trips, as he was convinced that I should get "scuppered" sooner or later if I persisted in going after lions with a "popgun," as he contemptuously termed my .303. Indeed, this was rather a bone of contention between us, he being a firm believer (and rightly) in a heavy weapon for big and dangerous game, while I always did my best to defend the .303 which I was in the habit of using. On this occasion we effected a compromise for the day, I accepting the loan of his spare 12-bore rifle as a second gun in case I should get to close quarters. But my experience has been that it is always a very dangerous thing to rely on a borrowed gun or rifle, unless it has precisely the same action as one's own; and certainly in this instance it almost proved disastrous.

Having thus seen to our rifles and ammunition and taken care also that some brandy was put in the luncheon-basket in case of an accident, we set off early in the afternoon in Spooner's tonga, which is a two-wheeled cart with a hood over it. The party consisted of Spooner and myself, Spooner's Indian shikari Bhoota, my own gun-boy Mahina, and two other Indians, one of whom, Imam Din, rode in the tonga, while the other led a spare horse called "Blazeaway." Now it may seem a strange plan to go lion-hunting in a tonga, but there is no better way of getting about country like the Athi Plains, where—so long as it is dry—there is little or nothing to obstruct wheeled traffic. Once started, we rattled over the smooth expanse at a good rate, and on the way bagged a hartebeeste and a couple of gazelle, as fresh meat was badly needed in camp; besides, they offered most tempting shots, for they stood stock-still gazing at us, struck no doubt by the novel appearance of our conveyance. Next we came upon a herd of wildebeeste, and here we allowed Bhoota, who was a wary shikari and an old employee of Spooner's, to stalk a solitary bull. He was highly pleased at this opportunity, and did the job admirably.

At last we reached the spot where I had seen the two lions on the previous day—a slight hollow, covered with long grass; but there was now no trace of them to be discovered, so we moved further on and had another good beat round. After some little time the excitement began by our spying the black-tipped ears of a lioness projecting above the grass, and the next moment a very fine lion arose from beside her and gave us a full view of his grand head and mane. After staring fixedly at us in an inquiring sort of way as we slowly advanced upon them, they both turned and slowly trotted off, the lion stopping every now and again to gaze round in our direction. Very imposing and majestic he looked, too, as he thus turned his great shaggy head defiantly towards us, and Spooner had to admit that it was the finest sight he had ever seen. For a while we followed them on foot; but finding at length that they were getting away from us and would soon be lost to sight over a bit of rising ground, we jumped quickly into the tonga and galloped round the base of the knoll so as to cut off their retreat, the excitement of the rough and bumpy ride being intensified a hundred-fold by the probability of our driving slap into the pair on rounding the rise. On getting to the other side, however, they were nowhere to be seen, so we drove on as hard as we could to the top, whence we caught sight of them about four hundred yards away. As there seemed to be no prospect of getting nearer we decided to open fire at this range, and at the third shot the lioness tumbled over to my .303. At first I thought I had done for her, as for a few minutes she lay on the ground kicking and struggling; but in the end, although evidently badly hit, she rose to her feet and followed the lion, who had escaped uninjured, into some long grass from which we could not hope to dislodge them.

As it was now late in the afternoon, and as there seemed no possibility of inducing the lions to leave the thicket in which they had concealed themselves, we turned back towards camp, intending to come out again the next day to track the wounded lioness. I was now riding "Blazeaway" and was trotting along in advance of the tonga, when suddenly he shied badly at a hyena, which sprang up out of the grass almost from beneath his feet and quickly scampered off. I pulled up for a moment and sat watching the hyena's ungainly bounds, wondering whether he were worth a shot. Suddenly I felt "Blazeaway" trembling violently beneath me, and on looking over my left shoulder to discover the reason, I was startled to see two fine lions not more than a hundred yards away, evidently the pair which I had seen the day before and which we had really come in search of. They looked as if they meant to dispute our passage, for they came slowly towards me for about ten yards or so and then lay down, watching me steadily all the time. I called out to Spooner, "Here are the lions I told you about," and he whipped up the ponies and in a moment or two was beside me with the tonga.

By this time I had seized my .303 and dismounted, so we at once commenced a cautious advance on the crouching lions, the arrangement being that Spooner was to take the right-hand one and I the other. We had got to within sixty yards' range without incident and were just about to sit down comfortably to "pot" them, when they suddenly surprised us by turning and bolting off. I managed, however, to put a bullet into the one I had marked just as he crested a bank, and he looked very grand as he reared up against the sky and clawed the air on feeling the lead. For a second or two he gave me the impression that he was about to charge; but luckily he changed his mind and followed his companion, who had so far escaped scot free. I immediately mounted "Blazeaway" and galloped off in hot pursuit, and after about half a mile of very stiff going got up with them once more. Finding now that they could not get away, they halted; came to bay and then charged down upon me, the wounded lion leading. I had left my rifle behind, so all I could do was to turn and fly as fast as "Blazeaway" could go, praying inwardly the while that he would not put his foot into a hole. When the lions saw that they were unable to overtake me, they gave up the chase and lay down again, the wounded one being about two hundred yards in front of the other. At once I pulled up too, and then went back a little way, keeping a careful eye upon them; and I continued these tactics of riding up and down at a respectful distance until Spooner came up with the rifles, when we renewed the attack.

As a first measure I thought it advisable to disable the unhurt lion if possible, and, still using the .303, I got him with the second shot at a range of about three hundred yards. He seemed badly hit, for he sprang into the air and apparently fell heavily. I then exchanged my .303 for Spooner's spare 12-bore rifle, and we turned our attention to the nearer lion, who all this time had been lying perfectly still, watching our movements closely, and evidently just waiting to be down upon us the moment we came within charging distance. He was never given this opportunity, however, for we did not approach nearer than ninety yards, when Spooner sat down comfortably and knocked him over quite dead with one shot from his .577, the bullet entering the left shoulder obliquely and passing through the heart.

It was now dusk, and there was no time to be lost if we meant to bag the second lion as well. We therefore resumed our cautious advance, moving to the right, as we went, so as to get behind us what light there was remaining. The lion of course twisted round in the grass in such a way as always to keep facing us, and looked very ferocious, so that I was convinced that unless he were entirely disabled by the first shot he would be down on us like a whirlwind. All the same, I felt confident that, even in this event, one of us would succeed in stopping him before he could do any damage; but in this I was unfortunately to be proved mistaken.

Eventually we managed to get within eighty yards of the enraged animal, I being about five yards to the left front of Spooner, who was followed by Bhoota at about the same distance to his right rear. By this time the lion was beside himself with fury, growling savagely and raising quite a cloud of dust by lashing his tail against the ground. It was clearly high time that we did something, so asking Spooner to fire, I dropped on one knee and waited. Nor was I kept long in suspense, for the moment Spooner's shot rang out, up jumped the lion and charged down in a bee-line for me, coming in long, low bounds at great speed. I fired the right barrel at about fifty yards, but apparently missed; the left at about half that range, still without stopping effect. I knew then that there was no time to reload, so remained kneeling, expecting him to be on me the next moment. Suddenly, just as he was within a bound of me, he made a quick turn, to my right. "Good heavens," I thought, "he is going for Spooner." I was wrong in this, however, for like a flash he passed Spooner also, and with a last tremendous bound seized Bhoota by the leg and rolled over and over with him for some yards in the impetus of the rush. Finally he stood over him and tried to seize him by the throat, which the brave fellow prevented by courageously stuffing his left arm right into the great jaws. Poor Bhoota! By moving at the critical moment, he had diverted the lion's attention from me and had drawn the whole fury of the charge on to himself.

All this, of course, happened in only a second or two. In the short instant that intervened, I felt a cartridge thrust into my hand by Spooner's plucky servant, Imam Din, who had carried the 12-bore all day and who had stuck to me gallantly throughout the charge; and shoving it in, I rushed as quickly as I could to Bhoota's rescue. Meanwhile, Spooner had got there before me and when I came up actually had his left hand on the lion's flank, in a vain attempt to push him off Bhoota's prostrate body and so get at the heavy rifle which the poor fellow still stoutly clutched. The lion, however, was so busily engaged mauling Bhoota's arm that he paid not the slightest attention to Spooner's efforts. Unfortunately, as he was facing straight in my direction, I had to move up in full view of him, and the moment I reached his head, he stopped chewing the arm, though still holding it in his mouth, and threw himself back on his haunches, preparing for a spring, at the same time curling back his lips and exposing his long tusks in a savage snarl. I knew then that I had not a moment to spare, so I threw the rifle up to my shoulder and pulled the trigger. Imagine my utter despair and horror when it did not go off! "Misfire again," I thought, and my heart almost stopped beating. As I took a step backwards, I felt it was all over now for he would never give me time to extract the cartridge and load again. Still I took another step backwards, keeping my eyes fixed on the lion's, which were blazing with rage; and in the middle of my third step, just as the brute was gathering himself for his spring, it suddenly struck me that in my haste and excitement, I had forgotten that I was using a borrowed rifle and had not pulled back the hammer (my own was hammerless). To do this and put a bullet through the lion's brain was then the work of a moment; and he fell dead instantly right on the top of Bhoota.

We did not lose a moment in rolling his great carcase off Bhoota's body and quickly forced open the jaws so as to disengage the mangled arm which still remained in his mouth. By this time the poor shikari was in a fainting condition, and we flew to the tonga for the brandy flask which we had so providentially brought with us. On making a rough examination of the wounded man, we found that his left arm and right leg were both frightfully mauled, the latter being broken as well. He was lifted tenderly into the tonga—how thankful we now were to have it with us!—and Spooner at once set off with him to camp and the doctor.

Before following them home I made a hasty examination of the dead lion and found him to be a very good specimen in every way. I was particularly satisfied to see that one of the two shots I had fired as he charged down upon me had taken effect. The bullet had entered below the right eye, and only just missed the brain. Unfortunately it was a steel one which Spooner had unluckily brought in his ammunition bag by mistake; still one would have thought that a shot of this kind, even with a hard bullet, would at least have checked the lion for the moment. As a matter of fact, however, it went clean through him without having the slightest stopping effect. My last bullet, which was of soft lead, had entered close to the right eye and embedded itself in the brain. By this time it had grown almost dark, so I left the two dead lions where they lay and rode for camp, which I was lucky enough to reach without further adventure or mishap. I may mention here that early next morning two other lions were found devouring the one we had first shot; but they had not had time to do much damage, and the head, which I have had mounted, makes a very fine trophy indeed. The lion that mauled Bhoota was untouched.

On my arrival in camp I found that everything that was possible was being done for poor Bhoota by Dr. McCulloch, the same who had travelled up with me to Tsavo and shot the ostrich from the train on my first arrival in the country, and who was luckily on the spot. His wounds had been skilfully dressed, the broken leg put in splints, and under the influence of a soothing draught the poor fellow was soon sleeping peacefully. At first we had great hope of saving both life and limb, and certainly for some days he seemed to be getting on as well as could be expected. The wounds, however, were very bad ones, especially those on the leg where the long tusks had met through and through the flesh, leaving over a dozen deep tooth marks; the arm, though dreadfully mauled, soon healed. It was wonderful to notice how cheerfully the old shikari bore it all, and a pleasure to listen to his tale of how he would have his revenge on the whole tribe of lions as soon as he was able to get about again. But alas, his shikar was over. The leg got rapidly worse, and mortification setting in, it had to be amputated half way up the thigh.

Dr. Winston Waters performed the operation most skilfully, and curiously enough the operating table was canopied with the skin of the lion which had been responsible for the injury. Bhoota made a good recovery from the operation, but seemed to lose heart when he found that he had only one leg left, as according to his ideas he had now but a poor chance of being allowed to enter Heaven. We did all that was possible for him, and Spooner especially could not have looked after a brother more tenderly; but to our great sorrow he sank gradually, and died on July 19.

The hunt which had such a disastrous sequel proved to be the last occasion on which I met a lion in the open, as we got out of the hunting country shortly afterwards and for the rest of my stay in East Africa I had too much work to do to be able to go any distance in search of big game.

Towards the end of my stay in British East Africa, I dined one evening with Mr. Ryall, the Superintendent of the Police, in his inspection carriage on the railway. Poor Ryall! I little thought then what a terrible fate was to overtake him only a few months later in that very carriage in which we dined.

A man-eating lion had taken up his quarters at a little roadside station called Kimaa, and had developed an extraordinary taste for the members of the railway staff. He was a most daring brute, quite indifferent as to whether he carried off the station-master, the signalman, or the pointsman; and one night, in his efforts to obtain a meal, he actually climbed up on to the roof of the station buildings and tried to tear off the corrugated-iron sheets. At this the terrified baboo in charge of the telegraph instrument below sent the following laconic message to the Traffic Manager: "Lion fighting with station. Send urgent succour." Fortunately he was not victorious in his "fight with the station"; but he tried so hard to get in that he cut his feet badly on the iron sheeting, leaving

large blood-stains on the roof. Another night, however, he succeeded in carrying off the native driver of the pumping-engine,
and soon afterwards added several other victims to his list. On one
occasion an engine-driver arranged to sit up all night in a large
iron water-tank in the hope of getting a shot at him, and had a
loop-hole cut in the side of the tank from which to fire. But as
so often happens, the hunter became the hunted; the lion turned
up in the middle of the night, overthrew the tank and actually
tried to drag the driver out through the narrow circular hole in
the top through which he had squeezed in. Fortunately the tank
was just too deep for the brute to be able to reach the man at the
bottom; but the latter was naturally half paralysed with fear and
had to crouch so low down as to be unable to take anything like
proper aim. He fired, however, and succeeded in frightening the
lion away for the time being.

It was in a vain attempt to destroy this pest that poor Ryall
met his tragic and untimely end. On June 6, 1900, he was travelling up in his inspection carriage from Makindu to Nairobi,
accompanied by two friends, Mr. Huebner and Mr. Parenti. When
they reached Kimaa, which is about two hundred and fifty miles
from Mombasa, they were told that the man-eater had been seen
close to the station only a short time before their train arrived, so
they at once made up their minds to remain there for the night
and endeavour to shoot him. Ryall's carriage was accordingly
detached from the train and shunted into a siding close to the
station, where, owing to the unfinished state of the line, it did
not stand perfectly level, but had a pronounced list to one side. In
the afternoon the three friends went out to look for the lion, but,
finding no traces of him whatever, they returned to the carriage
for dinner. Afterwards they all sat up on guard for some time;
but the only noticeable thing they saw was what they took to be
two very bright and steady glow-worms. After-events proved that
these could have been nothing else than the eyes of the man-
eater steadily watching them all the time and studying their every

movement. The hour now growing late, and there being apparently no sign of the lion, Ryall persuaded his two friends to lie down, while he kept the first watch. Huebner occupied the high berth over the table on the one side of the carriage, the only other berth being on the opposite side of the compartment and lower down. This Ryall offered to Parenti, who declined it, saying that he would be quite comfortable on the floor and he accordingly lay down to sleep, with his feet towards the sliding door which gave admission the carriage.

It is supposed that Ryall, after watching for some considerable time, must have come to the conclusion that the lion was not going to make its appearance that night, for he lay down on the lower berth and dozed off. No sooner had he done so, doubtless, than the cunning man-eater began cautiously to stalk the three sleepers. In order to reach the little platform at the end of the carriage, he had to mount two very high steps from the railway line, but these he managed to negotiate successfully and in silence. The door from this platform into the carriage was a sliding one on wheels, which ran very easily on a brass runner; and as it was probably not quite shut, or at any rate not secured in any way, it was an easy matter for the lion to thrust in a paw and shove it open. But owing to the tilt of the carriage and to his great extra weight on the one side, the door slid to and snapped into the lock the moment he got his body right in, thus leaving him shut up with the three sleeping men in the compartment.

He sprang at once at Ryall, but in order to reach him had actually to plant his feet on Parenti, who, it will be remembered, was sleeping on the floor. At this moment Huebner was suddenly awakened by a loud cry, and on looking down from his berth was horrified to see an enormous lion standing with his hind feet on Parenti's body, while his forepaws rested on poor Ryall. Small wonder that he was panic-stricken at the sight. There was only one possible way of escape, and that was through the second sliding door communicating with the servants' quarters, which was opposite to that by which the lion had entered. But in order to reach this door Huebner had literally to jump on to the man-eater's back, for its great bulk filled up all the space beneath his berth. It sounds scarcely credible, but it appears that in the excitement and horror of the moment he actually did this, and fortunately the lion was too busily engaged with his victim to pay any attention to him. So he managed to reach the door in safety; but there, to his dismay, he found that it was held fast on the other side by the terrified coolies, who had been aroused by the disturbance caused by the lion's entrance. In utter desperation he made frantic efforts to open it, and exerting all his strength at last managed to pull it back sufficiently far to allow him to squeeze through, when the trembling coolies instantly tied it up again with their turbans. A moment afterwards a great crash was heard, and the whole carriage lurched violently to one side; the lion had broken through one of the windows, carrying off poor Ryall with him. Being now released, Parenti lost no time in jumping through the window on the opposite side of the carriage, and fled for refuge to one of the station buildings; his escape was little short of miraculous, as the lion had been actually standing on him as he lay on the floor. The carriage itself was badly shattered, and the wood-work of the window had been broken to pieces by the passage of the lion as he sprang through with his victim in his mouth.

All that can be hoped is that poor Ryall's death was instantaneous. His remains were found next morning about a quarter of a mile away in the bush, and were taken to Nairobi for burial. I am glad to be able to add that very shortly afterwards the terrible brute who was responsible for this awful tragedy was caught in an ingenious trap constructed by one of the railway staff. He was kept on view for several days, and then shot.

The Road to Tinkhamtown
by Corey Ford

IF YOU OWN A COPY OF THE JUNE 1970 ISSUE OF *FIELD & STREAM* magazine, consider yourself lucky. That was the seventy-fifth anniversary issue, a fine thing. But that's not the reason that issue was so precious. Illustrated with a painting by Howard Terpning, Corey Ford's story "The Road to Tinkhamtown" makes that issue a classic. A blurb written by the editors and displayed on the pages tells the story: "This story by the late Corey Ford, here published for the first time anywhere, is a moving tale which will not soon be forgotten. It is for all those who mourned his death that we present this farewell from the creator of 'The Lower Forty.'" A few months after he wrote this story in 1969, Ford passed away. He never saw "Tinkhamtown" in print. Ford's stories and his "Lower Forty" column were *Field & Stream* favorites. His setters provided the background of many of his tales. "Tinkhamtown" was his masterpiece, written in the evening of his life, written with skill and love, a dog story unlike any other. More than any story I know, this one brings to mind the great William Faulkner quote: "The past is never dead. It's not even past."

* * *

It was a long way, but he knew where he was going. He would follow the road through the woods and over the crest of a hill and down the hill to the stream, and cross the sagging timbers of the bridge, and on the other side would be the place called Tinkhamtown. He was going back to Tinkhamtown.

He walked slowly at first, his legs dragging with each step. He had not walked for almost a year, and his flanks had shriveled and wasted away from lying in bed so long; he could fit his fingers around his thigh, Doc Towle had said he would never walk again, but that was Doc for you, always on the pessimistic side. Why, now he was walking quite easily, once he had started. The strength was coming back into his legs, and he did not have to stop for breath so often. He tried jogging a few steps, just to show he could, but he slowed again because he had a long way to go.

It was hard to make out the old road, choked with alders and covered by matted leaves, and he shut his eyes so he could see it better. He could always see it when he shut his eyes. Yes, here was the beaver dam on the right, just as he remembered it, and the flooded stretch where he had picked his way from hummock to hummock while the dog splashed unconcernedly in front of him. The water had been over his boot tops in one place, and sure enough, as he waded it now his left boot filled with water again, the same warm squidgy feeling. Everything was the way it had been that afternoon, nothing had changed in ten years. Here was the blowdown across the road that he had clambered over, and here on a knoll was the clump of thorn apples where a grouse had flushed as they passed. Shad had wanted to look for it, but he had whistled him back. They were looking for Tinkhamtown.

He had come across the name on a map in the town library. He used to study the old maps and survey charts of the state; sometimes they showed where a farming community had flourished, a century ago, and around the abandoned pastures and in the orchards grown up to pine, the birds would be feeding undisturbed. Some of his best grouse covers had been located that way.

The map had been rolled up in a cardboard cylinder; it crackled with age as he spread it out. The date was 1857. It was the sector between Cardigan and Kearsarge Mountains, a wasteland of slash and second-growth timber without habitation today, but evidently it had supported a number of families before the Civil War. A road was marked on the map, dotted with Xs for homesteads, and the names of the owners were lettered beside them: Nason J. Tinkham, Allard R. Tinkham. Half the names were Tinkham In the center of the map—the paper was so yellow that he could barely make it out—was the word "Tinkhamtown."

He had a drawn a rough sketch on the back of an envelope, noting where the road left the highway and ran north to a fork and then turned east and crossed a stream that was not even named; and the next morning he and Shad had set out together to find the place. They could not drive very far in the jeep, because washouts had gutted the roadbed and laid bare the ledges and boulders. He had stuffed the sketch in his hunting-coat pocket, and hung his shotgun over his forearm and started walking, the setter trotting ahead with the bell on his collar tinkling. It was an old-fashioned sleigh bell, and it had a thin silvery note that echoed through the woods like peepers in the spring. He could follow the sound in the thickest cover, and when it stopped he would go to where he heard it last and Shad would be on point. After Shad's death, he had put the bell away. He'd never had another dog.

It was silent in the woods without the bell, and the way was longer than he remembered. He should have come to the big hill by now. Maybe he'd taken the wrong turn back at the fork. He thrust a hand into his hunting coat; the envelope with the sketch was still in the pocket. He sat down on a flat rock to get his bearings, and then he realized, with a surge of excitement, that he had stopped on this very rock for lunch ten years ago. Here was the waxed paper from his sandwich, tucked in a crevice, and here was the hollow in the leaves where Shad had stretched out beside him, the dog's soft muzzle flattened on his thigh. He looked up, and through the trees he could see the hill.

He rose and started walking again, carrying his shotgun. He had left the gun standing in its rack in the kitchen when he had been taken to the state hospital, but now it was hooked over his arm by the trigger guard; he could feel the solid heft of it. The woods grew more dense as he climbed, but here and there a shaft of sunlight slanted through the trees. "And there were forests ancient as the hills," he thought "enfolding sunny spots of greenery." Funny that should come back to him now; he hadn't read it since he was a boy. Other things were coming back to him, the smell of dank leaves and sweetfern and frosted apples, the sharp contrast of sub and cool shade, the November stillness before snow. He walked faster feeling the excitement swell within him.

He paused on the crest of the hill, straining his ears for the faint mutter of the stream below him, but he could not hear it because of the voices. He wished they would stop talking, so he could hear the stream. Someone was saying his name over and over, "Frank, Frank," and he opened his eyes reluctantly and worried, and there was nothing to worry about. He tried to tell her where he was going, but when he moved his lips the words would not form. "What did you say, Frank?" she asked, bending her head lower. "I don't understand." He couldn't make the words any clearer, and she straightened and said to Doc Towle: "It sounded like Tinkhamtown."

"Tinkhamtown?" Doc shook his head, "Never heard him mention any place by that name."

He smiled to himself. Of course he'd never mentioned it to Doc. Things like a secret grouse cover you didn't mention to anyone, not even to as close a friend as Doc was. No, he and Shad were the only ones who knew. They found it together, that long ago afternoon, and it was their secret.

They had come to the stream—he shut his eyes so he could see it again—and Shad had trotted across the bridge. He had followed more cautiously, avoiding the loose planks and walking along a beam with his shotgun held out to balance himself. On the other side of the stream the road mounted steeply to a clearing in the woods, and he halted before the split-stone foundations of a house, the first of the series of farms shown on the map. It must have been a long time since the building had fallen in; the cottonwoods growing in the cellar hole were twenty, maybe thirty years old. His boot overturned a rusted axe blade, and the handle of a china cup in the grass; that was all. Beside the doorstep was a lilac bush, almost as tall as the cottonwoods. He thought of the wife who had set it out, a little shrub then, and the husband who had chided her for wasting time on such frivolous things with all the farmwork to be done. But the work had come to nothing, and still the lilac bloomed each spring, the one thing that had survived.

Shad's bell was moving along the stone wall at the edge of the clearing, and he strolled after him, not hunting, wondering about the people who had gone away and left their walls to crumble and their buildings to collapse under the winter snows. Had they ever come back to Tinkhamtown? Were they here now, watching him unseen? His toe stubbed against a block of hewn granite hidden by briers, part of the sill of the old barn. Once it had been a tight barn, warm with cattle steaming in their stalls, rich with the blend of hay and manure and harness leather. He liked to think of it the way it was; it was more real than this bare rectangle of blocks and the emptiness inside. He'd always felt that way about the past. Doc used to argue that what's over is over, but he would insist Doc was wrong. Everything is the way it was, he'd tell Doc. The past never changes. You leave it and go on to the present, but it is still there, waiting for you to come back to it.

He had been so wrapped in his thoughts that he had not realized Shad's bell had stopped. He hurried across the clearing holding his gun ready. In a corner of the stone wall an ancient apple tree had littered the ground with fallen fruit, and beneath it Shad was standing motionless. The white fan of his tail was lifted a little and his backline was level, the neck craned forward, one foreleg cocked. His flanks were trembling with the nearness of grouse, and a thin skein of drool hung from his jowls. The dog did not move as he approached, but the brown eyes rolled back until their whites showed, looking for him. "Steady, boy," he called. His throat was tight, the way it always got when Shad was on point, and he had to swallow hard, "Steady, I'm coming."

"I think his lips moved just now," his sister's voice said. He did not open his eyes, because he was waiting for the grouse to get up in front of Shad, but he knew Doc Towle was looking at him. "He's sleeping," Doc said after a moment. "Maybe you better get some sleep yourself, Mrs. Duncombe." He heard Doc's heavy footsteps cross the room. "Call me if there's any change," Doc said, and closed the door, and in the silence he could hear his sister's chair creaking beside him, her silk dress rustling regularly as she breathed.

What was she doing here, he wondered. Why had she come all the way from California to see him? It was the first time they had seen each other since she had married and moved out West. She was his only relative, but they had never been very close; they had nothing in common, really. He heard from her now and then, but it was always the same letter: Why didn't he sell the old place, it was too big for him now that the folks had passed on, why didn't he take a small apartment in town where he wouldn't be alone? But he liked the big house, and he wasn't alone, not with Shad. He had closed off all the other rooms and moved into the kitchen so everything would be handy. His sister didn't approve of his bachelor ways, but it was very comfortable with his cot by the stove and Shad curled on the floor near him at night, whinnying and scratching the linoleum with his claws as he chased a bird in a dream. He wasn't alone when he heard that.

He had never married. He had looked after the folks as long as they lived; maybe that was why. Shad was a family. They were always together—Shad was short for Shadow—and there was a closeness between them that he did not feel for anyone else, not his sister or Doc even. He and Shad used to talk without words, each knowing what the other was thinking, and they could always find one another in the woods. He still remembered the little things about him: the possessive thrust of his jaw, the way he false-yawned when he was vexed, the setter stubbornness sometimes, the clownish grin when they were going hunting, the kind eyes. That was it: Shad was the kindest person he had ever known.

They had not hunted again after Tinkhamtown. The old dog had stumbled several times, walking back to the jeep, and he had to carry him in his arms the last hundred yards. It was hard to realize he was gone. He liked to think of him the way he was; it was like the barn, it was more real than the emptiness. Sometimes at night, lying awake with the pain in his legs, he would hear the scratch of claws on the linoleum, and he would turn on the light and the hospital room would be empty. But when he turned the light off he would hear the scratching again, and he would be content and drop off to sleep, or what passed for sleep in these days and nights that ran together without dusk or dawn.

Once he asked Doc point-blank if he would ever get well. Doc was giving him something for the pain, and he hesitated a moment and finished what he was doing and cleaned the needle and then looked at him and said: "I'm afraid not, Frank." They had grown up in the town together, and Doc knew him too well to lie. "I'm afraid there's nothing to do." Nothing to do but lie there and wait till it was over. "Tell me, Doc," he whispered, for his voice wasn't very strong, "what happens when it's over?" And Doc fumbled with the catch of his black bag and closed it and said well he supposed you went on to someplace else called the Hereafter. But he shook his head: He always argued with Doc. "No, it isn't someplace else," he told him, "it's someplace you've been where you want to be again." Doc didn't understand, and he couldn't explain it any better. He knew what he meant, but the shot was taking effect and he was tired.

He was tired now, and his legs ached a little as he started down the hill, trying to find the stream. It was too dark under the trees to see the sketch he had drawn, and he could not tell direction by the moss on the north side of the trunks. The moss grew all around them, swelling them out of size, and huge blowdowns blocked his way. Their upended roots were black and misshapen, and now instead of excitement he felt a surge of panic. He floundered through a pile of slash, his legs throbbing with pain as the sharp points stabbed him, but he did not have the strength to get to the other side and he had to back out again and circle. He did not know where he was going. It was getting late, and he had lost the way.

There was no sound in the woods, nothing to guide him, nothing but his sister's chair creaking and her breath catching now and then in a dry sob. She wanted him to turn back, and Doc wanted him to, they all wanted him to turn back. He thought of the big house; if he left it alone it would fall in with the winter snows and cottonwoods would grow in the cellar hole. And there were all the other doubts, but most of all there was the fear. He was afraid of the darkness, and being alone, and not knowing where he was going. It would be better to turn around and go back. He knew the way back.

And then he heard it, echoing through the woods like peepers in the spring, the thin silvery tinkle of a sleigh bell. He started running toward it, following the sound down the hill. His legs were strong again, and he hurdled the blowdowns, he leapt over fallen logs, he put one fingertip on a pile of slash and sailed over it like a grouse skimming. He was getting nearer and the sound filled his ears, louder than a thousand church bells ringing, louder than all the choirs in the sky, as loud as the pounding of his heart. The fear was gone; he was not lost. He had the bell to guide him now.

He came to the stream, and paused for a moment at the bridge. He wanted to tell them he was happy, if they only knew how happy he was, but when he opened his eyes he could not see them anymore. Everything else was bright, but the room was dark.

The bell had stopped and he looked across the stream. The other side was bathed in sunshine, and he could see the road mounting steeply, and the clearing in the woods, and the apple tree in a corner of the stone wall. Shad was standing motionless beneath it, the white fan of his tail lifted, his neck craned forward and one foreleg cocked. The whites of his eyes showed as he looked back, waiting for him.

"Steady," he called, "steady, boy." He started across the bridge. "I'm coming."

Tracks to Remember

by Tom Hennessey

THE LATE TOM HENNESSEY, OUTDOOR COLUMNIST FOR THE *Bangor Daily News*, wrote memorable pieces appreciated by Maine readers for many years. "Tracks to Remember" is a little gem of a whitetail hunting story and is one of the pieces collected in Tom's book *Feathers 'n Fins*, published by Amwell Press in 1989. Tom's talent does not end with his writing. He was an artist whose paintings, prints, and drawings were eagerly sought by collectors.

* * *

Steeple-like spruces were silhouetted against a sky of gunmetal gray as Hank Lyons slipped five 170-grain cartridges into the magazine of his .30–30 carbine. Fully loaded, the magazine held six of the flat-nosed .30s. Somewhere long ago—probably because he liked the lines, angles, and curve of its configuration—Hank had decided that five was his lucky number. With a flip of the lever action he chambered a round, then eased the cocked hammer onto the safety position. At a brisk pace, he began hiking the grown-up tote road that would cross a brook about a mile into the woods. You'd have thought it was springtime. Two days earlier, Ol' Man Winter had thrown one of his white-with-rage tantrums.

Shortly thereafter, he began running a temperature and now the woods were shrouded with ground fog. Every bough and branch wore beads of moisture. Arriving at the brook, Hank wasn't surprised to see that the log bridge had partially collapsed under the constant weight of time. The makeshift span had been old when, years before, he first crossed it while bird hunting. A short distance beyond the brook, several sets of deer tracks crisscrossed the road. "Does," Hank allowed. "At least a couple. Maybe a fawn with 'em—got to be a buck around somewhere." The tracks indicated that deer were using the mixed growth to the left of the road, and a fir thicket to the right. The mixed growth climbed a knoll whose top was crowned with apple trees glowing with "golden nuggets." Quietly, Hank worked his way up the slope until he had a commanding view of the area. "As good as any and better than most," he said as he brushed the snow from a wind-toppled spruce. Sitting among the boughs, he checked the hammer of the carbine. Hank Lyons could sit all day in a duck blind, but he found it difficult to stay anchored for more than an hour on a deer stand. For that reason he had waited until afternoon to enter the woods. Within an hour and a half at the most, dusk would demand his departure. Along the ice-rimmed brook, the ground fog was more concentrated. Thickening and thinning, it swirled like ghosts rising from snow-covered crypts. Directly across from where Hank was sitting—about sixty yards away—a leaning birch opened a white gash in the gray-green timber. Slightly to the right of the birch squatted the stub of what was once an immense pine. Now and then, the ground fog became so cottony that those objects were momentarily obscured from Hank's view. The wind must have been weary—it never so much as sighed in the tops of the spruces. "There ain't no sense in sittin' out a deer," Hank had been told early on, "if you can't sit still." That much he had learned. Any movement he made was slower than a Southern drawl. The carbine was cradled across his lap. Slush slid off a bough and stabbed coldly down his neck. Hurry up and wait. A drizzle that came close to rain began falling and water colored the woods a shade darker. It seemed that Hank watched the second-hand of his watch sweep the next half hour away. He had about convinced himself that he was wasting his time when he saw a flicker of movement. Near the tote road, the tip of a fir bough nodded. An instant later a dark-furred animal made a swift crossing and disappeared into the fir thicket. "Fisher," Hank observed. "Probably squirrel hunting. He'll do a hell of a lot better than I will." Again he glanced at his watch. Again he slowly scanned the steamy surroundings.

When his eyeballs locked up, he felt it all the way down to his toes. Squarely in front of the pine stub stood a deer—wearing horns. Just like that. No sight. No sound. Just there. When it comes to quiet, they'd put a shadow to shame. In a situation like that, it takes a second or so to sort things out. From its coiled-tight posture, Hank knew this was no young buck blinded by doe scent, and there was no mistaking that the eight-pointer sensed his presence. Statue-still, and with a tautness almost tangible, hunter and hunted stared.

"If I make a wrong move," Hank thought, "his mainspring will unwind all at once." Directly the buck eased his nose forward, slowly lowered his head and turned it to one side—like a bird dog sifting scent. Hank's thumb cocked the hammer of the carbine. To him, the muffled click sounded like a rock being dropped through shell ice. Taking a step backward, the buck blew. "Please, God." So slowly it was painful, Hank began lifting the carbine from his lap. To his left—thicker than smoke from a smudge—a bank of fog was following the brook. Like a curtain of white being drawn across a dimly lit stage, it drifted between them, obliterating the buck from Hank's view. Seizing the opportunity, he snapped the carbine to his shoulder, snugged his cheek onto the stock, and squinted through the drizzle-fuzzed sights. Long moments later, the birch leaned. "Right . . . about . . . " The pine stub squatted. Shocked, Hank lifted his head and stared into the dripping, dusky woods. No antlers. No ears. No rut-swollen neck. Not to be outdone, the woods-wise buck also had taken advantage of the well-timed "smoke screen." Springing to his feet, Hank searched for movement. Not a sign. Hoping for a last-chance shot, he hurried down the slope and crossed the brook. Locating the buck's tracks, he followed them. The wary whitetail had exited through the same door he used for his entrance. In the woods, dusk means darkness. Disappointed as he was, Hank, with a steamy expulsion of breath, conceded, "Just as well. If I wounded him I wouldn't have had time to trail him, and it's a pretty good bet the coyotes would catch up with him during the night—just as well." If you've never been in the woods on a wet November night, then you don't know the meaning of darkness. Hank's spirits were brightened, however, and his strides lengthened as he recalled the words of a now-departed deer hunter: "You'll soon forget the ones you drag out," his grandfather had said, "but the ones that outfox you will leave tracks on your mind."

Hunting the Arctic

by Caspar Whitney

HUNTING IN THE EXTREME NORTHERN REACHES OF THE ARCTIC demands the ultimate in skill and luck. In the pioneering years of such hunting in the early 1900s, failure could mean certain death.

* * *

We had passed through the "Land of Little Sticks," as the Indians so appropriately call that desolate waste which connects the edge of timber land with the Barren Grounds, and had been for several days making our way north on the lookout for any living thing that would provide us with a mouthful of food.

We had got into one of those pieces of this great barren area, which, broken by rocky ridges, of no great height but of frequent occurrence, are unspeakably harassing to the travelling snow-shoer. It was the third twelve hours of our fast, save for tea and the pipe, and all day we had been dragging ourselves wearily up one ridge and down another in the ever recurring and always disappointed hope that on each we should sight caribou or musk-oxen. The Indians were discouraged and sullen, as they usually did become on such occasions; and this troubled me really more than not finding food, for I was in constant dread of their growing disheartened and turning back to the woods. That was the possibility which, since the very starting day, had at all times and most seriously menaced the success of my venture; because we were pushing on in the early part of March, at a time when the storms are at their greatest severity, and when none had ever before ventured into the Barren Grounds. Therefore, in my fear lest the Indians turn back, I sought to make light of our difficulties by breaking into song when we stopped to "spell" our dogs, hoping by my assumed light-heartedness to shame the Indians out of showing their desire to turn homeward.

How much I felt like singing may be imagined.

So the day dragged on without sight of a moving creature, not even a fox, and it was past noon when we laboriously worked our way up one particular ridge which seemed to have an unusual amount of unnecessary and ragged rock strewn over its surface. I remember we scarcely ventured to look into the white silent country that stretched in front of us; disappointment had rewarded our long searchings so often that we had somehow come to accept it as a matter of course. Squatting down back of the sledge in shelter from the wind seemed of more immediate concern than looking ahead for meat: at least we were sure of the solace our pipes gave. Thus we smoked in silence, with no sign of interest in what the immediate country ahead might hold for us, until Beniah, the leader of my Indians, and an unusually good one, started to his feet with an exclamation and, hurriedly climbing on top a good-sized rock, stretched his arm ahead, obviously much stirred with excitement. He shouted, once and loud, "*ethan*," and then continued mumbling it as though to make his tongue sure of what his eyes beheld. We all gathered around him, climbing his rock or on other ones, in desperate earnestness to see what he saw in the direction he continued pointing. It was minutes before I could discern anything having life in the distance which reached away to the horizon all white and silent, and then I detected a kind of vapor arising apparently from some dark objects blurringly outlined against the snow about four miles away; it was the mist which arises from a herd of animals where the mercury is ranging between sixty and seventy degrees below zero, and on a clear day may be seen five miles away. Thoroughly aroused now, I got my field-glasses from my sledge and searched the dark objects under the mist. They were not caribou, of that I was certain; as to what they were I was equally uncertain, for the forms were strange to my eye. So I handed the glasses to Beniah, saying, "*ethan illa.*" Beniah took the glasses, but as it was the first time he had ever looked through a pair, their range and power seemed to excite him quite as much as did the appearance of the game itself. When he did find his tongue, he fairly shouted, "*ejerri.*" I had no accurate knowledge of what "*ejerri*" meant, but assumed we had sighted musk-oxen. Instantly all was excitement. The Indians set up a yell and rushed for their sledges, jabbering and laughing. It seemed incredible that these were the same men who so shortly before had sat silent with backs to the wind, dejected and indifferent.

Every one now busied himself turning loose his dogs,—a small matter for the Indians, with their simply sewn harness from which the dogs were easily slipped, but a rather complex job for me. My dog train had come from the Post, and its harness was made of buckles and straps and things not easily undone in freezing weather; so it happened that by the time my dogs were unhitched, the Indians and all their dogs were fully quarter of a mile nearer the musk-oxen than I and running for very dear life. My preconceived notions of the musk-ox hunting game were in a jiffy jolted to the point of destruction, as I now found myself in a situation neither expected nor joyful. It was natural to suppose some assistance would be given me in this strange environment, and that the consideration of a party of my own organizing and my own paying should be my killing the musk-ox for which I had come so long a distance. But we were a long way from the Post and interpreters and restraining influences; and at this moment of readjustment I speedily realized that it was to be a survival of the fittest on this expedition, and if I got a musk-ox it would be of my own getting. It comforted me to know that, even though somewhat tucked up as to stomach, due to three days' hard travel on only tea, I was in fine physical condition, and up to making the effort of my life.

By the time I had run about two miles I had caught the last of the Indians, who were stretched out in a long column, with two leading by half a mile. Within another mile I had passed all the stragglers, and was running practically even with the second Indian, who was two or three hundred yards behind the leading one. This Indian, Seco by name, was one of the best snow-shoe runners I ever encountered. He gave evidence of his endurance and speed on many another occasion than this one, for always there was a run of four miles or more after every musk-ox herd we sighted, and invariably a foot-race between Seco and me preceded final leadership. I may add incidentally that he always beat me, although we made some close finishes during the fifty-seven days we roamed this God-forgotten bit of the earth.

On this particular day, though I passed the second Indian, Seco kept well in the lead, with practically all the dogs just ahead of him. It was the roughest going I had ever experienced, for the course lay over a succession of low but sharp, rocky ridges covered with about a foot of snow, and, on the narrow tripping shoes used in the Barren Grounds, I broke through the crust where it was soft, or jammed my shoes between the wind-swept rocks that lay close together, or caught in those I attempted to clear in my stride. It was a species of hurdle racing to test the bottom of a well-fed, conditioned athlete; how it wore on a tea diet I need not say.

After we had been running for about an hour, it seemed to me as though we should never see the musk-oxen. Ridge after ridge we crossed and yet not a sight of the coveted quarry. Seco still held a lead of about one hundred yards, and I remember I wondered in my growing fatigue why on earth that Indian maintained such a pace, for I could not help feeling that when the musk-oxen finally had been caught up, he would stop until I, and all the Indians and all the dogs had come up, so as to more certainly assure the success of the hunt: but it was not the first time I had been with Indian hunters, and I knew well enough not to take any chances.

In another half hour's running, as I worked up the near side of a rather higher and broader ridge than any we had crossed, I heard the dogs barking, and speeding to the top, what was my disappointment, not to say distress, at beholding twenty-five to thirty musk-oxen just startled into running along a ridge about a quarter of a mile beyond Seco, who, with his dogs, was in full chase after them about fifty yards ahead of me. What I thought at that time of the Northland Indian hunting methods, and of Seco and all my other Indians in particular, did the situation and my condition of mind scant justice then—and would not make goodly reading here. Had I been on an ordinary hunting expedition, disgust with the whole fool business would, I doubt not, have been paramount, but the thought of the distance I had come and the privations undergone for no other reason than to get a musk-ox, made me the more determined to succeed despite obstacles of any and all kinds. So I went on. The wind was blowing a gale from the south when I reached the top of the ridge along which I had seen the musk-oxen run, and the main herd had disappeared over the northern end of it, and were a mile away to the north, travelling with heads carried well out, though not lowered, at an astonishing pace and ease over the rocks. Four had separated from the main body and were going almost due east on the south side of the ridge. I determined to stalk these four, because I could keep the north side of the ridge, out of sight, and to leeward, feeling certain they would sooner or later turn north to rejoin the main herd. It seemed my best chance. I perfectly realized the risk I ran in separating from the Indians; but at that moment nothing appeared so important as getting a musk-ox, for which I had now travelled nearly twelve hundred miles on snowshoes.

I have done a deal of hunting in my life, over widely separated and trackless sections, and had my full share of hard trips; but never shall I forget the run along that ridge. It called for more heart and more strength than any situation I ever faced. Already I had run, I suppose, about five miles when I started after those four musk-oxen; and when the first enthusiasm had passed, it seemed as though I must give it up. Such fatigue I had never dreamed of. I have no idea how much farther I ran,—three or four more miles, likely,—but I do remember that after a time the fancy possessed me that those four musk-oxen and I were alone on earth, that they knew I was after their heads, and were luring me deep into a strange land to lose me; thus in the great silent land we raced grimly, with death trailing the steps of each. The dead-white surface reaching out before me without ending seemed to rise and to fall as though I travelled a rocking ship; and the snow and the rocks danced around my whirling head in a grinning, glistening maze. When I fell, which frequently I did, it seemed such a long time before I again stood on my feet; and what I saw appeared as though seen through the small end of field-glasses.

I was in a dripping perspiration and had dropped my fur capote and cartridge-belt after thrusting half a dozen shells into my pocket. On and on I ran, wondering in a semi-dazed way if the musk-oxen were really on the other side of the ridge. Finally the ridge took a sharp turn to the north, and as I reached the top of it, there—about one hundred yards ahead—were two of the musk-oxen running slowly but directly from me. Instantly the blood coursed through my veins and the mist cleared from my eyes; dropping on one knee I swung my rifle into position, but my hand was so tremulous and my heart thumped so heavily that the front sight wobbled all over the horizon. I realized that this might be the only shot I should get,—for Indians had gone into the Barren Grounds in more propitious seasons, and not seen even one herd,—yet with the musk-oxen going away from me all the while, every instant of time seemed an insuperable age. The agony of those few seconds I waited so as to steady my hand! Once or twice I made another attempt to aim, but still the hand was too uncertain. I did not dare risk a shot. When I had rested a minute or two, that seemed fully half an hour,—at last the fore sight held true for an instant; and I pressed the trigger.

The exultation of that moment when I saw one of the two musk-oxen stagger, and then fall, I know I shall never again experience.

The report of my rifle startled the other musk-ox into a wild gallop over a ridge, and I followed as rapidly as I could, so soon as I made sure that the other was really down. As I went over the ridge I caught sight of the remaining musk-ox, and shot simultaneously with two reports on my left, which I later discovered to have come from the second Indian whom I had passed in closing upon Seco on the run to the first view of the musk-oxen, and who now hove in sight with one dog, as the second musk-ox dropped.

I found on returning to my kill that it was a cow, needless to say a sore disappointment; and so, although pretty well tuckered out, I again started to the north in the hope that I might get wind of the other two of the four after which I had originally started, or find tracks of stragglers from the main herd. Several miles I went on, but finding no tracks, and darkness coming down, I turned to make my way back, knowing that the Indians would follow up and camp by the slain musk-oxen for the night. But as I journeyed I suddenly realized that, except for going in a southerly direction, I really had no definite idea of the exact direction in which I was travelling, and with night setting in and a chilling wind blowing I knew that to lose myself might easily mean death. So I turned about on my tracks and followed them back first to where I had turned south, and thence on my back tracks to where the muskox lay. It was a long and puzzling task, for the wind had always partly, and for distances entirely, obliterated the earlier marks of my snowshoes.

Nine o'clock came before I finally reached the place where the dead quarry lay; and there I found the Indians gnawing on raw and half-frozen musk-ox fat. Seco, badly frozen and hardly able to crawl from fatigue, did not turn up until midnight; and it was not until he arrived that we lighted our little fire of sticks and had our tea.

Then in a sixty-seven degrees below zero temperature we rolled up in our furs, while the dogs howled and fought over the carcass of my first musk-ox.

Except in the summer, when the caribou are running in vast herds, venture into the Barren Grounds entails a struggle with both cold and hunger. It is either a feast or a famine; more frequently the latter than the former. So there was nothing extraordinary in being upon our third day without food at the first musk-ox killing to which I have referred. Yet the lack of nourishment was not perhaps as trying as the wind, which seemed to sweep directly from the frozen seas, so strong that we had to bend low in pushing forward against it, and so bitter as to cut our faces cruelly. Throughout my journey into this silent land of the lone North the wind caused me more real suffering than the semi-starvation state in which we were more or less continuously. Indeed, for the first few weeks I had utmost difficulty in travelling; the wind appeared to take the very breath out of my body and the activity out of my muscles. I was physically in magnificent shape, for I had spent a couple of weeks at Fort Resolution, on Great Slave Lake, and what with plenty of caribou meat and a daily run of from ten to twenty miles on snowshoes by way of keeping in training, I was about as fit as I have been at any time in my life. Therefore the severe struggle with the wind impressed me the more. But the novelty wore off in a couple of weeks, and though the conditions were always trying, they became more endurable as I grew accustomed to the daily combat.

One of the first lessons I learned was to keep my face free from covering, and also as clean shaven as was possible under such circumstances. It makes me smile now to remember the elaborate hood arrangement which was knitted for me in Canada, and that then seemed to me one of the most important articles of my equipment. It covered the entire head, ears, and neck, with openings only for eyes and mouth, and in town I had viewed it as a great find; but I threw it away before I got within a thousand miles of the Barren Grounds. The reason is obvious: my breath turned the front of the hood into a sheet of ice before I had run three miles; and as there was no fire in the Barren Grounds to thaw it, of course it was an impossible thing to wear in that region and a poor thing in any region of low temperature. After other experiments, I found the simplest and most comfortable headgear to be my own long hair, which hung even with my jaw, bound about just above the ears by a handkerchief, and the open hood of my caribou-skin capote drawn forward overall.

It is well known, I suppose, that the Barren Grounds are devoid absolutely not only of trees but even of brush, except for some scattered, stunted bushes that in summer are to be found in occasional spots at the water's edge, but may not be depended upon for fuel. From Great Slave Lake north to the timber's edge is about three hundred miles; beyond that is a stretch of country perhaps of another hundred miles, suggestively called the Land of Little Sticks by the Indians, over which are scattered and widely separated little patches of small pine, sometimes of an acre in extent, sometimes a little less and sometimes a little more. They seem to be a chain of wooded islands in this desert that connect the main timber line (which, by the way, does not end abruptly, but straggles out for many miles, growing thinner and thinner until it ends, and the Land of Little Sticks begins) with the last free growth; and I never found them nearer together than a good day's journey. About three or four days' travel takes you through this Land of Little Sticks and brings you to the last wood. The last wood that I found was a patch of about four or five acres with trees two or three inches in diameter at their largest, although one or two isolated ones were perhaps as large as five or six inches. Here you take the firewood for your trip into the Barrens.

"Yonder They Are!"

by Lamar Underwood

The first article I ever sold to a magazine was about quail hunting in my native Georgia. Hugh Grey, editor of *Field & Stream*, liked it so much he assigned a photographer to meet me in Georgia and improve my rather weak selection of photographs to accompany the story. Dade Thornton took the photos, and the article appeared in *Field & Stream* in the September 1959 edition. Today, I still find myself with an urge to write about quail hunting. "Yonder They Are!" is my latest.

* * *

There are words that strike a quail hunter's ears like claps of thunder, promising the end of a parching drought.

"Duke's acting birdy . . . lots of scent . . . they've been here . . . careful now."

The heartbeat leaps, pulling nerve ends taunt. Legs that were feeling tired become sprightly with new bursts of energy. The hands on the double gun caress the familiar shapes of walnut and steel with anticipation.

Then comes the cry: "Point!"

When that single word rings out in bobwhite quail country, in pinelands or tawny sedge patches or brush-tangled field edges, the stage is set for the bird hunter's ultimate reward. The pointer or setter is locked in a trance-like staunch pose. As he steps ahead of the dog, the hunter walks like he's afraid he's about to step on a land mine. He trembles when one boot snags on a briar, then breaks free. The other boot crunches on dry weeds, a sound too loud. His grip on the gun tightens. There's a wobbly feeling in his knees.

This is it!

This is the reason he owns a bird dog; or why he dreamed of this hunt over countless hours of planning and research and bleary-eyed surfing on the Internet; or even why he bought an airline ticket.

"Live in the moment." *Where had he first heard that?* he wonders as he creeps ahead. Anyway, it was true. He knew that. And the moment is now!

The explosion that follows is a feathery eruption of brownish hurtling bodies, startling fast as they vault toward the stubby black-jack oaks at the edge of the field. As the gun comes to his shoulder, the hunter sees the birds are already among the oaks, twisting into narrow corridors. He pokes the barrel toward one image. No time to aim, swing the gun. Just stab at it. Wham! He sees bark and twigs scattering. The oaks are swallowing the birds. There's a final fleeting image. Another stab. Wham! Suddenly the oaks are empty; the double gun is empty; the dog is scouring the grass for dead birds in vain.

Not every scenario that begins with the shout "Point!" turns out as described here. For openers, the birds might run ahead of the dog's initial point. [That's exactly the reason savvy hunters do not take off their safety until birds are in the air. They might trip or stumble as they move ahead of the dog for running birds.] The "Point!" may not be for a covey at all, but a single bird, hunted after a covey has been scattered. The covey rise itself may vary in intensity, depending on the size of the covey and whether or not these are wild birds or pen-raised for preserve hunting. Once you have put up a covey of wild birds, you'll never again wonder if there's a difference between wild and pen-raised.

For this aging tramper of stubble and tangles, the issue—wild or pen-raised—isn't worth worrying about. My boots are laced; my briar-guarded trousers are cut a little short at the ankles to clear the weeds. My 20-gauge side-by-side is an old friend, and the game pocket of my shooting vest still has feathers from the day of my last hunt. I'm going quail hunting. I'll hunt where I can, when I can, with the vision of staunch and gallant dogs and whirring wings leading me on like a kid at Christmas. The boy who first hunted bobwhite quail in Georgia pinelands in the late 1940s is still very much alive inside me, calling for me to find another covey, to experience yet again the classic upland scene that is bobwhite quail hunting.

I use the word "Point!" with a touch of hesitation. For while "Point!" resounded from the magazine and book pages of my youth—and still does today—the elders who took this lad quail hunting used a simpler and more colorful expression to announce that Mack, or Lily, or Queen had locked up on birds. The exalted cry that rang through the crisp air was, "Yonder they are!"

For me, there is pure magic in that phrase. So much so that I still use it today. Even though the years have carried me far from my southern accent, the heritage is still there. And when we're in the field together, on a preserve or one of those elusive and almost-rare wild-bird hunts, you'll be happier than a pig in slop when you hear my voice ring out, "Yonder they are!"

If our dog can remain a statue, as expected and trained, and if the birds hold tight as quail-hunting literature and legend suggest, our "Yonder" is about to turn into a rush of excitement few bird-hunting episodes can equal. The good covey rise is indeed quail hunting's moment of truth, an event conjured in dreams, relived in the paintings of talented artists, and sought by folks like us who appreciate dog work and a game bird with the qualities of bobwhite quail. When things are right, they come in coveys; they offer single-bird shots that are like flushing small ruffed grouse in tight cover; and they're so good on the table that they inspire culinary artistry in enough ways to fill a cookbook.

The two equally challenging acts of traditional bobwhite hunting—covey rises then prying loose single birds—have lost some of their distinct differences in today's released-bird shooting. In preserve opportunities at their lovingly managed best, covey rises come in spurts of six or eight birds at best. Of course, there are exceptions. In a superb moment you might see a dozen birds bouncing from the sedge grass.

The sudden vision of multiple targets over your gun barrels is so unusual that it's startling. The confidence and cool reflexes of a crack shot are lost in a heartbeat. Pick a bird! Stay with it! The commands whip through your thoughts, but the sight of so many birds in the air at once is overwhelming, your dream come alive. Breaking that vision down to one bird, staying with it, is hard to do. Without you even realizing it, your head is lifting slightly as you peer down the gun barrel in elation. Your timing is shattered. Your gun is slow—glacier-slow it seems—obeying the commands your reflexes dictate.

Three seconds! That's all you have. Mississippi one . . . Mississippi two. By Mississippi three your smooth swing has degenerated into a panicked throw shot—a stab, a poke, a desperate jab at a disappearing brownish blur.

For sure, covey rises take some getting used to. For openers, take the fact that most of the great quail paintings you've admired over the years show the covey leaping from almost right under the dogs' noses. Sometimes they do. But often they can be 15 or even 20 yards in front of the point. Wild birds particularly. You're behind from the git-go with the need of speed.

Perhaps the "covey" you're expecting turns out to be four or five birds. A paltry bunch if you were expecting an honest-to-God covey. Good dog work and shooting action, yes. But not the covey rise of 12 or 15 birds of quail hunting's halcyon days. Back then, coveys of five or six birds were left for seed; the singles were not pursued. Now the average shooting preserve party tries to hunt down every escaping single, like they're dollar bills getting away. Which, of course, they are.

Thinking about what used to be isn't good for the quail hunter's morale. Better instead to loosen up and do yourself the favor of enjoying whatever turns you on in the great outdoors. If the fish aren't hitting top-water—a passion for all anglers—you'll go deep. Lures, baits, rigs—whatever the hell will make fish strike. If a K-Mart is standing where your grand-dad once kept his hunting coat puffy with Bobs, you'll press on to find new grounds to re-kindle the flame.

Of course quail hunting was better when Nash Buckingham was tramping behind his setters and pointers. Truth is, not many people who lived back then were able to get in on the fun. Except for a few lucky farmers, tending the fields, quail hunting has never come easy. The inspirations that drive us to the sport—the dog work, the game bird itself, the pastoral surroundings where quail are found—these visions must be nourished with effort and money. What we seek is irresistible. It can't be replaced by golf or football games or even fishing. We can enjoy those things if we like them, but the love of following pointing dogs in treks toward whirring wings is a force like no other.

We yield, we respond, doing whatever it takes to keep alive a certain part of our guarded world of dreams and memories we refuse to allow to wither away. If you are a bird hunter to the core, no matter what you have loved and lost over the years, that part of you never dies.

So we're out there, tramping again. As noted bobwhite storyteller Havilah Babcock so wisely wrote, "Birds, like gold, are where you find them. They can be a lot of other places too."

Sometimes those "other places" seem beyond the radar noses of our canine companions. Whether working in "Hunt Close" sweeps, or bending out to promising horizons, they simply can't find the birds. Indeed, boots are made for walking, and ours get in some overtime while doubt creeps into our minds about the ground we're hunting, the vagaries of scenting conditions, and the mysterious movements of bobwhite coveys. At such times it pays to be persistent, but also patient.

Aboard in the uplands (is there anywhere else you'd rather be?), enjoying the good dog work, no matter how fruitless, we become part of a setting where things might happen that we will remember the rest of our lives. The air has the tawny sharpness we missed all summer; the sun is warm on our bird vests; winter visitors like mallards flash past, and we hear the jabbering of familiar crows. Sometimes we look over the treetops ahead and see a hawk floating in circles, a sight that immediately triggers the frightening notion that the winged hunter has found and spooked our birds.

Finding the mother lodes of birds on land we can hunt rests on a game plan with two critical elements: the choke-bore noses of pointing dogs and our tactics in using them.

Bird dogs are not created equal. Some seem to have an uncanny ability. Their noses are radar-sharp. They work the terrain with careful, methodical sweeps, bending back or off to the sides to check out birdy-looking copses. They do not plunge into tangles of briars and field-edge bushes; nor do they ignore them. They circle such thick spots, probing all sides for precious scent.

It is more likely on my hunts that such a dog was trained— "broke" to use that terrible word—on a farm or in a suburban back yard where a copy of the late Dick Wolter's mellow *Gun Dog* book was on hand, than on the prairies of Saskatchewan or Alberta frequented by professional trainers. Big-going field trial dogs, trained by pros and destined to hunt leased land and plantations, get in many weeks of work with sharp-tail grouse long before open quail season dawns in places like in Texas or Georgia.

While there is something undeniably exciting about the vision of a pointer or setter slamming into a wall of scent at full gallop, such events are often a speck on the horizon, a jeep or horseback ride away. Our "Gun Dog" pointer or setter, plodding along, will be working where our legs can take us, within sensible range. We won't be walking past many coveys without contacting them. We hope.

Sometimes, even with the best dogs money can buy or we can train, we bobwhite hunters are up against a stacked deck. Take a morning when you open the dog box over iron-hard ground with a stinging wind out of the northeast. Scenting conditions will be somewhere between nil and none. Rain is another deal-breaker. Although a little moisture is good for scent, days when the world around you is like one vast soaked sponge will not be fun. Preserve shooting can be ridiculous in the rain, with the birds mobbing up in briar-choked nooks the dogs can't reach. When you do get these soaked fugitives up, their flight may be nothing more than a short hop, dangerously close to the dogs' noses. I'll take a pass on preserve birds in the rain, unless I'm gunning where the operator's birds are proven fliers, in all weathers.

Successful quail hunters have a mental map marking the home ranges of every covey. My own "Treasure Island" sketches of bobwhite heaven focus on Bob's predictable schedule: feeding somewhere in the morning; loafing, dusting, catching insects in some secluded spot in midday; feeding in the late afternoon; then roosting in some weedy field with no trees overhead.

A gleaner from the moment they are born, bobwhites possess tough gizzards and ample crops to enable them to snatch whatever tidbits they can find from the ground under their feet. Special treats like golden corn kernels, soybean, and wheat seeds, are backed up by a multitude of seed-bearing wild plants. Acorns are shattered and consumed eagerly. Bugs that fail to scamper from Bob's path are quickly pecked. The food chain in all seasons stretches thorough a landscape of brushy edges alongside crop fields, pinelands with broom sedge and gallberry patches, meadows and old fields lush with weeds. Swampy wall-like tangles where enemy predators thrive may be nearby, but where they choke out the open country, they doom Bob's chances.

Over most of the bird's natural range, wild bobwhite populations are devastated by crop fields cut clean as billiard tables and bordered by dense walls of brush and briars, heaven for predators. So clean do today's combines leave fields like corn and soybeans, "A chicken following behind one would starve to death," as one of my Georgia uncles puts it. Even the most efficient combines spill some grain—particularly where they make sharp turns—and Bobs risk a few moments of exposure in the fields for these treats. They fly—not walk as in bobwhite literature!—into the field from nearby cover, feed quickly (the big yellow corn kernels are favorite), then fly back to safety. Of course, they are spooky as hawks out in the open.

In good quail country the croplands are bordered by the reaches of open pinelands with broom sedge, old fields of ragweed—cover a dog can hunt through. To make the picture perfect, add in patches of sunflowers, millet, or lespedeza. These Valhallas are maintained on plantations, shooting preserves, and private farms where the owners care about bobwhite coveys.

Perhaps it is on such a place that good luck smiles on us. Up ahead, pointer Mack's ground-eating strides have broken into a stalking, tip-toeing creep. Then he stops altogether, right at the field's edge, a figure as locked and solid as granite.

My heart surges. Hands tighten on the smoothbore. Then, from the Southern boy who will always live inside me, my call rings out, "Yonder they are!"

Hunting the Grisly

by Theodore Roosevelt

THE MISSPELLING OF "GRIZZLY" WILL BE OVERLOOKED. PRESI-
dent Theodore Roosevelt's adventures with the great bears stand
as he wrote them, with passion and experience.

* * *

If out in the late fall or early spring, it is often possible to follow
a bear's trail in the snow; having come upon it either by chance
or hard hunting, or else having found where it leads from some
carcass on which the beast has been feeding. In the pursuit one
must exercise great caution, as at such times the hunter is easily
seen a long way off, and game is always especially watchful for any
foe that may follow its trail.

Once I killed a grisly in this manner. It was early in the fall,
but snow lay on the ground, while the gray weather boded a storm.
My camp was in a bleak, wind-swept valley, high among the
mountains which form the divide between the headwaters of the
Salmon and Clarke's Fork of the Columbia. All night I had lain
in my buffalo-bag, under the lea of a windbreak of branches, in
the clump of fir-trees, where I had halted the preceding evening.
At my feet ran a rapid mountain torrent, its bed choked with
ice-covered rocks; I had been lulled to sleep by the stream's splashing murmur, and the loud moaning of the wind along the naked

cliffs. At dawn I rose and shook myself free of the buffalo robe, coated with hoar-frost. The ashes of the fire were lifeless; in the dim morning the air was bitter cold. I did not linger a moment, but snatched up my rifle, pulled on my fur cap and gloves, and strode off up a side ravine; as I walked I ate some mouthfuls of venison, left over from supper.

Two hours of toil up the steep mountain brought me to the top of a spur. The sun had risen, but was hidden behind a bank of sullen clouds. On the divide I halted, and gazed out over a vast landscape, inconceivably wild and dismal. Around me towered the stupendous mountain masses which make up the backbone of the Rockies. From my feet, as far as I could see, stretched a rugged and barren chaos of ridges and detached rock masses. Behind me, far below, the stream wound like a silver ribbon, fringed with dark conifers and the changing, dying foliage of poplar and quaking aspen. In front the bottoms of the valleys were filled with the somber evergreen forest, dotted here and there with black, ice-skimmed tarns; and the dark spruces clustered also in the higher gorges, and were scattered thinly along the mountain sides. The snow which had fallen lay in drifts and streaks, while, where the wind had scope it was blown off, and the ground left bare.

For two hours I walked onwards across the ridges and valleys. Then among some scattered spruces, where the snow lay to the depth of half a foot, I suddenly came on the fresh, broad trail of a grisly. The brute was evidently roaming restlessly about in search of a winter den, but willing, in passing, to pick up any food that lay handy. At once I took the trail, travelling above and to one side, and keeping a sharp look-out ahead. The bear was going across wind, and this made my task easy. I walked rapidly, though cautiously; and it was only in crossing the large patches of bare ground that I had to fear making a noise. Elsewhere the snow muffled my footsteps, and made the trail so plain that I scarcely had to waste a glance upon it, bending my eyes always to the front.

At last, peering cautiously over a ridge crowned with broken rocks, I saw my quarry, a big, burly bear, with silvered fur. He had halted on an open hillside, and was busily digging up the caches of some rock gophers or squirrels. He seemed absorbed in his work, and the stalk was easy. Slipping quietly back, I ran towards the end of the spur, and in ten minutes struck a ravine, of which one branch ran past within seventy yards of where the bear was working. In this ravine was a rather close growth of stunted evergreens, affording good cover, although in one or two places I had to lie down and crawl through the snow. When I reached the point for which I was aiming, the bear had just finished rooting, and was starting off. A slight whistle brought him to a standstill, and I drew a bead behind his shoulder, and low down, resting the rifle across the crooked branch of a dwarf spruce. At the crack he ran off at speed, making no sound, but the thick spatter of blood splashes, showing clear on the white snow, betrayed the mortal nature of the wound. For some minutes I followed the trail; and then, topping a ridge, I saw the dark bulk lying motionless in a snow drift at the foot of a low rock-wall, from which he had tumbled.

The usual practice of the still-hunter who is after grisly is to toll it to baits. The hunter either lies in ambush near the carcass, or approaches it stealthily when he thinks the bear is at its meal.

One day while camped near the Bitter Root Mountains in Montana I found that a bear had been feeding on the carcass of a moose which lay some five miles from the little open glade in which my tent was pitched, and I made up my mind to try to get a shot at it that afternoon. I stayed in camp till about three o'clock, lying lazily back on the bed of sweet-smelling evergreen boughs, watching the pack ponies as they stood under the pines on the edge of the open, stamping now and then, and switching their tails. The air was still, the sky a glorious blue; at that hour in the afternoon even the September sun was hot. The smoke from the smouldering logs of the campfire curled thinly upwards. Little chipmunks scuttled out from their holes to the packs, which lay in a heap on the ground, and then scuttled madly back again. A couple of drab-colored whisky-jacks, with bold mien and fearless bright eyes, hopped and fluttered round, picking up the scraps, and uttering an extraordinary variety of notes, mostly discordant; so tame were they that one of them lit on my outstretched arm as I half dozed, basking in the sunshine.

When the shadows began to lengthen, I shouldered my rifle and plunged into the woods. At first my route lay along a mountain side; then for half a mile over a windfall, the dead timber piled about in crazy confusion. After that I went up the bottom of a valley by a little brook, the ground being carpeted with a sponge of soaked moss. At the head of this brook was a pond covered with waterlilies; and a scramble through a rocky pass took me into a high, wet valley, where the thick growth of spruce was broken by occasional strips of meadow. In this valley the moose carcass lay, well at the upper end.

In moccasined feet I trod softly through the soundless woods. Under the dark branches it was already dusk, and the air had the cool chill of evening. As I neared the clump where the body lay, I walked with redoubled caution, watching and listening with strained alertness. Then I heard a twig snap; and my blood leaped, for I knew the bear was at his supper. In another moment I saw his shaggy, brown form. He was working with all his awkward giant strength, trying to bury the carcass, twisting it to one side and the other with wonderful ease. Once he got angry and suddenly gave it a tremendous cuff with his paw; in his bearing he had something half humorous, half devilish. I crept up within forty yards; but for several minutes he would not keep his head still. Then something attracted his attention in the forest, and he stood motionless looking towards it, broadside to me, with his forepaws planted on the carcass. This gave me my chance. I drew a very fine bead between his eye and ear; and pulled trigger. He dropped like a steer when struck with a poleaxe.

If there is a good hiding-place handy it is better to lie in wait at the carcass. One day on the headwaters of the Madison, I found that a bear was coming to an elk I had shot some days before; and I at once determined to ambush the beast when he came back that evening. The carcass lay in the middle of a valley a quarter of a mile broad. The bottom of this valley was covered by an open forest of tall pines; a thick jungle of smaller evergreens marked where the mountains rose on either hand. There were a number of large rocks scattered here and there, one, of very convenient shape, being only some seventy or eighty yards from the carcass. Up this I clambered. It hid me perfectly, and on its top was a carpet of soft pine needles, on which I could lie at my ease.

Hour after hour passed by. A little black woodpecker with a yellow crest ran nimbly up and down the tree-trunks for some time and then flitted away with a party of chickadees and nut-hatches. Occasionally a Clarke's crow soared about overhead or clung in any position to the swaying end of a pine branch, chattering and screaming. Flocks of crossbills, with wavy flight and plaintive calls, flew to a small mineral lick nearby, where they scraped the clay with their queer little beaks.

As the westering sun sank out of sight beyond the mountains these sounds of birdlife gradually died away. Under the great pines the evening was still with the silence of primeval desolation. The sense of sadness and loneliness, the melancholy of the wilderness, came over me like a spell. Every slight noise made my pulses throb as I lay motionless on the rock gazing intently into the gathering gloom. I began to fear that it would grow too dark to shoot before the grisly came.

Suddenly and without warning, the great bear stepped out of the bushes and trod across the pine needles with such swift and silent footsteps that its bulk seemed unreal. It was very cautious, continually halting to peer around; and once it stood up on its hind legs and looked long down the valley towards the red west. As it reached the carcass I put a bullet between its shoulders.

It rolled over, while the woods resounded with its savage roaring. Immediately it struggled to its feet and staggered off; and fell again to the next shot, squalling and yelling. Twice this was repeated; the brute being one of those bears which greet every wound with a great outcry, and sometimes seem to lose their feet when hit—although they will occasionally fight as savagely as their more silent brethren. In this case the wounds were mortal, and the bear died before reaching the edge of the thicket.

I spent much of the fall of 1889 hunting on the headwaters of the Salmon and Snake in Idaho, and along the Montana boundary line from the Big Hole Basin and the head of the Wisdom River to the neighborhood of Red Rock Pass and to the north and west of Henry's Lake. During the last fortnight my companion was the old mountain man, already mentioned, named Griffeth or Griffin—I cannot tell which, as he was always called either "Hank" or "Griff." He was a crabbedly honest old fellow, and a very skilful hunter; but he was worn out with age and rheumatism, and his temper had failed even faster than his bodily strength. He showed me a greater variety of game than I had ever seen before in so short a time; nor did I ever before or after make so successful a hunt. But he was an exceedingly disagreeable companion on account of his surly, moody ways. I generally had to get up first, to kindle the fire and make ready breakfast, and he was very quarrelsome. Finally, during my absence from camp one day, while not very far from Red Rock pass, he found my whisky-flask, which I kept purely for emergencies, and drank all the contents. When I came back he was quite drunk. This was unbearable, and after some high words I left him, and struck off homeward through the woods on my own account. We had with us four pack and saddle horses; and of these I took a very intelligent and gentle little bronco mare, which possessed the invaluable trait of always staying near camp, even when not hobbled. I was not hampered with much of an outfit, having only my buffalo sleeping-bag, a fur coat, and my washing kit, with a couple of spare pairs of socks and some handkerchiefs. A frying-pan, some salt pork, and a hatchet, made up a light pack, which, with the bedding, I fastened across the stock saddle by means of a rope and a spare packing cinch. My cartridges and knife were in my belt; my compass and matches, as always, in my pocket. I walked, while the little mare followed almost like a dog, often without my having to hold the lariat which served as halter.

The country was for the most part fairly open, as I kept near the foothills where glades and little prairies broke the pine forest. The trees were of small size. There was no regular trail, but the course was easy to keep, and I had no trouble of any kind save on the second day. That afternoon I was following a stream which at last "canyoned up," that is sank to the bottom of a canyon-like ravine impossible for a horse. I started up a side valley, intending to cross from its head coulies to those of another valley which would lead in below the canyon.

However, I got enmeshed in the tangle of winding valleys at the foot of the steep mountains, and as dusk was coming on I halted and camped in a little open spot by the side of a small, noisy brook, with crystal water. The place was carpeted with soft, wet, green moss, dotted red with the kinnikinnic berries, and at its edge, under the trees where the ground was dry, I threw down the buffalo bed on a mat of sweet-smelling pine needles. Making camp took but a moment. I opened the pack, tossed the bedding on a smooth spot, knee-haltered the little mare, dragged up a few dry logs, and then strolled off, rifle on shoulder, through the frosty gloaming, to see if I could pick up a grouse for supper.

For half a mile I walked quickly and silently over the pine needles, across a succession of slight ridges separated by narrow, shallow valleys. The forest here was composed of lodge-pole pines, which on the ridges grew close together, with tall slender trunks, while in the valleys the growth was more open. Though the sun was behind the mountains there was yet plenty of light by which to shoot, but it was fading rapidly.

At last, as I was thinking of turning towards camp, I stole up to the crest of one of the ridges, and looked over into the valley some sixty yards off. Immediately I caught the loom of some large, dark object; and another glance showed me a big grisly walking slowly off with his head down. He was quartering to me, and I fired into his flank, the bullet, as I afterwards found, ranging forward and piercing one lung. At the shot he uttered a loud, moaning grunt and plunged forward at a heavy gallop, while I raced obliquely down the hill to cut him off. After going a few hundred feet he reached a laurel thicket, some thirty yards broad, and two or three times as long which he did not leave. I ran up to the edge and there halted, not liking to venture into the mass of twisted, close-growing stems and glossy foliage. Moreover, as I halted, I heard him utter a peculiar, savage kind of whine from the heart of the brush. Accordingly, I began to skirt the edge, standing on tiptoe and gazing earnestly to see if I could not catch a glimpse of his hide. When I was at the narrowest part of the thicket, he suddenly left it directly opposite, and then wheeled and stood broadside to me on the hillside, a little above. He turned his head stiffly towards me; scarlet strings of froth hung from his lips; his eyes burned like embers in the gloom.

I held true, aiming behind the shoulder, and my bullet shattered the point or lower end of his heart, taking out a big nick. Instantly the great bear turned with a harsh roar of fury and challenge, blowing the blood foam from his mouth, so that I saw the gleam of his white fangs; and then he charged straight at me, crashing and bounding through the laurel bushes, so that it was hard to aim. I waited until he came to a fallen tree, raking him as he topped it with a ball, which entered his chest and went through the cavity of his body, but he neither swerved nor flinched, and at the moment I did not know that I had struck him. He came steadily on, and in another second was almost upon me. I fired for his forehead, but my bullet went low, entering his open mouth, smashing his lower jaw and going into the neck. I leaped to one side almost as I pulled trigger; and through the hanging smoke the first thing I saw was his paw as he made a vicious side blow at me. The rush of his charge carried him past. As he struck he lurched forward, leaving a pool of bright blood where his muzzle hit the ground; but he recovered himself and made two or three jumps onwards, while I hurriedly jammed a couple of cartridges into the magazine, my rifle holding only four, all of which I had fired. Then he tried to pull up, but as he did so his muscles seemed suddenly to give way, his head drooped, and he rolled over and over like a shot rabbit. Each of my first three bullets had inflicted a mortal wound.

It was already twilight, and I merely opened the carcass, and then trotted back to camp. Next morning I returned and with much labor took off the skin. The fur was very fine, the animal being in excellent trim, and unusually bright-colored. Unfortunately, in packing it out I lost the skull, and had to supply its place with one of plaster. The beauty of the trophy, and the memory of the circumstances under which I procured it, make me value it perhaps more highly than any other in my house.

This is the only instance in which I have been regularly charged by a grisly. On the whole, the danger of hunting these great bears has been much exaggerated. At the beginning of the present century, when white hunters first encountered the grisly, he was doubtless an exceedingly savage beast, prone to attack without provocation, and a redoubtable foe to persons armed with the clumsy, small-bore muzzle-loading rifles of the day. But at present bitter experience has taught him caution. He has been hunted for the bounty, and hunted as a dangerous enemy to stock, until, save in the very wildest districts, he has learned to be more wary than a deer and to avoid man's presence almost as carefully as the most timid kind of game. Except in rare cases he will not attack of his own accord, and, as a rule, even when wounded his object is escape rather than battle.

Still, when fairly brought to bay, or when moved by a sudden fit of ungovernable anger, the grisly is beyond peradventure a very dangerous antagonist. The first shot, if taken at a bear a good distance off and previously unwounded and unharried, is not usually fraught with much danger, the startled animal being at the outset bent merely on flight. It is always hazardous, however, to track a wounded and worried grisly into thick cover, and the man who habitually follows and kills this chief of American game in dense timber, never abandoning the bloody trail whithersoever it leads, must show no small degree of skill and hardihood, and must not too closely count the risk to life or limb. Bears differ widely in temper, and occasionally one may be found who will not show fight, no matter how much he is bullied; but, as a rule, a hunter must be cautious in meddling with a wounded animal which has retreated into a dense thicket, and had been once or twice roused; and such a beast, when it does turn, will usually charge again and again, and fight to the last with unconquerable ferocity. The short distance at which the bear can be seen through the underbrush, the fury of his charge, and his tenacity of life make it necessary for the hunter on such occasions to have steady nerves and a fairly quick and accurate aim. It is always well to have two men in following a wounded bear under such conditions. This is not necessary, however, and a good hunter, rather than lose his quarry, will, under ordinary circumstances, follow and attack it, no matter how tangled the fastness in which it has sought refuge; but he must act warily and with the utmost caution and resolution, if he wishes to escape a terrible and probably fatal mauling. An experienced hunter is rarely rash, and never heedless; he will not, when alone, follow a wounded bear into a thicket, if by that exercise of patience, skill, and knowledge of the game's habits he can avoid the necessity; but it is idle to talk of the feat as something which ought in no case to be attempted. While danger ought never to be needlessly incurred, it is yet true that the keenest zest in sport comes from its presence, and from the consequent exercise of the qualities necessary to overcome it. The most thrilling moments of an American hunter's life are those in which, with every sense on the alert, and with nerves strung to the highest point, he is following alone into the heart of its forest fastness the fresh and bloody footprints of an angered grisly; and no other triumph of American hunting can compare with the victory to be thus gained.

These big bears will not ordinarily charge from a distance of over a hundred yards; but there are exceptions to this rule. In the fall of 1890 my friend Archibald Rogers was hunting in Wyoming, south of the Yellowstone Park, and killed seven bears. One, an old he, was out on a bare tableland, grubbing for roots, when he was spied. It was early in the afternoon, and the hunters, who were on a high mountain slope, examined him for some time through their powerful glasses before making him out to be a bear. They then stalked up to the edge of the wood which fringed on the tableland on one side, but could get no nearer than about three hundred yards, the plains being barren of all cover. After waiting for a couple of hours Rogers risked the shot, in despair of getting nearer, and wounded the bear, though not very seriously. The animal made off, almost broadside to, and Rogers ran forward to intercept it. As soon as it saw him it turned and rushed straight for him, not heeding his second shot, and evidently bent on charging home. Rogers then waited until it was within twenty yards, and brained it with his third bullet.

In fact bears differ individually in courage and ferocity precisely as men do, or as the Spanish bulls, of which it is said that not more than one in twenty is fit to stand the combat of the arena. One grisly can scarcely be bullied into resistance; the next may fight to the end, against any odds, without flinching, or even attack unprovoked. Hence men of limited experience in this sport, generalizing from the actions of the two or three bears each has happened to see or kill, often reach diametrically opposite conclusions as to the fighting temper and capacity of the quarry. Even old hunters—who indeed, as a class, are very narrow-minded and opinionated—often generalize just as rashly as beginners. One will portray all bears as very dangerous; another will speak and act as if he deemed them of no more consequence than so many rabbits. I knew one old hunter who had killed a score without ever seeing one show fight. On the other hand, Dr. James C. Merrill, U. S. A., who has had about as much experience with bears as I have had, informs me that he has been charged with the utmost determination three times. In each case the attack was delivered before the bear was wounded or even shot at, the animal being roused by the approach of the hunter from his day bed, and charging headlong at them from a distance of twenty or thirty paces. All three bears were killed before they could do any damage. There was a very remarkable incident connected with the killing of one of them. It occurred in the northern spurs of the Bighorn range. Dr. Merrill, in company with an old hunter, had climbed down into a deep, narrow canyon. The bottom was threaded with well-beaten elk trails. While following one of these the two men turned a corner of the canyon and were instantly charged by an old she-grisly, so close that it was only by good luck that one of the hurried shots disabled her and caused her to tumble over a cut bank where she was easily finished. They found that she had been lying directly across the game trail, on a smooth well beaten patch of bare earth, which looked as if it had been dug up, refilled, and trampled down. Looking curiously at this patch they saw a bit of hide only partially covered at one end; digging down they found the body of a well grown grisly cub. Its skull had been crushed, and the brains licked out, and there were signs of other injuries. The hunters pondered long over this strange discovery, and hazarded many guesses as to its meaning. At last they decided that probably the cub had been killed, and its brains eaten out, either by some old male-grisly or by a cougar, that the mother had returned and driven away the murderer, and that she had then buried the body and lain above it, waiting to wreak her vengeance on the first passer-by.

Old Tazewell Woody, during his thirty years' life as a hunter in the Rockies and on the great plains, killed very many grislies. He always exercised much caution in dealing with them; and, as it happened, he was by some suitable tree in almost every case when he was charged. He would accordingly climb the tree (a practice of which I do not approve however); and the bear would look up at him and pass on without stopping. Once, when he was hunting in the mountains with a companion, the latter, who was down in a valley, while Woody was on the hillside, shot at a bear. The first thing Woody knew the wounded grisly, running up-hill, was almost on him from behind. As he turned it seized his rifle in its jaws. He wrenched the rifle round, while the bear still gripped it, and pulled trigger, sending a bullet into its shoulder; whereupon it struck him with its paw, and knocked him over the rocks. By good luck he fell in a snowbank and was not hurt in the least. Meanwhile the bear went on and they never got it.

Once he had an experience with a bear which showed a very curious mixture of rashness and cowardice. He and a companion were camped in a little tepee or wigwam, with a bright fire in front of it, lighting up the night. There was an inch of snow on the ground. Just after they went to bed a grisly came close to camp. Their dog rushed out and they could hear it bark round in the darkness for nearly an hour; then the bear drove it off and came right into camp. It went close to the fire, picking up the scraps of meat and bread, pulled a haunch of venison down from a tree, and passed and repassed in front of the tepee, paying no heed whatever to the two men, who crouched in the doorway talking to one another. Once it passed so close that Woody could almost have touched it. Finally his companion fired into it, and off it ran, badly wounded, without an attempt at retaliation. Next morning they followed its tracks in the snow, and found it a quarter or a mile away. It was near a pine and had buried itself under the loose earth, pine needles, and snow; Woody's companion almost walked over it, and putting his rifle to its ear blew out its brains.

In all his experience Woody had personally seen but four men who were badly mauled by bears. Three of these were merely wounded. One was bitten terribly in the back. Another had an arm partially chewed off. The third was a man named George Dow, and the accident happened to him on the Yellowstone about the year 1878. He was with a pack animal at the time, leading it on a trail through a wood. Seeing a big she-bear with cubs he yelled at her; whereat she ran away, but only to cache her cubs, and in a minute, having hidden them, came racing back at him. His pack animal being slow he started to climb a tree; but before he could get far enough up she caught him, almost biting a piece out of the calf of his leg, pulled him down, bit and cuffed him two or three times, and then went on her way.

The only time Woody ever saw a man killed by a bear was once when he had given a touch of variety to his life by shipping on a New Bedford whaler which had touched at one of the Puget Sound ports. The whaler went up to a part of Alaska where bears were very plentiful and bold. One day a couple of boats' crews landed; and the men, who were armed only with an occasional harpoon or lance, scattered over the beach, one of them, a Frenchman, wading into the water after shellfish. Suddenly a bear emerged from some bushes and charged among the astonished sailors, who scattered in every direction; but the bear, said Woody, "just had it in for that Frenchman," and went straight at him. Shrieking with terror he retreated up to his neck in the water; but the bear plunged in after him, caught him, and disembowelled him. One of the Yankee mates then fired a bomb lance into the bear's hips, and the savage beast hobbled off into the dense cover of the low scrub, where the enraged sailor folk were unable to get at it.

The truth is that while the grisly generally avoids a battle if possible, and often acts with great cowardice, it is never safe to take liberties with him; he usually fights desperately and dies hard when wounded and cornered, and exceptional individuals take the aggressive on small provocation.

During the years I lived on the frontier I came in contact with many persons who had been severely mauled or even crippled for life by grislies; and a number of cases where they killed men outright were also brought under my ken. Generally these accidents, as was natural, occurred to hunters who had roused or wounded the game.

A fighting bear sometimes uses his claws and sometimes his teeth. I have never known one to attempt to kill an antagonist by hugging, in spite of the popular belief to this effect; though he will sometimes draw an enemy towards him with his paws the better to reach him with his teeth, and to hold him so that he cannot escape from the biting. Nor does the bear often advance on his hind legs to the attack; though, if the man has come close to him in thick underbrush, or has stumbled on him in his lair unawares, he will often rise up in this fashion and strike a single blow. He will also rise in clinching with a man on horseback. In 1882 a mounted Indian was killed in this manner on one of the river bottoms some miles below where my ranch house now stands, not far from the junction of the Beaver and Little Missouri. The bear had been hunted into a thicket by a band of Indians, in whose company my informant, with whom I afterward did some trading, was travelling. One of them in the excitement of the pursuit rode across the end of the thicket; as he did so the great beast sprang at him with wonderful quickness, rising on its hind legs, and knocking over the horse and rider with a single sweep of its terrible forepaws. It then turned on the fallen man and tore him open, and though the other Indians came promptly to his rescue and slew his assailant, they were not in time to save their comrade's life.

A bear is apt to rely mainly on his teeth or claws according to whether his efforts are directed primarily to killing his foe or to making good his own escape. In the latter event he trusts chiefly to his claws. If cornered, he of course makes a rush for freedom, and in that case he downs any man who is in his way with a sweep of his great paw, but passes on without stopping to bite him. If while sleeping or resting in thick brush someone suddenly stumbles on him close up he pursues the same course, less from anger than from fear, being surprised and startled. Moreover, if attacked at close quarters by men and dogs he strikes right and left in defence.

Sometimes what is called a charge is rather an effort to get away. In localities where he has been hunted, a bear, like every other kind of game, is always on the look-out for an attack, and is prepared at any moment for immediate flight. He seems ever to have in his mind, whether feeding, sunning himself, or merely roaming around, the direction—usually towards the thickest cover or most broken ground—in which he intends to run if molested. When shot at he instantly starts towards this place; or he may be so confused that he simply runs he knows not whither; and in either event he may take a line that leads almost directly to or by the hunter, although he had at first no thought of charging. In such a case he usually strikes a single knock-down blow and gallops on without halting, though that one blow may have taken life. If the claws are long and fairly sharp (as in early spring, or even in the fall, if the animal has been working over soft ground) they add immensely to the effect of the blow, for they cut like blunt axes. Often, however, late in the season, and if the ground has been dry and hard, or rocky, the claws are worn down nearly to the quick, and the blow is then given mainly with the underside of the paw; although even under this disadvantage a thump from a big bear will down a horse or smash in a man's breast. The hunter Hofer once lost a horse in this manner. He shot at and wounded a bear which rushed off, as ill luck would have it, past the place where his horse was picketed; probably more in fright than in anger it struck the poor beast a blow which, in the end, proved mortal.

If a bear means mischief and charges not to escape but to do damage, its aim is to grapple with or throw down its foe and bite him to death. The charge is made at a gallop, the animal sometimes coming on silently, with the mouth shut, and sometimes with the jaws open, the lips drawn back and teeth showing, uttering at the same time a succession of roars or of savage rasping snarls. Certain bears charge without any bluster and perfectly straight; while others first threaten and bully, and even when charging stop to growl, shake the head and bite at a bush or knock holes in the ground with their forepaws. Again, some of them charge home with a ferocious resolution which their extreme tenacity of life renders especially dangerous; while others can be turned or driven back even by a shot which is not mortal. They show the same variability in their behavior when wounded. Often a big bear, especially if charging, will receive a bullet in perfect silence, without flinching or seeming to pay any heed to it; while another will cry out and tumble about, and if charging, even though it may not abandon the attack, will pause for a moment to whine or bite at the wound.

Sometimes a single bite causes death. One of the most successful bear hunters I ever knew, an old fellow whose real name I never heard as he was always called Old Ike, was killed in this way in the spring or early summer of 1886 on one of the headwaters of the Salmon. He was a very good shot, had killed nearly a hundred bears with the rifle, and, although often charged, had never met with any accident, so that he had grown somewhat careless. On the day in question he had met a couple of mining prospectors and was travelling with them, when a grisly crossed his path. The old hunter immediately ran after it, rapidly gaining, as the bear did not hurry when it saw itself pursued, but slouched slowly forwards, occasionally turning its head to grin and growl. It soon went into a dense grove of young spruce, and as the hunter reached the edge it charged fiercely out. He fired one hasty shot, evidently wounding the animal, but not seriously enough to stop or cripple it; and as his two companions ran forward they saw the bear seize him with its wide-spread jaws, forcing him to the ground. They shouted and fired, and the beast abandoned the fallen man on the instant and sullenly retreated into the spruce thicket, whither they dared not follow it. Their friend was at his last gasp; for the whole side of the chest had been crushed in by the one bite, the lungs showing between the rent ribs.

Very often, however, a bear does not kill a man by one bite, but after throwing him lies on him, biting him to death. Usually, if no assistance is at hand, such a man is doomed; although if he pretends to be dead, and has the nerve to lie quiet under very rough treatment, it is just possible that the bear may leave him alive, perhaps after half burying what it believes to be the body. In a very few exceptional instances men of extraordinary prowess with the knife have succeeded in beating off a bear, and even in mortally wounding it, but in most cases a single-handed struggle, at close quarters, with a grisly bent on mischief, means death.

Occasionally the bear, although vicious, is also frightened, and passes on after giving one or two bites; and frequently a man who is knocked down is rescued by his friends before he is killed, the big beast mayhap using his weapons with clumsiness. So a bear may kill a foe with a single blow of its mighty forearm, either crushing in the head or chest by sheer force of sinew, or else tearing open the body with its formidable claws; and so on the other hand he may, and often does, merely disfigure or maim the foe by a hurried stroke. Hence it is common to see men who have escaped the clutches of a grisly, but only at the cost of features marred beyond recognition, or a body rendered almost helpless for life. Almost every old resident of western Montana or northern Idaho has known two or three unfortunates who have suffered in this manner. I have myself met one such man in Helena, and another in Missoula; both were living at least as late as 1889, the date at which I last saw them. One had been partially scalped by a bear's teeth; the animal was very old and so the fangs did not enter the skull. The other had been bitten across the face, and the wounds never entirely healed, so that his disfigured visage was hideous to behold.

Most of these accidents occur in following a wounded or worried bear into thick cover; and under such circumstances an animal apparently hopelessly disabled, or in the death throes, may with a last effort kill one or more of its assailants. In 1874 my wife's uncle, Captain Alexander Moore, U. S. A., and my friend Captain Bates, with some men of the 2nd and 3rd Cavalry, were scouting in Wyoming, near the Freezeout Mountains. One morning they roused a bear in the open prairie and followed it at full speed as it ran towards a small creek. At one spot in the creek beavers had built a dam, and as usual in such places there was a thick growth of bushes and willow saplings. Just as the bear reached the edge of this little jungle it was struck by several balls, both of its forelegs being broken. Nevertheless, it managed to shove itself forward on its hind-legs, and partly rolled, partly pushed itself into the thicket, the bushes though low being so dense that its body was at once completely hidden. The thicket was a mere patch of brush, not twenty yards across in any direction. The leading troopers reached the edge almost as the bear tumbled in. One of them, a tall and powerful man named Miller, instantly dismounted and prepared to force his way in among the dwarfed willows, which were but breast-high. Among the men who had ridden up were Moore and Bates, and also the two famous scouts, Buffalo Bill—long a companion of Captain Moore,—and California Joe, Custer's faithful follower. California Joe had spent almost all his life on the plains and in the mountains, as a hunter and Indian fighter; and when he saw the trooper about to rush into the thicket he called out to him not to do so, warning him of the danger. But the man was a very reckless fellow and he answered by jeering at the old hunter for his over-caution in being afraid of a crippled bear. California Joe made no further effort to dissuade him, remarking quietly: "Very well, sonny, go in; it's your own affair." Miller then leaped off the bank on which they stood and strode into the thicket, holding his rifle at the port. Hardly had he taken three steps when the bear rose in front of him, roaring with rage and pain. It was so close that the man had no chance to fire. Its forearms hung useless and as it reared unsteadily on its hind-legs, lunging forward at him, he seized it by the ears and strove to hold it back. His strength was very great, and he actually kept the huge head from his face and braced himself so that he was not overthrown; but the bear twisted its muzzle from side to side, biting and tearing the man's arms and shoulders. Another soldier jumping down slew the beast with a single bullet, and rescued his comrade; but though alive he was too badly hurt to recover and died after reaching the hospital. Buffalo Bill was given the bearskin, and I believe has it now.

The instances in which hunters who have rashly followed grislies into thick cover have been killed or severely mauled might be multiplied indefinitely. I have myself known of eight cases in which men have met their deaths in this manner.

It occasionally happens that a cunning old grisly will lie so close that the hunter almost steps on him; and he then rises suddenly with a loud, coughing growl and strikes down or seizes the man before the latter can fire off his rifle. More rarely a bear which is both vicious and crafty deliberately permits the hunter to approach fairly near to, or perhaps pass by, its hiding-place, and then suddenly charges him with such rapidity that he has barely time for the most hurried shot. The danger in such a case is of course great.

Ordinarily, however, even in the brush, the bear's object is to slink away, not to fight, and very many are killed even under the most unfavorable circumstances without accident. If an unwounded bear thinks itself unobserved it is not apt to attack; and in thick cover it is really astonishing to see how one of these large animals can hide, and how closely it will lie when there is danger. About twelve miles below my ranch there are some large river bottoms and creek bottoms covered with a matted mass of cottonwood, box-alders, bull-berry bushes, rosebushes, ash, wild plums, and other bushes. These bottoms have harbored bears ever since I first saw them; but, though often in company with a large party, I have repeatedly beaten through them, and though we must at times have been very near indeed to the game, we never so much as heard it run.

When bears are shot, as they usually must be, in open timber or on the bare mountain, the risk is very much less. Hundreds may thus be killed with comparatively little danger; yet even under these circumstances they will often charge, and sometimes make their charge good. The spice of danger, especially to a man armed with a good repeating rifle, is only enough to add zest to the chase, and the chief triumph is in outwitting the wary quarry and getting within range. Ordinarily the only excitement is in the stalk, the bear doing nothing more than keep a keen look-out and manifest the utmost anxiety to get away. As is but natural, accidents occasionally occur; yet they are usually due more to some failure in man or weapon than to the prowess of the bear. A good hunter whom I once knew, at a time when he was living in Butte, received fatal injuries from a bear he attacked in open woodland. The beast charged after the first shot, but slackened its pace on coming almost up to the man. The latter's gun jambed, and as he was endeavoring to work it he kept stepping slowly back, facing the bear which followed a few yards distant, snarling and threatening. Unfortunately, while thus walking backwards the man struck a dead log and fell over it, whereupon the beast instantly sprang on him and mortally wounded him before help arrived.

On rare occasions men who are not at the time hunting it fall victims to the grisly. This is usually because they stumble on it unawares and the animal attacks them more in fear than in anger. One such case, resulting fatally, occurred near my own ranch. The man walked almost over a bear while crossing a little point of brush, in a bend of the river, and was brained with a single blow of the paw. In another instance which came to my knowledge the man escaped with a shaking up, and without even a fight. His name was Perkins, and he was out gathering huckleberries in the woods on a mountain side near Pend'Oreille Lake. Suddenly he was sent flying head over heels, by a blow which completely knocked the breath out of his body; and so instantaneous was the whole affair that all he could ever recollect about it was getting a vague glimpse of the bear just as he was bowled over. When he came to he found himself lying some distance down the hill-side, much shaken, and without his berry pail, which had rolled a hundred yards below him, but not otherwise the worse for his misadventure; while the footprints showed that the bear, after delivering the single hurried stoke at the unwitting disturber of its day-dreams, had run off up-hill as fast as it was able.

A she-bear with cubs is a proverbially dangerous beast; yet even under such conditions different grislies act in directly opposite ways. Some she-grislies, when their cubs are young, but are able to follow them about, seem always worked up to the highest pitch of anxious and jealous rage, so that they are likely to attack unprovoked any intruder or even passer-by. Others when threatened by the hunter leave their cubs to their fate without a visible qualm of any kind, and seem to think only of their own safety.

In 1882 Mr. Casper W. Whitney, now of New York, met with a very singular adventure with a she-bear and cub. He was in Harvard when I was, but left it and, like a good many other Harvard men of that time, took to cow-punching in the West. He went on a ranch in Rio Arriba County, New Mexico, and was a keen hunter, especially fond of the chase of cougar, bear, and elk. One day while riding a stony mountain trail he saw a grisly cub watching him from the chaparral above, and he dismounted to try to capture it; his rifle was a 40–90 Sharp's. Just as he neared the cub, he heard a growl and caught a glimpse of the old she, and he at once turned up-hill, and stood under some tall, quaking aspens. From this spot he fired at and wounded the she, then seventy yards off; and she charged furiously. He hit her again, but as she kept coming like a thunderbolt he climbed hastily up the aspen, dragging his gun with him, as it had a strap. When the bear reached the foot of the aspen she reared, and bit and clawed the slender trunk, shaking it for a moment, and he shot her through the eye. Off she sprang for a few yards, and then spun round a dozen times, as if dazed or partially stunned; for the bullet had not touched the brain. Then the vindictive and resolute beast came back to the tree and again reared up against it; this time to receive a bullet that dropped her lifeless. Mr. Whitney then climbed down and walked to where the cub had been sitting as a looker-on. The little animal did not move until he reached out his hand; when it suddenly struck at him like an angry cat, dove into the bushes, and was seen no more.

In the summer of 1888 an old-time trapper, named Charley Norton, while on Loon Creek, of the middle fork of the Salmon, meddled with a she and her cubs. She ran at him and with one blow of her paw almost knocked off his lower jaw; yet he recovered, and was alive when I last heard of him.

Yet the very next spring the cowboys with my own wagon on the Little Missouri round-up killed a mother bear which made but little more fight than a coyote. She had two cubs, and was surprised in the early morning on the prairie far from cover. There were eight or ten cowboys together at the time, just starting off on a long circle, and of course they all got down their ropes in a second, and putting spurs to their fiery little horses started toward the bears at a run, shouting and swinging their loops round their heads. For a moment the old she tried to bluster and made a half-hearted threat of charging; but her courage failed before the rapid onslaught of her yelling, rope-swinging assailants; and she took to her heels and galloped off, leaving the cubs to shift for themselves. The cowboys were close behind, however, and after half a mile's run she bolted into a shallow cave or hole in the side of a butte, where she stayed cowering and growling, until one of the men leaped off his horse, ran up to the edge of the hole, and killed her with a single bullet from his revolver, fired so close that the powder burned her hair. The unfortunate cubs were roped, and then so dragged about that they were speedily killed instead of being brought alive to camp, as ought to have been done.

In the cases mentioned above the grisly attacked only after having been itself assailed, or because it feared an assault, for itself or for its young. In the old days, however, it may almost be said that a grisly was more apt to attack than to flee. Lewis and Clarke and the early explorers who immediately succeeded them, as well as the first hunters and trappers, the "Rocky Mountain men" of the early decades of the present century, were repeatedly assailed in this manner; and not a few of the bear hunters of that period found that it was unnecessary to take much trouble about approaching their quarry, as the grisly was usually prompt to accept the challenge and to advance of its own accord, as soon as it discovered the foe. All this is changed now. Yet even at the present day an occasional vicious old bear may be found, in some far-off and little-trod fastness, which still keeps up the former habit of its kind. All old hunters have tales of this sort to relate, the prowess, cunning, strength, and ferocity of the grisly being favorite topics for campfire talk throughout the Rockies; but in most cases it is not safe to accept these stories without careful sifting.

Still it is just as unsafe to reject them all. One of my own cowboys was once attacked by a grisly, seemingly in pure wantonness. He was riding up a creek bottom and had just passed a clump of rose and bull-berry bushes when his horse gave such a leap as almost to unseat him, and then darted madly forward. Turning round in the saddle to his utter astonishment he saw a large bear galloping after him, at the horse's heels. For a few jumps the race was close, then the horse drew away and the bear wheeled and went into a thicket of wild plums. The amazed and indignant cowboy, as soon as he could rein in his steed, drew his revolver and rode back to and around the thicket, endeavoring to provoke his late pursuer to come out and try conclusions on more equal terms; but prudent Ephraim had apparently repented of his freak of ferocious bravado, and declined to leave the secure shelter of the jungle.

Other attacks are of a much more explicable nature. Mr. Huff-man, the photographer of Miles City, informed me once when butchering some slaughtered elk he was charged twice by a she-bear and two well-grown cubs. This was a piece of sheer bul-lying, undertaken solely with the purpose of driving away the man and feasting on the carcasses; for in each charge the three bears, after advancing with much blustering, roaring, and growling, halted just before coming to close quarters. In another instance a gentleman I once knew, a Mr. S. Carr was charged by a grisly from mere ill temper at being disturbed at mealtime. The man was rid-ing up a valley; and the bear was at an elk carcass, near a clump of firs. As soon as it became aware of the approach of the horseman, while he was yet over a hundred yards distant, it jumped on the carcass, looked at him a moment, and then ran straight for him. There was no particular reason why it should have charged, for it was fat and in good trim, though when killed its head showed scars made by the teeth of rival grislies. Apparently it had been living so well, principally on flesh, that it had become quarrel-some; and perhaps its not over sweet disposition had been soured by combats with others of its own kind. In yet another case, a grisly charged with even less excuse. An old trapper, from whom I occasionally bought fur, was toiling up a mountain pass when he spied a big bear sitting on his haunches on the hillside above. The trapper shouted and waved his cap; whereupon, to his amazement, the bear uttered a loud "wough" and charged straight down on him—only to fall a victim to misplaced boldness.

I am even inclined to think that there have been wholly exceptional occasions when a grisly has attacked a man with the deliberate purpose of making a meal of him; when, in other words, it has started on the career of a man-eater. At least, on any other theory I find it difficult to account for an attack which once came to my knowledge. I was at Sand point, on Pend'Oreille Lake, and met some French and Meti trappers, then in town with their bales of beaver, otter, and sable. One of them, who gave his name as Baptiste Lamoche, had his head twisted over to one side, the result of the bite of a bear. When the accident occurred he was out on a trapping trip with two companions. They had pitched camp right on the shore of a cove in a little lake, and his comrades were off fishing in a dugout or pirogue. He himself was sitting near the shore, by a little lean-to, watching some beaver meat which was sizzling over the dying embers. Suddenly, and without warning, a great bear, which had crept silently up beneath the shadows of the tall evergreens, rushed at him, with a guttural roar, and seized him before he could rise to his feet. It grasped him with its jaws at the junction of the neck and shoulder, making the teeth meet through bone, sinew, and muscle; and turning, tracked off towards the forest, dragging with it the helpless and paralyzed victim. Luckily the two men in the canoe had just paddled round the point, in sight of, and close to, camp. The man in the bow, seeing the plight of their comrade, seized his rifle and fired at the bear. The bullet went through the beast's lungs, and it forthwith dropped its prey, and running off some two hundred yards, lay down on its side and died. The rescued man recovered full health and strength, but never again carried his head straight.

Old hunters and mountain-men tell many stories, not only of malicious grislies thus attacking men in camp, but also of their even dogging the footsteps of some solitary hunter and killing him when the favorable opportunity occurs. Most of these tales are mere fables; but it is possible that in altogether exceptional instances they rest on a foundation of fact. One old hunter whom I knew told me such a story. He was a truthful old fellow and there was no doubt that he believed what he said, and that his companion was actually killed by a bear; but it is probable that he was mistaken in reading the signs of his comrade's fate, and that the latter was not dogged by the bear at all, but stumbled on him and was slain in the surprise of the moment.

At any rate, cases of wanton assaults by grislies are altogether out of the common. The ordinary hunter may live out his whole life in the wilderness and never know aught of a bear attacking a man unprovoked; and the great majority of bears are shot under circumstances of no special excitement, as they either make no fight at all, or, if they do fight, are killed before there is any risk of their doing damage. If surprised on the plains, at some distance from timber or from badly broken ground, it is no uncommon feat for a single horseman to kill them with a revolver. Twice of late years it has been performed in the neighborhood of my ranch. In both instances the men were not hunters out after game, but simply cowboys, riding over the range in early morning in pursuance of their ordinary duties among the cattle. I knew both men and have worked with them on the round-up. Like most cowboys, they carried 44-calibre Colt revolvers, and were accustomed to and fairly expert in their use, and they were mounted on ordinary cow-ponies—quick, wiry, plucky little beasts. In one case the bear was seen from quite a distance, lounging across a broad tableland. The cowboy, by taking advantage of a winding and rather shallow coulie, got quite close to him. He then scrambled out of the coulie, put spurs to his pony, and raced up to within fifty yards of the astonished bear ere the latter quite understood what it was that was running at him through the gray dawn. He made no attempt at fight, but ran at top speed towards a clump of brush not far off at the head of a creek. Before he could reach it, however, the galloping horsemen was alongside, and fired three shots into his broad back. He did not turn, but ran on into the bushes and then fell over and died.

In the other case the cowboy, a Texan, was mounted on a good cutting pony, a spirited, handy, agile little animal, but excitable, and with a habit of dancing, which rendered it difficult to shoot from its back. The man was with the round-up wagon, and had been sent off by himself to make a circle through some low, barren buttes, where it was not thought more than a few head of stock would be found. On rounding the corner of a small washout he almost ran over a bear which was feeding on the carcass of a steer that had died in an alkali hole. After a moment of stunned surprise the bear hurled himself at the intruder with furious impetuosity; while the cowboy, wheeling his horse on its haunches and dashing in the spurs, carried it just clear of his assailant's headlong rush. After a few springs he reined in and once more wheeled half round, having drawn his revolver, only to find the bear again charging and almost on him. This time he fired into it, near the joining of the neck and shoulder, the bullet going downwards into the chest hollow; and again by a quick dash to one side he just avoided the rush of the beast and the sweep of its mighty forepaw. The bear then halted for a minute, and he rode close by it at a run, firing a couple of shots, which brought on another resolute charge. The ground was somewhat rugged and broken, but his pony was as quick on its feet as a cat, and never stumbled, even when going at full speed to avoid the bear's first mad rushes. It speedily became so excited, however, as to render it almost impossible for the rider to take aim. Sometimes he would come up close to the bear and wait for it to charge, which it would do, first at a trot, or rather rack, and then at a lumbering but swift gallop; and he would fire one or two shots before being forced to run. At other times, if the bear stood still in a good place, he would run by it, firing as he rode. He spent many cartridges, and though most of them were wasted occasionally a bullet went home. The bear fought with the most savage courage, champing its bloody jaws, roaring with rage, and looking the very incarnation of evil fury. For some minutes it made no effort to flee, either charging or standing at bay. Then it began to move slowly towards a patch of ash and wild plums in the head of a coulie, some distance off. Its pursuer rode after it, and when close enough would push by it and fire, while the bear would spin quickly round and charge as fiercely as ever, though evidently beginning to grow weak. At last, when still a couple of hundred yards from cover the man found he had used up all his cartridges, and then merely followed at a safe distance. The bear no longer paid heed to him, but walked slowly forwards, swaying its great head from side to side, while the blood streamed from between its half-opened jaws. On reaching the cover he could tell by the waving of the bushes that it walked to the middle and then halted. A few minutes afterwards some of the other cowboys rode up, having been attracted by the incessant firing. They surrounded the thicket, firing and throwing stones into the bushes. Finally, as nothing moved, they ventured in and found the indomitable grisly warrior lying dead.

Cowboys delight in nothing so much as the chance to show their skill as riders and ropers; and they always try to ride down and rope any wild animal they come across in favorable ground and close enough up. If a party of them meets a bear in the open they have great fun; and the struggle between the shouting, galloping, rough-riders and their shaggy quarry is full of wild excitement and not unaccompanied by danger. The bear often throws the noose from his head so rapidly that it is a difficult matter to catch him; and his frequent charges scatter his tormentors in every direction while the horses become wild with fright over the roaring, bristling beast—for horses seem to dread a bear more than any other animal. If the bear cannot reach cover, however, his fate is sealed. Sooner or later, the noose tightens over one leg, or perchance over the neck and fore-paw, and as the rope straightens with a "plunk," the horse braces itself desperately and the bear tumbles over. Whether he regains his feet or not the cowboy keeps the rope taut; soon another noose tightens over a leg, and the bear is speedily rendered helpless.

I have known of these feats being performed several times in northern Wyoming, although never in the immediate neighborhood of my ranch. Mr. Archibald Roger's cowhands have in this manner caught several bears, on or near his ranch on the Gray Bull, which flows into the Bighorn; and those of Mr. G. B. Grinnell have also occasionally done so. Any set of moderately good ropers and riders, who are accustomed to back one another up and act together, can accomplish the feat if they have smooth ground and plenty of room. It is, however, indeed a feat of skill and daring for a single man; and yet I have known of more than one instance in which it has been accomplished by some reckless knight of the rope and the saddle. One such occurred in 1887 on the Flathead Reservation, the hero being a half-breed; and another in 1890 at the mouth of the Bighorn, where a cowboy roped, bound, and killed a large bear single-handed.

My friend General "Red" Jackson, of Bellemeade, in the pleasant mid-county of Tennessee, once did a feat which casts into the shade even the feats of the men of the lariat. General Jackson, who afterwards became one of the ablest and most renowned of the Confederate cavalry leaders, was at the time a young officer in the Mounted Rifle Regiment, now known as the 3rd United States Cavalry. It was some years before the Civil War, and the regiment was on duty in the Southwest, then the debatable land of Comanche and Apache. While on a scout after hostile Indians, the troops in their march roused a large grisly which sped off across the plain in front of them. Strict orders had been issued against firing at game, because of the nearness of the Indians. Young Jackson was a man of great strength, a keen swordsman, who always kept the finest edge on his blade, and he was on a swift and mettled Kentucky horse, which luckily had but one eye. Riding at full speed he soon overtook the quarry. As the horse hoofs sounded nearer, the grim bear ceased its flight, and whirling round stood at bay, raising itself on its hind-legs and threatening its pursuer with bared fangs and spread claws. Carefully riding his horse so that its blind side should be towards the monster, the cavalryman swept by at a run, handling his steed with such daring skill that he just cleared the blow of the dreaded forepaw, while with one mighty sabre stroke he cleft the bear's skull, slaying the grinning beast as it stood upright.

The White Goat and His Country

by Owen Wister

EDITOR'S NOTE: THE AUTHOR OF THE FIRST POPULAR WESTERN novel, *The Virginian*, shows his prose skills in this portrait of early mountain goat hunting. From *The Virginian*, Mr. Wister (1860–1938) is famous for the expression, "When you call me that, smile!" Also in *The Virginian*, he wrote, "When a man ain't got no ideas of his own, he'd ought to be kind o' careful who he borrows 'em from." He was a good friend of Theodore Roosevelt and shared hunting adventures with him.

* * *

In a corner of what is occasionally termed "Our Empire of the Northwest," there lies a country of mountains and valleys where, until recently, citizens have been few. At the present time certain mines, and uncertain hopes, have gathered an eccentric population and evoked some sudden towns. The names which several of these bear are tolerably sumptuous: Golden, Oro, and Ruby, for instance; and in them dwell many colonels and judges, and people who own one suit of clothes and half a name (colored by adjuncts, such as Hurry Up Ed), and who sleep almost anywhere. These communities are brisk, sanguine, and nomadic, full of good will and crime; and in each of them you will be likely to find a weekly newspaper, and an editor who is busy writing things about the neighboring editors. The flume slants down the hill bearing water to the concentrator; buckets unexpectedly swing out from the steep pines into mid-air, sailing along their wire to the mill; little new staring shanties appear daily; somebody having trouble in a saloon upsets a lamp, and half the town goes to ashes, while the colonels and Hurry Up Eds carouse over the fireworks till morning. In a short while there are more little shanties than ever, and the burnt district is forgotten. All this is going on not far from the mountain goat, but it is a forlorn distance from the railroad; and except for the stage line which the recent mining towns have necessitated, my route to the goat country might have been too prolonged and uncertain to attempt.

I stepped down one evening from the stage, the last public conveyance I was to see, after a journey that certainly has one good side. It is completely odious; and the breed of sportsmen that takes into camp every luxury excepting, perhaps, cracked ice, will not be tempted to infest the region until civilization has smoothed its path. The path, to be sure, does not roughen until one has gone along it for twenty-eight hundred miles. You may leave New York in the afternoon, and arrive very early indeed on the fifth day at Spokane. Here the luxuries begin to lessen, and a mean once-a-day train trundles you away on a branch west of Spokane at six in the morning into a landscape that wastes into a galloping consumption. Before noon the last sick tree, the ultimate starved blade of wheat, has perished from sight, and you come to the end of all things, it would seem; a domain of wretchedness unspeakable. Not even a warm, brilliant sun can galvanize the corpse of the bare ungainly earth. The railroad goes no further,—it is not surprising,—and the stage arranges to leave before the train arrives. Thus you spend sunset and sunrise in the moribund terminal town, the inhabitants of which frankly confess that they are not staying from choice. They were floated here by a boom-wave, which left them stranded. Kindly they were, and anxious to provide the stranger with what comforts existed.

Geographically I was in the "Big Bend" country, a bulk of land looped in by the Columbia River, and highly advertised by railroads for the benefit of "those seeking homes." Fruit and grain no doubt grow somewhere in it. What I saw was a desert cracked in two by a chasm sixty-five miles long. It rained in the night, and at seven next morning, bound for Port Columbia, we wallowed northward out of town in the sweating canvas-covered stage through primeval mud. After some eighteen miles we drew out of the rain area, and from around the wheels there immediately arose and came among us a primeval dust, monstrous, shapeless, and blind. First your power of speech deserted you, then your eyesight went, and at length you became uncertain whether you were alive. Then hilarity at the sheer discomfort overtook me, and I was joined in it by a brother American; but two drummers on the back seat could not understand, and seemed on the verge of tears. The landscape was entirely blotted out by the dust. Often you could not see the roadside,—if the road had any side. We may have been passing homes and fruit-trees, but I think not. I remember wondering if [we'd be] getting goat after all—But they proved well worth it.

Toward evening we descended into the sullen valley of the Columbia, which rushes along, sunk below the level of the desert we had crossed. High sterile hills flank its course, and with the sweeping, unfriendly speed of the stream, its bleak shores seemed a chilly place for home-seekers. Yet I blessed the change. A sight of running water once more, even of this overbearing flood, and of hills however dreary, was exhilaration after the degraded, stingy monotony of the Big Bend. The alkali trails in Wyoming do not seem paradises till you bring your memory of them here. Nor am I alone in my estimate of this impossible hole. There is a signpost sticking up in the middle of it, that originally told the traveler it was thirty-five miles to Central Ferry. But now the traveler has retorted; and three different handwritings on this sign-post reveal to you that you have had predecessors in your thought, comrades who shared your sorrows:

Forty-five miles to water. Seventy-five miles to wood.

And then the last word:

Two and one-half miles to hell.

Perhaps they were home-seekers.

We halted a moment at the town of Bridgeport, identified by one wooden store and an inchoate hotel. The rest may be seen upon blue-print maps, where you would suppose Bridgeport was a teeming metropolis. At Port Columbia, which we reached by a land-slide sort of road that slanted the stage over and put the twin drummers in mortal fear, we slept in one of the two buildings which indicate that town. It is another important center,—in blue print,—but invisible to the naked eye. In the morning, a rope ferry floated the new stage and us travelers across the river. The Okanagon flows south from lakes and waters above the British line, and joins the Columbia here. We entered its valley at once, crossed it soon by another rope ferry, and keeping northward, with the river to the east between us and the Colville Reservation, had one good meal at noon, and entering a smaller valley, reached Ruby that evening. Here the stage left me to continue its way to Conconally, six miles further on. With the friends who had come to meet me, I ascended out of Ruby the next day over the abrupt hill westward, and passing one night out in my blankets near a hospitable but limited cabin (its flowing-haired host fed us, played us the fiddle, and would have had us sleep inside), arrived bag and baggage the fourth day from the railroad at the forks of the Methow River— the next tributary of the Columbia below the Okanagon.

Here was a smiling country, winning the heart at sight. An ample beauty was over everything Nature had accomplished in this place; the pleasant trees and clear course of the stream, a fertile soil on the levels, the slopes of the foothills varied and gentle, unencumbered by woods, the purple cloak of forest above these on the mountains, and rising from the valley's head a crown of white, clean frozen pcaks. These are known to some as the Isabella Range and Mount Gardner, though the maps do not name them. Moreover, I heard that now I was within twenty-five miles of goats; and definite ridges were pointed out as the promised land.

Many things were said to me, first and last. I remember a ragged old trapper, lately come over the mountains from the Skagit River. Goats, did I say? On top there the goats had tangled your feet walking in the trail. He had shot two in camp for staring at him. Another accurate observer had seen three hundred on a hill just above Early Winter as he was passing by. The cabined dwellers on the Methow tied their horses to the fence and talked to me—so I had come from the East after goats, had I?—and in the store of the Man at the Forks I became something of a curiosity. Day by day I sat on the kegs of nails, or lay along the counter devoted to his dry-goods, and heard what passed. Citizens and denizens—for the Siwash with his family and horses was having his autumn hunt in the valley—knocked at the door to get their mail, or buy tobacco, or sell horns and fur, or stare for an hour and depart with a grunt; and the grave Man at the Forks stood behind one counter while I lay on the other, acquiring a miscellaneous knowledge. One old medical gentleman had slain all wild animals without weapons, and had been the personal friend of so many distinguished historical characters that we computed he was nineteen about the time of Bunker Hill. They were hospitable with their information, and I followed my rule of believing everything that I hear. And they were also hospitable with whatever they possessed. The memory of those distant dwellers among the mountains, young and old, is a friendly one, like the others I carry, whether of Wind or Powder Rivers, or the Yellowstone, or wherever Western trails have led me.

Yet disappointment and failure were the first things. There was all the zeal you could wish. We had wedged painfully into a severe country—twelve miles in two days, and trail-cutting between—when sickness turned us back, goatless. By this time October was almost gone, and the last three days of it went in patching up our disintegrated outfit. We needed other men and other horses; and while these were being sought, nothing was more usual than to hear "if we'd only been along with So-and-So, he saw goats" here and there, and apparently everywhere. We had, it would seem, ingeniously selected the only place where there were none. But somehow the services of So-and-So could not be procured. He had gone to town; or was busy getting his winter's meat; or his married daughter had just come to visit him, or he had married somebody else's daughter. I cannot remember the number of obstacles always lying between ourselves and So-and-So.

At length we were once more in camp on a stream named the Twispt. In the morning—new stroke of misfortune—one of us was threatened with illness, and returned to the Forks. We three, the guide, the cook, and myself, went on, finally leaving the narrow valley, and climbing four hours up a mountain at the rate of about a mile an hour. The question was, had winter come in the park above, for which we were heading? On top, we skirted a bare ridge from which everything fell precipitously away, and curving round along a steep hollow of the hill, came to an edge and saw the snow lying plentifully among the pines through which we must go down into the bottom of the park. But on the other side, where the sun came, there was little or none, and it was a most beautiful place. At the head of it was a little frozen lake fringed with tamarack, and a stream flowed down from this through scattered birches and pines, with good pasture for the horses between. The park sank at its outlet into a tall impassable cañon through which the stream joined the Twispt, miles below. It was a little lap of land clear at the top of the mountains, the final peaks and ridges of which rose all around, walling it in completely. You must climb these to be able to see into it, and the only possible approach for packhorses was the pine-tree slant, down which we came. Of course there was no trail.

We prospected before venturing, and T——, the guide, shook his head. It was only a question of days—possibly of hours—when snow must shut the place off from the world until spring. But T—— appreciated the three thousand miles I had come for goats; and if the worst came to the worst, said he, we could "make it in" to the Forks on foot, leading the horses, and leaving behind all baggage that weighed anything. So we went down. Our animals slipped a little, the snow balling their feet; but nothing happened, and we reached the bottom and chose a camp in a clump of tamarack and pine. The little stream, passing through shadows here, ran under a lid of frozen snow easily broken, and there was plenty of wood, and on the ground only such siftings of snow as could be swept clean for the tent. The saddles were piled handily under a tree, a good fireplace was dug, we had a comfortable supper; and nothing remained but that the goats should be where they ought to be—on the ridges above the park.

I have slept more soundly; doubt and hope kept my thoughts active. Yet even so, it was pleasant to wake in the quiet and hear the bell on our horse, Duster, occasionally tankle somewhere on the hill. My watch I had forgotten to place at T——'s disposal, so he was reduced to getting the time of day from the stars. He consulted the Great Bear, and seeing this constellation at an angle he judged to indicate five o'clock, he came back into the tent, and I heard him wake the cook, who crawled out of his blankets.

"Why, it's plumb night," the cook whined.

"Make the breakfast," said T——.

I opened my eyes, and shut them immediately in despair at the darkness that I saw. Presently I heard the fire and the pans, and knew that the inevitable had come. So I got my clothes on, and we looked at my watch. It was only 4.30 A. M. T——and the Great Bear had made half an hour's miscalculation, and the face of the cook was so grievous that I secretly laughed myself entirely awake. "Plumb night" lasted some time longer. I had leisure to eat two plates of oatmeal and maple syrup, some potato-and-onion soup, bacon, and coffee, and digest these, before dawn showed.

T—— and I left camp at 6.40 A. M. The day was a dark one. On the high peaks behind camp great mounds of cloud moved and swung, and the sky was entirely overcast. We climbed one of the lower ridges, not a hard climb nor long, but very sliding, and often requiring hands and feet to work round a ledge. From the top we could see the open country lying comfortably below and out of reach of the howling wind that cut across the top of the mountain, straight from Puget Sound, bringing all that it could carry of the damp of the Pacific. The ridges and summits that surrounded our park continually came into sight and disappeared again among the dense vapors which bore down upon them.

We went cautiously along the narrow top of crumbling slate, where the pines were scarce and stunted, and had twisted themselves into corkscrews so they might grip the ground against the tearing force of storms. We came on a number of fresh goat-tracks in the snow or the soft shale. These are the reverse of those of the mountain sheep, the V which the hoofs make having its open end in the direction the animal is going. There seemed to be several, large and small; and the perverted animals invariably chose the sharpest slant they could find to walk on, often with a decent level just beside it that we were glad enough to have. If there were a precipice and a sound flat top, they took the precipice, and crossed its face on juts that did not look as if your hat would hang on them. In this I think they are worse than the mountain sheep, if that is possible. Certainly they do not seem to come down into the high pastures and feed on the grass levels as the sheep will.

T—— and I hoped we should find a bunch, but that was not to be, in spite of the indications. As we continued, I saw a singular-looking stone lying on a little ledge some way down the mountain ahead. I decided it must be a stone, and was going to speak of it, when the stone moved, and we crouched in the slanting gravel. T—— had been making up his mind it was a stone. The goat turned his head our way, but did not rise. He was two hundred yards across a split in the mountain, and the wind blowing hard. T—— wanted me to shoot, but I did not dare to run such a chance. I have done a deal of missing at two hundred yards, and much nearer, too. So I climbed, or crawled, out of sight, keeping any stone or little bush between me and the goat, till I got myself where a buttress of rock hid me, and then I ran along the ridge and down and up the scoop in it made by the split of the mountain, and so came cautiously to where I could peer over and see the goat lying turned away from me, with his head commanding the valley. He was on a tiny shelf of snow, beside him was one small pine, and below that the rock fell away steeply into the gorge. Ought I to have bellowed at him, and at least have got him on his legs? I know it would have been more honorable. He looked white, and huge, and strange; and somehow I had a sense of personality about him more vivid than any since I watched my first silver-tip lift a rotten log, and, sitting on his hind legs, make a breakfast on beetles, picking them off the log with one paw.

I fired, aiming behind the goat's head. He did not rise, but turned his head round. The white bead of my Lyman sight had not showed well against the white animal, and I thought I had missed him. Then I fired again, and he rolled very little—six inches—and lay quiet. He could not have been more than fifty yards away, and my first shot had cut through the back of his neck and buried itself in mortal places, and the second in his head merely made death instantaneous. Shooting him after he had become alarmed might have lost him over the edge; even if a first shot had been fatal, it could not have been fatal soon enough. Two struggles on that snow would have sent him sliding through space. As it was, we had a steep, unsafe scramble down through the snow to where he lay stretched out on the little shelf by the tree.

He was a fair-sized billy, and very heavy. The little lifting and shoving we had to do in skinning him was hard work. The horns were black, slender, slightly spreading, curved backward, pointed, and smooth. They measured six inches round the base, and the distance from one point to the other, measured down one horn, along the skull, and up the other, was twenty-one and a half inches. The hoofs were also black and broad and large, wholly unlike a tame goat's. The hair was extraordinarily thick, long, and of a weather-beaten white; the eye large and deep-brown.

I had my invariable attack of remorse on looking closely at the poor harmless old gentleman, and wondered what achievement, after all, could be discerned in this sort of surprise and murder. We did not think of securing any of his plentiful fat, but with head and hide alone climbed back up the ticklish slant, hung the trophies on a tree in a gap on the camp side of the ridge, and continued our hunt. It was not ten o'clock yet, and we had taken one hour to skin the goat. We now hunted the higher ridges behind camp until 1 P. M., finding tracks that made it seem as if a number of goats must be somewhere nearby. But the fog came down and shut everything out of sight; moreover, the wind on top blew so that we could not have seen had it been clear.

We returned to camp, and found it greatly improved. The cook had carpentered an important annex to the tent. By slanting pine-logs against a ridgepole and nailing them, he had built a room, proof against wind and rain, and in it a table. One end was against the opening of the tent, the other at the fire. The arrangement was excellent, and timely also. The storm revived during the night, and it rained fitfully. The roar of the wind coming down from the mountain into our park sounded like a Niagara, and its approach was tremendous. We had built up a barrier of pine-brush, and this, with a clump of trees, sheltered us well enough; but there were wild moments when the gust struck us, and the tent shuddered

and strained, until that particular breeze passed on with a dimin-
ishing roar down the cañon.

The next morning the rain kept us from making an early start,
and we did not leave camp until eight. Now and then a drizzle
fell from the mist, and the banks of clouds were still driving
across the higher peaks, but during the day the sun slowly got the
better of them. Again we saw a solitary goat, this time far below
down the ridge we had chosen. Like the sheep, these animals
watch the valley. There is no use in attempting to hunt them
from there. Their eyes are watchful and keen, and the chances
are that if you are working up from below and see a goat on the
hill, he will have been looking at you for some time. Once he is
alarmed, ten minutes will be enough for him to put a good many
hours of climbing between himself and you. His favorite trick is
to remain stock-still, watching you till you pass out of his sight
behind something, and then he makes off so energetically that
when you see him next he will be on some totally new mountain. But his intelligence does not seem to grasp more than the
danger from below. While he is steadfastly on the alert against
this, it apparently does not occur to him that anything can come
down upon him. Consequently from above you may get very near
before you are noticed. The chief difficulty is the noise of falling
stones your descent is almost sure to make. The character of these
mountainsides is such that even with the greatest care in stepping
we sent a shower rattling down from time to time. We had a
viciously bad climb. We went down through tilted funnels of crag,
avoiding jumping off places by crossing slides of brittle slate and
shale, hailing a dead tree as an oasis. And then we lost count, and
T——came unexpectedly on the goat, which was up and away
and was shot by T—— before I could get a sight of him. I had
been behind some twenty yards, both of us supposing we had to
go considerably further. T—— was highly disgusted. "To think of
me managing such a botch as that," he said, "when you've come so

far"; and he wanted me to tell the people that I had shot the goat myself. He really cared more than I did.

This goat was also a billy, and larger than the first. We sat skinning him where he had fallen at the edge of a grove of tamarack, and T——conversed about the royal family of England. He remarked that he had always rather liked "that chap Lorne."

I explained to him that "that chap Lorne" had made himself ridiculous forever at the Queen's Jubilee. Then, as T——did not know, I told him how the marquis had insisted on riding in the procession upon a horse, against which the Prince of Wales, aware of the tame extent of his horsemanship, had warned him. In the middle of the pageant, the Queen in her carriage, the crowned heads of Europe escorting her on horseback, and the whole world looking on—at this picturesque moment, Lorne fell off. I was not sure that T—— felt fully how inappropriate a time this was for a marquis to tumble from his steed.

"I believe the Queen sent somebody," I continued.

"Where?" said T——.

"To him. She probably called the nearest king and said: 'Frederick, Lorne's off. Go and see if he's hurt.'"

"'And if he ain't hurt, *hurt him*,'" said T——, completing her Majesty's thought.

This second billy seemed to me twice the size of a domestic goat. He was certainly twice the weight. His hide alone weighed thirty pounds, as far as one could determine by balancing it against weights that we knew, such as a sack of flour or sugar. But I distrust the measurements of wild animals made by guesswork on a mountain-top during the enthusiastic state of the hunter's mind which follows at once upon a lucky shot. Therefore, I can positively vouch for this only, that all the goats which I have seen struck me as being larger and heavier animals than the goat of civilization. After all, the comparison is one into which we are misled by the name. This is an antelope; and though, through certain details of his costume, he is able to masquerade as a goat, it must be remembered that he is of a species wholly distinct. We took the web tallow, and the tallow of one kidney. The web was three quarters of an inch thick.

Neither elk, nor any animal I have seen, except bear, has such quantities of fat, and I do not think even a bear has a thicker hide. On the rump it was as thick as the sole of my boot, and the masses of hair are impenetrable to anything but modern firearms. An arrow might easily stick harmless; and I am told that carnivorous animals who prey upon the deer in these mountains respectfully let the goat alone. Besides his defensive armor, he is an ugly customer in attack. He understands the use of his thin, smooth horns, and, driving them securely into the belly of his enemy, jumps back and leaves him a useless, ripped-open sack. Male and female have horns of much the same size; and in taking a bite out of one of either sex, as T—— said, a mountain lion would get only a mouthful of hair.

But modern firearms have come to be appreciated by the wild animals; and those which were once unquestionably dangerous to pioneers, now retreat before the Winchester rifle. Only a bear with cubs to defend remains formidable.

I said this to T——, who told me a personal experience that tends to destroy even this last chance for the sportsman to be doughty. T—— came on a bear and cubs in the spring, and of course they made off, but his dog caught and held one little cub which cried out like a child—and its contemptible mama hurried straight on and away.

Not so a goat mama of which T—— also told me. Some prospectors came on a bunch of goats when the kids were young enough to be caught. One of the men captured a kid, and was walking off with it, when the mother took notice and charged furiously down on him. He flew by in ignominious sight of the whole camp with the goat after him, till he was obliged to drop the kid, which was then escorted back to its relatives by its most competent parent.

Yet no room for generalizing is here. We cannot conclude that the *Ursus* family fails to think blood as thick as other people do. These two incidents merely show that the race of bears is capable of producing unmaternal females, while, on the other hand, we may expect occasionally to find in a nanny-goat a Mother of the Gracchi.

I wished to help carry the heavy hide of the second billy; but T—— inflicted this upon himself, "every step to camp," he insisted, "for punishment at disappointing you." The descent this day had been bad enough, taking forty minutes for some four hundred yards. But now we were two hours getting up, a large part of the way on hands and knees. I carried the two rifles and the glass, going in front to stamp some sort of a trail in the sliding rocks, while T—— panted behind me, bearing the goat-hide on his back.

Our next hunt was from seven till four, up and down, in the presence of noble and lonely mountains. The straight peaks which marshal round the lake of Chelan were in our view nearby, beyond the valley of the Twisp, and the whole Cascade range rose endlessly, and seemed to fill the world. Except in Switzerland, I have never seen such an unbroken area of mountains. And all this beauty going begging, while each year our American citizens of the East, more ignorant of their own country and less identified with its soil than any race upon earth, herd across the sea to the tables d'hôte they know by heart! But this is wandering a long way from goats, of which this day we saw none.

A gale set in after sunset. This particular afternoon had been so mellow, the sun had shone so clear from a stable sky, that I had begun to believe the recent threats of winter were only threats, and that we had some open time before us still. Next morning we waked in midwinter, the flakes flying thick and furious over a park that was no longer a pasture, but a blind drift of snow. We lived in camp, perfectly comfortable. Down at the Forks I had had made a rough imitation of a Sibley stove. All that its forger had to go on was my unprofessional and inexpert description, and a lame sketch in pencil; but he succeeded so well that the hollow iron cone and joints of pipe he fitted together turned out most efficient. The sight of the apparatus packed on a horse with the panniers was whimsical, and until he saw it work I know that T—— despised it. After that, it commanded his respect. All this stormy day it roared and blazed, and sent a lusty heat throughout the tent. T—— cleaned the two goat-heads, and talked Shakespeare and Thackeray to me. He quoted Henry the Fourth, and regretted that Thackeray had not more developed the character of George Warrington. Warrington was the *man* in the book. When night came the storm was gone.

By eight the next morning we had sighted another large solitary billy. But he had seen us down in the park from his ridge. He had come to the edge, and was evidently watching the horses. If not quick-witted, the goat is certainly wary; and the next time we saw him he had taken himself away down the other side of the mountain, along a spine of rocks where approach was almost impossible. We watched his slow movements through the glass, and were both reminded of a bear. He felt safe, and was stepping deliberately along, often stopping, often walking up some small point and surveying the scenery. He moved in an easy, rolling fashion, and turned his head importantly. Then he lay down in the sun, but saw us on our way to him, and bounced off. We came to the place where he had jumped down sheer twenty feet at least. His hoof-tracks were on the edge, and in the gravel below the heavy scatter he made in landing; and then,—hasty tracks round a corner of rock, and no more goat that day.

I had become uneasy about the weather. It was all sunshine again, and though our first goat was irretrievably gone, we had the afternoon before us. Nevertheless, when I suggested we should spend it in taking the shoes off the horses, so they might be able to walk homeward without falling in the snow, T—— thought it our best plan. We wanted to find a bunch of goats now, nannies and kids, as well as billies. It had been plain that these ridges here contained very few, and those all hermits; males who from age, or temperament, or disappointment in love, had retired from society, and were spending the remainder of their days in a quiet isolation and whatever is the goat equivalent for reading Horace. It was well enough to have begun with these philosophers, but I wanted new specimens.

We were not too soon. A new storm had set in by next morning, and the unshod horses made their journey down the mountain, a most odious descent for man and beast, in the sliding snow. But down on the Twispt it was yet only autumn, with no snow at all. This was a Monday, the 7th of November, and we made haste to the Forks, where I stopped a night to read a large, accumulated mail, and going on at once, overtook my outfit, which had preceded me on the day before.

Our new camp—and our last one—was up the Methow, twenty-three miles above the Forks, in a straight line. Here the valley split at right angles against a tall face of mountain, and each way the stream was reduced to a brook one could cross afoot. The new valley became steep and narrow almost at once, and so continued to the divide between Columbia water and tributaries of the Skagit. We lived comfortably in an old cabin built by prospectors. The rain filtered through the growing weeds and sand on the roof and dropped on my head in bed; but not much, and I was able to steer it off by a rubber blanket. And of course there was no glass in the windows; but to keep out wind and wet we hung gunny sacks across those small holes, and the big stone fireplace was magnificent.

By ten next morning T—— and I saw "three hundred" goats on the mountain opposite where we had climbed. Just here I will risk a generalization. When a trapper tells you he has seen so many hundred head of game, he has not counted them, but he believes what he says. The goats T——and I now looked at were a mile away in an airline, and they seemed numberless. The picture which the white, slightly moving dots made, like mites on a cheese, inclined one to a large estimate of them, since they covered the whole side of a hill. The more we looked the more we found; besides the main army there were groups, caucuses, families sitting apart over some discourse too intimate for the general public; and beyond these single animals could be discerned, moving, gazing, browsing, lying down.

"Megod and Begod," said T—— (he occasionally imitated a brogue for no hereditary reason), "there's a hundred thousand goats!"

"Let's count 'em," I suggested, and we took the glasses. There were thirty-five.

We found we had climbed the wrong hill, and the day was too short to repair this error. Our next excursion, however, was successful. The hill where the goats were was not two miles above camp,—you could have seen the animals from camp but for the curve in the cañon,—yet we were four hours and a half climbing the ridge, in order to put ourselves above them. It was a hard climb, entirely through snow after the first. On top the snow came at times considerably above the knees. But the judicious T—— (I have never hunted with a more careful and thorough man) was right in the route he had chosen, and after we had descended again to the edge of the snow, we looked over a rock, and saw, thirty yards below us, the nanny and kid for which we had been aiming. I should have said earlier that the gathering of yesterday had dispersed during the night, and now little bunches of three and four goats could be seen up and down the cañon. We were on the exact ground they had occupied, and their many tracks were plain. My first shot missed—thirty yards!—and as nanny and kid went bounding by on the hill below, I knocked her over with a more careful bullet, and T—— shot the kid. The little thing was not dead when we came up, and at the sight of us it gave a poor little thin bleat that turns me remorseful whenever I think of it. We had all the justification that any code exacts. We had no fresh meat, and among goats the kid alone is eatable; and I justly desired specimens of the entire family.

We carried the whole kid to camp, and later its flesh was excellent. The horns of the nanny, as has been said before, are but slightly different from those of the male. They are, perhaps, more slender, as is also the total makeup of the animal. In camp I said to T—— that I desired only one more of those thirty-five goats, a billy; and that if I secured him the next day, that should be the last. Fortune was for us. We surprised a bunch of several. They had seen me also, and I was obliged to be quick. This resulted in some shots missing, and in two, perhaps three, animals going over ledges with bullets in them, leaving safe behind the billy I wanted. His conduct is an interesting example of the goat's capacity to escape you and die uselessly, out of your reach.

I had seen him reel at my first shot, but he hurried around a corner, and my attention was given to others. As I went down, I heard a shot, and came round the corner on T——, who stood some hundred yards further along the ledge beside a goat. T—— had come on him lying down. He had jumped up and run apparently unhurt, and T—— had shot him just as he reached the end of the ledge. Beyond was a fall into inaccessible depths. Besides T——'s shot we found two of mine—one clean through from the shoulder—the goat had faced me when I fired first—to the ham, where the lead was flat against the bone. This goat was the handsomest we had, smaller than the other males, but with horns of a better shape, and with hair and beard very rich and white. Curiously enough, his lower jaw between the two front teeth had been broken a long time ago, probably from some fall. Yet this accident did not seem to have interfered with his feeding, for he was in excellent plump condition.

This completely satisfied me, and I willingly decided to molest no more goats. I set neither value nor respect on numerical slaughter. One cannot expect Englishmen to care whether American big game is exterminated or not; that Americans should not care is a disgrace. The pervading spirit of the far West as to game, as to timber, as to everything that a true American should feel it his right to use and his duty to preserve for those coming after, is—"What do I care, so long as it lasts my time?"

There remain a few observations to make, and then I have said the little that I know about goats. Their horns are not deciduous, so far at least as I could learn, and the books say this also. But I read a somewhat inaccurate account of the goat's habits in wintertime. It was stated that at that season, like mountain sheep, he descends and comes into the valleys. This does not seem to be the case. He does not depend upon grass, if indeed he eats grass at all. His food seems to be chiefly the short, almost lichen-like moss that grows on the faces and at the base of the rocks and between them in the crevices. The community of goats I watched was feeding; afterward, when on the spot where they had been, I found there was no grass growing anywhere near, and signs pointed to its having been the moss and rock plants that they had been eating. None of the people in the Methow country spoke of seeing goats come out of the mountains during winter. I have not sufficient data to make the assertion, but I am inclined to believe that the goat keeps consistently to the hills, whatever the season may be, and in this differs from the mountain sheep as he differs in appearance, temperament, and in all characteristics excepting the predilection for the inclined plane; and in this habit he is more vertical than the sheep.

Lest the region I hunted in may have remained vague to Eastern readers, it is as well to add that in an airline I was probably some thirty miles below the British border, and some hundred and twenty east of Puget Sound.

Owen Wister.

That Twenty-Five-Pound Gobbler

by Archibald Rutledge

THIS EDITOR HAS ALWAYS LOOKED UPON THE WORKS OF Archibald Rutledge (1883–1973) with great awe. His prose and poetry set in the South Carolina Lowcountry call out the life I spent as a youth in southeast Georgia. My days afield could not match the great Archibald Rutledge adventures from Hampton and the Santee River area, but I found much reading that bonded me with Mr. Rutledge. Poet laureate of South Carolina and author of so many stories and books too lengthy to mention in the limited space here, Rutledge was a man who led two lives. In one life he grew up on Hampton Plantation and returned there for lengthy Christmas vacations every year. His other life was as an English professor at Mercersburg Academy in Pennsylvania.

* * *

I suppose that there are other things which make a hunter uneasy, but of one thing I am very sure: that is to locate and to begin to stalk a deer or a turkey, only to find that another hunter is doing precisely the same thing at the same time. The feeling I had was worse than uneasy. It is, in fact, as inaccurate as if a man should say, after listening to a comrade swearing roundly, "Bill is expressing himself uneasily."

To be frank, I was jealous; and all the more so because I knew that Dade Saunders was just as good a turkey-hunter as I am— and maybe a good deal better. At any rate, both of us got after the same whopping gobbler. We knew this turkey and we knew each other; and I am positive that the wise old bird knew both of us far better than we knew him.

But we hunters have ways of improving our acquaintance with creatures that are over-wild and shy. Both Dade and I saw him, I suppose, a dozen times; and twice Dade shot at him. I had never fired at him, for I did not want to cripple, but to kill; and he never came within a hundred yards of me. Yet I felt that the gobbler ought to be mine; and for the simple reason that Dade Saunders was a shameless poacher and a hunter-out-of-season.

I have in mind the day when I came upon him in the pine-lands in mid-July, when he had in his wagon five bucks in the velvet, all killed that morning. Now, this isn't a fiction story; this is fact. And after I have told you of those bucks, I think you'll want me to beat Dade to the great American bird.

This wild turkey had the oddest range that you could imagine. You hear of turkeys ranging "original forests," "timbered wilds," and the like. Make up your mind that if wild turkeys have a chance they are going to come near civilization. The closer they are to man, the farther they are away from their other enemies. Near civilization they at least have (but for the likes of Dade Saunders) the protection of the law. But in the wilds what protection do they have from wildcats, from eagles, from weasels (I am thinking of young turkeys as well as old), and from all their other predatory persecutors?

Well, as I say, time and again I have known wild turkeys to come, and to seem to enjoy coming, close to houses. I have stood on the porch of my plantation home and have watched a wild flock feeding under the great live-oaks there. I have repeatedly flushed wild turkeys in an autumn cornfield. I have shot them in rice stubble.

Of course they do not come for sentiment. They are after grain. And if there is any better wild game than a rice-field wild turkey, stuffed with peanuts, circled with browned sweet potatoes, and fragrant with a rich gravy that plantation cooks know how to make, I'll follow you to it.

The gobbler I was after was a haunter of the edges of civilization. He didn't seem to like the wild woods. I think he got hungry there. But on the margins of fields that had been planted he could get all he wanted to eat of the things he most enjoyed. He particularly liked the edges of cultivated fields that bordered either on the pinewoods or else on the marshy rice-lands.

One day I spent three hours in the gaunt chimney of a burned rice-mill, watching this gobbler feeding on such edges. Although I was sure that sooner or later he would pass the mouth of the chimney, giving me a chance for a shot, he kept just that distance between us that makes a gun a vain thing in a man's hands. But though he did not give me my chance, he let me watch him all I pleased. This I did through certain dusty crevices between the bricks of the old chimney.

If I had been taking a post-graduate course in caution, this wise old bird would have been my teacher. Whatever he happened to be doing, his eyes and his ears were wide with vigilance. I saw him first standing beside a fallen pine log on the brow of a little hill where peanuts had been planted. I made the shelter of the chimney before he recognized me. But he must have seen the move I made.

I have hunted turkeys long enough to be thoroughly rid of the idea that a human being can make a motion that a wild turkey cannot see. One of my woodsman friends said to me, "Why, a gobbler can see anything. He can see a jaybird turn a somersault on the verge of the horizon." He was right.

Watching from my cover I saw this gobbler scratching for peanuts. He was very deliberate about this. Often he would draw back one huge handful (or footful) of viney soil, only to leave it there while he looked and listened. I have seen a turkey do the same thing while scratching in leaves. Now, a buck while feeding will alternately keep his head up and down; but a turkey gobbler keeps his down very little. That bright black eye of his, set in that sharp bluish head, is keeping its vision on every object on the landscape.

My gobbler (I called him mine from the first time I saw him) found many peanuts, and he relished them. From that feast he walked over into a patch of autumn-dried crabgrass. The long pendulous heads of this grass, full of seeds, he stripped skilfully. When satisfied with this food, he dusted himself beside an old stump. It was interesting to watch this; and while he was doing it I wondered if it was not my chance to leave the chimney, make a detour, and come up behind the stump. But of course just as I decided to do this, he got up, shook a small cloud of dust from his feathers, stepped off into the open, and there began to preen himself.

A short while thereafter he went down to a marshy edge, there finding a warm sandy hole on the sunny side of a briar patch, where he continued his dusting and loafing. I believe that he knew the stump, which shut off his view of what was behind it, was no place to choose for a midday rest.

All this time I waited patiently; interested, to be sure, but I would have been vastly more so if the lordly old fellow had turned my way. This I expected him to do when he got tired of loafing. Instead, he deliberately walked into the tall ranks of the marsh, which extended riverward for half a mile. At that I hurried forward, hoping to flush him on the margin; but he had vanished for that day. But though he had escaped me, the sight of him had made me keen to follow him until he expressed a willingness to accompany me home.

Just as I was turning away from the marsh I heard a turkey call from the shelter of a big live-oak beside the old chimney. I knew that it was Dade Saunders, and that he was after my gobbler.

I walked over to where he was making his box-call plead. He expressed no surprise on seeing me. We greeted each other as two hunters, who are not over-friendly, greet when they find themselves after the same game.

"I seen his tracks," said Dade. "I believe he limps in the one foot since I shot him last Sunday will be a week."

"He must be a big bird," I said; "you were lucky to have a shot."

Dade's eyes grew hungrily bright.

"He's the biggest in these woods, and I'll git him yet. You jest watch me."

"I suppose you will, Dade. You are the best turkey-hunter of these parts."

I hoped to make him overconfident; and praise is a great corrupter of mankind. It is not unlikely to make a hunter miss a shot. I remember that a friend of mine once said laughingly: "If a man tells me I am a good shot, I will miss my next chance, as sure as guns; but if he cusses me and tells me I'm not worth a darn, then watch me shoot!"

Dade and I parted for the time. I went off toward the marsh, whistling an old song. I wanted to have the gobbler put a little more distance between himself and the poacher. Besides, I felt that it was right of me to do this: for while I was on my own land, my visitor was trespassing. I hung around in the scrub–oak thickets for awhile; but no gun spoke out, I knew that the old gobbler's intelligence plus my whistling game had "foiled the relentless" Dade. It was a week later that the three of us met again.

Not far from the peanut field there is a plantation corner. Now, most plantation corners are graveyards; that is, cemeteries of the old days, where slaves were buried. Pathways have to be cut through the jungle-like growths to enable the cortege to enter.

Such a place is a wilderness for sure. Here grow towering pines, mournful and moss-draped. Here are hollies, canopied with jasmine-vines; here are thickets of myrtle, sweet gum, and young pines. If a covey of quail goes into such a place, you might as well whistle your dog off and go after another lot of birds.

Here deer love to come in the summer, where they can hide from the heat and the gauze-winged flies. Here in the winter is a haunt for woodcock, a good range (for great live-oaks drop their sweet acorns) for wild turkeys, and a harbor for foxes. In those great pines and oaks turkeys love to roost. It was on the borders of just such a corner that I roosted the splendid gobbler.

It was a glowing December sunset. I had left the house an hour before to stroll the plantation roads, counting (as I always do) the number of deer and turkey tracks that had recently been made in the soft damp sand. Coming near the dense corner, I sat against the bole of a monster pine. I love to be a mere watcher in woodlands as well as a hunter.

About two hundred yards away there was a little sunny hill, grown to scrub-oaks. They stood sparsely; that enabled me to see well what I now saw. Into my vision, with the rays of the sinking sun gleaming softly on the bronze of his neck and shoulders, the great gobbler stepped with superb beauty. Though he deigned to scratch once or twice in the leaves, and peck indifferently at what he thus uncovered, I knew he was bent on roosting; for not only was it nearly his bedtime, but he seemed to be examining with critical judgment every tall tree in his neighborhood.

He remained in my sight ten minutes; then he stepped into a patch of gallberries. I sat where I was. I tried my best to be as silent and as motionless as the bodies lying in the ancient graves behind me. The big fellow kept me on the anxious bench for five minutes. Then he shot his great bulk into the air, beating his ponderous way into the huge pine that seemed to sentry that whole wild tract of woodland.

I marked him when he came to his limb. He sailed up to it and alighted with much scraping of bark with his No. 10 shoes. There was my gobbler poised against the warm red sky of that winter twilight. It was hard to take my sight from him; but I did so in order to get my bearings in relation to his position. His flight had brought him nearer to me than he had been on the ground. But he was still far out of gun-range.

There was no use for me to look into the graveyard, for a man cannot see a foot into such a place. I glanced down the dim pine-wood road. A moving object along its edge attracted my attention. It skulked. It seemed to flit like a ghostly thing from pine to pine. But, though I was near a cemetery, I knew I was looking at no "haunt." It was Dade Saunders.

He had roosted the gobbler, and he was trying to get up to him. Moreover, he was at least fifty yards closer to him than I was. I felt like shouting to him to get off my land; but then a better thought came. I pulled out my turkey call.

The first note was good, as was intended. But after that there came some heart-stilling squeaks and shrills. In the dusk I noted two things; I saw Dade make a furious gesture, and at almost the same instant the old gobbler launched out from the pine, winging a lordly way far across the graveyard thicket. I walked down slowly and peeringly to meet Dade.

"Your call's broke," he announced.

"What makes you think so?" I asked.

"Sounds awful funny to me," he said; "more than likely it might scare a turkey. Seen him lately?" he asked.

"You are better at seeing that old bird than I am, Dade."

Thus I put him off; and shortly thereafter we parted. He was sure that I had not seen the gobbler; and that suited me all right.

Then came the day of days. I was up at dawn, and when certain red lights between the stems of the pines announced daybreak, I was at the far southern end of the plantation, on a road on either side of which were good turkey woods. I just had a notion that my gobbler might be found there, as he had of late taken to roosting in a tupelo swamp near the river, and adjacent to these woodlands.

Where some lumbermen had cut away the big timber, sawing the huge short-leaf pines close to the ground, I took my stand (or my seat) on one of these big stumps. Before me was a tangle of undergrowth; but it was not very thick or high. It gave me the screen I wanted; but if my turkey came out through it, I could see to shoot.

It was just before sunrise that I began to call. It was a little early in the year (then the end of February) to lure a solitary gobbler by a call; but otherwise the chance looked good. And I am vain enough to say that my willow box was not broken that morning. Yet it was not I but two Cooper's hawks that got the old wily rascal excited.

They were circling high and crying shrilly over a certain stretch of deep woodland; and the gobbler, undoubtedly irritated by the sounds, or at least not to be outdone by two mere marauders on a domain which he felt to be his own, would gobble fiercely every time one of the hawks would cry. The hawks had their eye on a building site; wherefore their excited maneuvering and shrilling continued; and as long as they kept up their screaming, so long did the wild gobbler answer in rivalry or provoked superiority, until his wattles must have been fiery red and near to bursting.

I had an idea that the hawks were directing some of their crying at the turkey, in which case the performance was a genuine scolding match of the wilderness. And before it was over, several gray squirrels had added to the already raucous debate their impatient coughing barks. This business lasted nearly an hour, until the sun had begun to make the thickets "smoke off" their shining burden of morning dew.

I had let up on my calling for awhile; but when the hawks had at last been silenced by the distance, I began once more to plead. Had I had a gobbler-call, the now enraged turkey would have come to me as straight as a surveyor runs a line. But I did my best with the one I had. I had answered by one short gobble, then by silence.

I laid down my call on the stump and took up my gun. It was in such a position that I could shoot quickly without much further motion. It is a genuine feat to shoot a turkey on the ground after he has made you out. I felt that a great moment was coming.

But you know how hunter's luck sometimes turns. Just as I thought it was about time for him to be in the pine thicket ahead of me, when, indeed, I thought I had heard his heavy but cautious step, from across the road, where lay the companion tract of turkey-woods to the one I was in, came a delicately pleading call from a hen turkey. The thing was irresistible to the gobbler; but I knew it to be Dade Saunders. What should I do?

At such a time a man has to use all the headwork he has. And in hunting I had long since learned that that often means not to do a darn thing but to sit tight. All I did was to put my gun to my face. If the gobbler was going to Dade, he might pass me. I had started him coming; if Dade kept him going, he might run within hailing distance. Dade was farther back in the woods than I was. I waited.

No step was heard. No twig was snapped. But suddenly, fifty yards ahead of me, the great bird emerged from the thicket of pines. For an instant the sun gleamed on his royal plumage. My gun was on him, but the glint of the sun along the barrel dazzled me. I stayed my finger on the trigger. At that instant he made me out. What he did was smart. He made himself so small that I believed it to be a second turkey. Then he ran crouching through the vines and huckleberry bushes.

Four times I thought I had my gun on him, but his dodging was that of an expert. He was getting away; moreover, he was making straight for Dade. There was a small gap in the bushes sixty yards from me, off to my left. He had not yet crossed that. I threw my gun in the opening. In a moment he flashed into it, running like a racehorse. I let him have it. And I saw him go down.

Five minutes later, when I had hung him on a scrub-oak, and was admiring the entire beauty of him, a knowing, cat-like step sounded behind me.

"Well, sir," said Dade, a generous admiration for the beauty of the great bird overcoming other less kindly emotions, "so you beat me to him."

There was nothing for me to do but to agree. I then asked Dade to walk home with me so that we might weigh him. He carried the scales well down at the 25-pound mark. An extraordinary feature of his manly equipment was the presence of three separate beards, one beneath the other, no two connected. And his spurs were respectable rapiers.

"Dade," I said, "what am I gong to do with this gobbler? I am alone here on the plantation."

The pineland poacher did not solve my problem for me.

"I tell you," said I, trying to forget the matter of the five velveted bucks, "some of the boys from down the river are going to come up on Sunday to see how he tastes. Will you join us?"

You know Dade Saunders' answer; for when a hunter refuses an invitation to help eat a wild turkey, he can be sold to a circus.

CHAPTER 12

In Buffalo Days

by George Bird Grinnell

GEORGE BIRD GRINNELL (1849–1938) WAS AN AMERICAN
anthropologist, historian, naturalist, and writer. Grinnell was
prominent in movements to preserve wildlife and conservation in
the American West. Grinnell wrote articles to help spread aware-
ness of the conservation of buffalo. For many years, he published
articles and lobbied for congressional support for the endangered
American buffalo. In 1887, Grinnell was a founding member, with
Theodore Roosevelt, of the Boone and Crockett Club, dedicated
to the restoration of America's wildlands.

* * *

On the floor, on either side of my fireplace, lie two buffalo skulls.
They are white and weathered, the horns cracked and bleached
by the snows and frosts and the rains and heats of many winters
and summers. Often, late at night, when the house is quiet, I sit
before the fire, and muse and dream of the old days; and as I
gaze at these relics of the past, they take life before my eyes. The
matted brown hair again clothes the dry bone, and in the empty
orbits the wild eyes gleam. Above me curves the blue arch; away
on every hand stretches the yellow prairie, and scattered near and
far are the dark forms of buffalo. They dot the rolling hills, quietly

feeding like tame cattle, or lie at ease on the slopes, chewing the cud and half asleep. The yellow calves are close by their mothers; on little eminences the great bulls paw the dust, and mutter and moan, while those whose horns have grown one, two, and three winters are mingled with their elders.

Not less peaceful is the scene near some riverbank, when the herds come down to water. From the high prairie on every side they stream into the valley, stringing along in single file, each band following the deep trail worn in the parched soil by the tireless feet of generations of their kind. At a quick walk they swing along, their heads held low. The long beards of the bulls sweep the ground; the shuffling tread of many hoofs marks their passing, and above each long line rises a cloud of dust that sometimes obscures the westering sun.

Life, activity, excitement, mark another memory as vivid as these. From behind a near hill mounted men ride out and charge down toward the herd. For an instant the buffalo pause to stare, and then crowd together in a close throng, jostling and pushing one another, a confused mass of horns, hair, and hoofs. Heads down and tails in air, they rush away from their pursuers, and as they race along herd joins herd, till the black mass sweeping over the prairie numbers thousands. On its skirts hover the active, nimble horsemen, with twanging bowstrings and sharp arrows piercing many fat cows. The naked Indians cling to their naked horses as if the two were parts of one incomparable animal, and swing and yield to every motion of their steeds with the grace of perfect horsemanship. The ponies, as quick and skillful as the men, race up beside the fattest of the herd, swing off to avoid the charge of a maddened cow, and, returning, dart close to the victim, whirling hither and yon, like swallows on the wing. And their riders, with the unconscious skill, grace, and power of matchless archery, are drawing their bows to the arrow's head, and driving the feathered shaft deep through the bodies of the buffalo. Returning on their tracks, they skin the dead, then load the meat and robes on their horses, and with laughter and jest ride away.

After them, on the deserted prairie, come the wolves to tear at the carcasses. The rain and the snow wash the blood from the bones, and fade and bleach the hair. For a few months the skeleton holds together; then it falls apart, and the fox and the badger pull about the whitening bones and scatter them over the plain. So this cow and this bull of mine may have left their bones on the prairie, where I found them and picked them up to keep as mementos of the past, to dream over, and in such reverie to see again the swelling hosts which yesterday covered the plains, and to-day are but a dream.

So the buffalo passed into history. Once an inhabitant of this continent from the Arctic slope to Mexico, and from Virginia to Oregon, and, within the memory of men yet young, roaming the plains in such numbers that it seemed as if it could never be exterminated, it has now disappeared as utterly as has the bison from Europe. For it is probable that the existing herds of that practically extinct species, now carefully guarded in the forests of Grodno, about equal in numbers the buffalo in the Yellowstone Park; while the wild bison in the Caucasus may be compared with the "wood" buffalo which survive in the Peace River district. In view of the former abundance of our buffalo, this parallel is curious and interesting.

The early explorers were constantly astonished by the multitudinous herds which they met with, the regularity of their movements, and the deep roads which they made in traveling from place to place. Many of the earlier references are to territory east of the Mississippi, but even within the last fifteen years buffalo were to be seen on the Western plains in numbers so great that an entirely sober and truthful account seems like fable. Describing the abundance of buffalo in a certain region, an Indian once said to me, in the expressive sign-language of which all old frontiersmen have some knowledge: "The country was one robe."

Much has been written about their enormous abundance in the old days, but I have never read anything that I thought an exaggeration of their numbers as I have seen them. Only one who has actually spent months in traveling among them in those old days can credit the stories told about them. The trains of the Kansas Pacific Railroad used frequently to be detained by herds which were crossing the tracks in front of the engines; and in 1870, trains on which I was traveling were twice so held, in one case for three hours. When railroad travel first began on this road, the engineers tried the experiment of running through these passing herds; but after their engines had been thrown from the tracks they learned wisdom, and gave the buffalo the right of way. Two or three years later, in the country between the Platte and Republican rivers, I saw a closely massed herd of buffalo so vast that I dared not hazard a guess as to its numbers; and in later years I have traveled, for weeks at a time, in northern Montana without ever being out of sight of buffalo. These were not in close herds, except now and then when alarmed and running, but were usually scattered about, feeding or lying down on the prairie at a little distance from one another, much as domestic cattle distribute themselves in a pasture or on the range. As far as we could see on every side of the line of march, and ahead, the hillsides were dotted with dark forms, and the field-glass revealed yet others stretched out on every side, in one continuous host, to the most distant hills. Thus was gained a more just notion of their numbers than could be had in any other way, for the sight of this limitless territory occupied by these continuous herds was far more impressive than the spectacle of a surging, terrified mass of fleeing buffalo, even though the numbers which passed rapidly before the observer's gaze in a short time were very great.

The former range of the buffalo has been worked out with painstaking care by Dr. Allen, to whom we owe an admirable monograph on this species. He concludes that the northern limit of this range was north of the Great Slave Lake, in latitude about 63° N.; while to the south it extended into Mexico as far as latitude 25° N. To the west it ranged at least as far as the Blue Mountains of Oregon, while on the east it was abundant in the western portions of New York, Pennsylvania, Virginia, North and South Carolinas, and Georgia. In the interior the buffalo were very abundant, and occupied Ohio, Kentucky, West Virginia, Tennessee, West Georgia, Illinois, Indiana, and Iowa, parts of Michigan, Wisconsin, and Minnesota, the whole of the great plains, from southern Texas north to their northern limit, and much of the Rocky Mountains. In Montana, Idaho, Wyoming, and most of New Mexico they were abundant, and probably common over a large part of Utah, and perhaps in northern Nevada. So far as now known, their western limit was the Blue Mountains of Oregon and the eastern foothills of the Sierra Nevada.

Thus it will be seen that the buffalo once ranged over a large part of the American continent,—Dr. Allen says one third of it,—but it must not be imagined that they were always present at the same time in every part of their range. They were a wandering race, sometimes leaving a district and being long absent, and again returning and occupying it for a considerable period. What laws or what impulses governed these movements we cannot know. Their wandering habits were well understood by the Indians of the Western plains, who depended upon the buffalo for food. It was their custom to follow the herds about, and when, as sometimes occurred, these moved away and could not be found, the Indians were reduced to great straits for food, and sometimes even starved to death.

Under natural conditions the buffalo was an animal of rather sluggish habits, mild, inoffensive, and dull. In its ways of life and intelligence it closely resembled our domestic cattle. It was slow to learn by experience, and this lack of intelligence greatly hastened the destruction of the race. Until the very last years of its existence as a species, it did not appear to connect the report of firearms with any idea of danger to itself, and though constantly pursued, did not become wild. If he used skill and judgment in shooting, a hunter who had "got a stand" on a small bunch could kill them all before they had moved out of rifle-shot. It was my fortune, one summer, to hunt for a camp of soldiers, and more than once I have lain on a hill above a little herd of buffalo, shot down what young bulls I needed to supply the camp, and then walked down to the bunch and, by waving my hat and shouting, driven off the survivors, so that I could prepare the meat for transportation to camp. This slowness to take the alarm, or indeed to realize the presence of danger, was characteristic of the buffalo almost up to the very last. A time did come when they were alarmed readily enough, but this was not until all the large herds had been broken up and scattered, and the miserable survivors had been so chased and harried that at last they learned to start and run even at their own shadows.

Another peculiarity of the buffalo was its habit, when stampeded, of dashing blindly forward against, over, or through anything that might be in the way. When running, a herd of buffalo followed its leaders, and yet these leaders lost the power of stopping, or even of turning aside, because they were constantly crowded upon and pushed forward by those behind. This explains why herds would dash into mire or quicksands, as they often did, and thus perish by the thousand. Those in front could not stop, while those behind could not see the danger toward which they were rushing. So, too, they ran into rivers, or into traps made for them by the Indians, or against railroad cars, or even dashed into the rivers and swam blindly against the sides of steamboats. If an obstacle lay squarely across their path, they tried to go through it, but if it lay at an angle to their course, they would turn a little to follow it, as will be shown further on.

The buffalo calf is born from April to June, and at first is an awkward little creature, looking much like a domestic calf, but with a shorter neck. The hump at first is scarcely noticeable, but develops rapidly. They are odd-looking and very playful little animals. They are easily caught and tamed when quite young, but when a few months old they become as shy as the old buffalo, and are much more swift of foot.

Although apparently very sluggish, buffalo are really extremely active, and are able to go at headlong speed over a country where no man would dare to ride a horse. When alarmed they will throw themselves down the almost vertical side of a cañon and climb the opposite wall with cat-like agility. Sometimes they will descend cut banks by jumping from shelf to shelf of rock like the mountain sheep. To get at water when thirsty, they will climb down bluffs that seem altogether impracticable for such great animals. Many years ago, while descending the Missouri River in a flatboat with two companions, I landed in a wide bottom to kill a mountain sheep. As we were bringing the meat to the boat, we saw on the opposite side of the river, about half-way down the bluffs, which were here about fifteen hundred feet high, a large buffalo bull. The bluffs were almost vertical, and this old fellow was having some difficulty in making his way down to the water. He went slowly and carefully, at times having pretty good going, and at others slipping and sliding for thirty or forty feet, sending the clay and stones rolling ahead of him in great quantities. We watched him for a little while, and then it occurred to some malicious spirit among us that it would be fun to see whether the bull could go up where he had come down. A shot was fired so as to strike near him,—for no one wanted to hurt the old fellow,—and as soon as the report reached his ears, he turned about and began to scramble up the bluffs. His first rush carried him, perhaps, a hundred feet vertically, and then he stopped and looked around. He seemed not to have the slightest difficulty in climbing up, nor did he use any caution, or appear to pick his way at all. A second shot caused another rush up the steep ascent, but this time he went only half as far as before, and again stopped. Three or four other shots drove him by shorter and shorter rushes up the bluffs, until at length he would go no further, and subsequent shots only caused him to shake his head angrily. Plainly he had climbed until his wind had given out, and now he would stand and fight. Our fun was over, and looking back as we floated down the river, our last glimpse was of the old bull, still standing on his shelf, waiting with lowered head for the unknown enemy that he supposed was about to attack him.

It is not only under the stress of circumstances that the bison climbs. The mountain buffalo is almost as active as the mountain sheep, and was often found in places that tested the nerve and activity of a man to reach; and even the buffalo of the plains had a fondness for high places, and used to climb up on to broken buttes or high rocky points. In recent years I have often noticed the same habit among range cattle and horses.

The buffalo were fond of rolling in the dirt, and to this habit, practised when the ground was wet, are due the buffalo wallows which so frequently occur in the old ranges, and which often contain water after all other moisture, except that of the streams, is dried up. These wallows were formed by the rolling of a succession of buffalo in the same moist place, and were frequently quite deep. They have often been described. Less well known was the habit of scratching themselves against trees and rocks. Sometimes a solitary erratic boulder, five or six feet high, may be seen on the bare prairie, the ground immediately around it being worn down two or three feet below the level of the surrounding earth. This is where the buffalo have walked about the stone, rubbing against it, and, where they trod, loosening the soil, which has been blown away by the wind, so that in course of time a deep trench was worn about the rock. Often single trees along streams were worn quite smooth by the shoulders and sides of the buffalo.

When the first telegraph line was built across the continent, the poles used were light and small, for transportation over the plains was slow and expensive, and it was not thought necessary to raise the wires high above the ground. These poles were much resorted to by the buffalo to scratch against, and before long a great many of them were pushed over. A story, now of considerable antiquity, is told of an ingenious employee of the telegraph company, who devised a plan for preventing the buffalo from disturbing the poles. This he expected to accomplish by driving into them spikes which should prick the animals when they rubbed against them. The result somewhat astonished the inventor, for it was discovered that where formerly one buffalo rubbed against the smooth telegraph poles, ten now struggled and fought for the chance to scratch themselves against the spiked poles, the iron furnishing just the irritation which their tough hides needed.

It was in spring, when its coat was being shed, that the buffalo, odd-looking enough at any time, presented its most grotesque appearance. The matted hair and wool of the shoulders and sides began to peel off in great sheets, and these sheets, clinging to the skin and flapping in the wind, gave it the appearance of being clad in rags.

The buffalo was a timid creature, but brought to bay would fight with ferocity. There were few sights more terrifying to the novice than the spectacle of an old bull at bay: his mighty bulk, a quivering mass of active, enraged muscle; the shining horns; the little, spiky tail; and the eyes half hidden beneath the shaggy frontlet, yet gleaming with rage, combined to render him an awe-inspiring object. Nevertheless, owing to their greater speed and activity, the cows were much more to be feared than the bulls.

It was once thought that the buffalo performed annually extensive migrations, and it was even said that those which spent the summer on the banks of the Saskatchewan wintered in Texas. There is no reason for believing this to have been true. Undoubtedly there were slight general movements north and south, and east and west, at certain seasons of the year; but many of the accounts of these movements are entirely misleading, because greatly exaggerated. In one portion of the northern country I know that there was a decided east and west seasonal migration, the herds tending in spring away from the mountains, while in the autumn they worked back again, seeking shelter in the rough, broken country of the foot-hills from the cold west winds of the winter.

The buffalo is easily tamed when caught as a calf, and in all its ways of life resembles the domestic cattle. It at once learns to respect a fence, and, even if at large, manifests no disposition to wander.

Three years ago there were in this country about two hundred and fifty domesticated buffalo, in the possession of about a dozen individuals. Of these the most important herd was that of Hon. C. J. Jones, of Garden City, Kansas, which, besides about fifty animals captured and reared by himself, included also the Bedson herd of over eighty, purchased in Manitoba. The Jones herd at one time consisted of about one hundred and fifty head. Next came that of Charles Allard and Michel Pablo, of the Flathead Agency in Montana, which in 1888 numbered thirty-five, and has now increased to about ninety. Mr. Jones's herd has been broken up, and he now retains only about forty-five head, of which fifteen are breeding cows. He tells me that within the past year or two he has sold over sixty pure buffalo, and that nearly as many more have died through injuries received in transporting them by rail.

Mr. Jones is the only individual who, of recent years, has made any systematic effort to cross the buffalo with our own domestic cattle. As far back as the beginning of the present century, this was successfully done in the West and Northwest; and in Audubon and Bachman's "Quadrupeds of America" may be found an extremely interesting account, written by Robert Wickliffe, of Lexington, Kentucky, giving the results of a series of careful and successful experiments which he carried on for more than thirty years. These experiments showed that the cross for certain purposes was a very valuable one, but no systematic efforts to establish and perpetuate a breed of buffalo cattle were afterward made until within the past ten years. Mr. Jones has bred buffalo bulls to Galloway, Polled Angus, and ordinary range cows, and has succeeded in obtaining calves from all. Such half-breeds are of very large size, extremely hardy, and, as a farmer would say, "easy keepers." They are fertile among themselves or with either parent. A half-breed cow of Mr. Jones's that I examined was fully as large as an ordinary work-ox, and in spring, while nursing a calf, was fat on grass. She lacked the buffalo hump, but her hide would have made a good robe. The great size and tremendous frame of these crossbred cattle should make them very valuable for beef, while their hardiness would exempt them from the dangers of winter,— so often fatal to domestic range cattle,—and they produce a robe which is quite as valuable as that of the buffalo, and more beautiful because more even all over. If continued, these attempts at crossbreeding may do much to improve our Western range cattle.

Mr. Jones has sold a number of buffalo to persons in Europe, where there is a considerable demand for them. It is to be hoped that no more of these domesticated buffalo will be allowed to leave the country where they were born. Indeed, it would seem quite within the lines of the work now being carried on by the Agricultural Department, for the government to purchase all the domesticated American buffalo that can be had, and to start, in some one of the Western States, an experimental farm for buffalo breeding and buffalo crossing. With a herd of fifty pure-bred buffalo cows and a sufficient number of bulls, a series of experiments could be carried on which might be of great value to the cattle-growers of our western country. The stock of pure buffalo could be kept up and increased; surplus bulls, pure and half bred, could be sold to farmers; and, in time, the new race of buffalo cattle might become so firmly established that it would endure.

To undertake this with any prospect of success, such a farm would have to be managed by a man of intelligence and of wide experience in this particular field; otherwise all the money invested would be wasted. Mr. Jones is perhaps the only man living who knows enough of this subject to carry on an experimental farm with success.

Although only one species of buffalo is known to science, old mountaineers and Indians tell of four kinds. These are, besides the ordinary animal of the plains, the "mountain buffalo," sometimes called "bison," which is found in the timbered Rocky Mountains; the "wood buffalo" of the Northwest, which inhabits the timbered country to the west and north of Athabasca Lake; and the "beaver buffalo." The last named has been vaguely described to me by northern Indians as small and having a very curly coat. I know of only one printed account of it, and this says that it had "short, sharp horns which were small at the root and curiously turned up and bent backward, not unlike a ram's, but quite unlike the bend of the horn in the common buffalo." It is possible that this description may refer to the muskox, and not to a buffalo. The "mountain" and "wood" buffalo seem to be very much alike in habit and appearance. They are larger, darker, and heavier than the animal of the plains, but there is no reason for thinking them specifically distinct from it. Such differences as exist are due to conditions of environment.

The color of the buffalo in its new coat is a dark liver-brown. This soon changes, however, and the hides, which are at their best in November and early December, begin to grow paler toward spring; and when the coat is shed, the hair and wool from young animals is almost a dark smoky-gray. The calf when just born is of a bright yellow color, almost a pale red on the line of the back. As it grows older it becomes darker, and by late autumn is almost as dark as the adults. Variations from the normal color are very rare, but pied, spotted, and roan animals are sometimes killed. Blue or mouse-colored buffalo were occasionally seen, and a bull of this color was observed in the National Park last January. White buffalo—though often referred to as mythical—sometimes occurred. These varied from gray to cream-white. The rare and valuable "silk" or "beaver" robe owes its name to its dark color and its peculiar sheen or gloss. White or spotted robes were highly valued by the

Indians. Among the Blackfeet they were presented to the Sun as votive offerings. Other tribes kept them in their sacred bundles.

Apart from man, the buffalo had but few natural enemies. Of these the most destructive were the wolves, which killed a great many of them. These, however, were principally old, straggling bulls, for the calves were protected by their mothers, and the females and young stock were so vigorous and so gregarious that they had but little to fear from this danger. It is probable that, notwithstanding the destruction which they wrought, the wolves performed an important service for the buffalo race, keeping it vigorous and healthy by killing weak, disabled, and superannuated animals, which could no longer serve any useful purpose in the herd, and yet consumed the grass which would support a healthy breeding animal. It is certainly true that sick buffalo, or those out of condition, were rarely seen.

The grizzly bear fed to some extent on the carcasses of buffalo drowned in the rivers or caught in the quicksands, and occasionally they caught living buffalo and killed them. A Blackfoot Indian told me of an attempt of this kind which he witnessed. He was lying hidden by a buffalo trail in the Bad Lands, near a little creek, waiting for a small bunch to come down to water, so that he might kill one. The buffalo came on in single file as usual, the leading animal being a young heifer. When they had nearly reached the water, and were passing under a vertical clay wall, a grizzly bear, lying hid on a shelf of this wall, reached down, and with both paws caught the heifer about the neck and threw himself upon her. The others at once ran off, and a short struggle ensued, the bear trying to kill the heifer, and she to escape. Almost at once, however, the Indian saw a splendid young bull come rushing down the trail toward the scene of conflict, and charge the bear, knocking him down. A fierce combat ensued. The bull would charge the bear, and when he struck him fairly would knock him off his feet, often inflicting severe wounds with his sharp horns. The bear struck at the bull, and tried to catch him by the head or shoulders, and to hold him, but this he could not do. After fifteen or twenty minutes of fierce and active fighting, the bear had received all the punishment he cared for, and tried to escape, but the bull would not let him go, and kept up the attack until he had killed his adversary. Even after the bear was dead the bull would gore the carcass and sometimes lift it clear of the ground on his horns. He seemed insane with rage, and, notwithstanding the fact that most of the skin was torn from his head and shoulders, appeared to be looking about for something else to fight. The Indian was very much afraid lest the bull should discover and kill him, and was greatly relieved when he finally left the bear and went off to join his band. This Blackfoot had never heard of Uncle Remus's tales, but he imitated Brer Rabbit—laid low and said nothing.

To the Indians the buffalo was the staff of life. It was their food, clothing, dwellings, tools. The needs of a savage people are not many, perhaps, but whatever the Indians of the plains had, that the buffalo gave them. It is not strange, then, that this animal was reverenced by most plains tribes, nor that it entered largely into their sacred ceremonies, and was in a sense worshiped by them. The Pawnees, in explaining their religious customs, say, "Through the corn and the buffalo we worship the Father." The Blackfeet ask, "What one of all the animals is most sacred?" and the reply given is, "The buffalo."

The robe was the Indian's winter covering and his bed, while the skin, freed from the hair and dressed, constituted his summer sheet or blanket. The dressed hide was used for moccasins, leggings, shirts, and women's dresses. Dressed cowskins formed the lodges, the warmest and most comfortable portable shelters ever devised. Braided strands of rawhide furnished them with ropes and lines, and these were made also from the twisted hair. The green hide was sometimes used as a kettle, in which to boil meat, or, stretched over a frame of boughs, gave them coracles, or boats, for crossing rivers. The tough, thick hide of the bull's neck, allowed to shrink smooth, made a shield which would turn a lance-thrust, an arrow, or even the ball from an old-fashioned smooth-bore gun. From the rawhide, the hair having been shaved off, were made parfleches—envelop-like cases which served for trunks or boxes—useful to contain small articles. The cannon-bones and ribs were used to make implements for dressing hides; the shoulder-blades lashed to sticks made hoes and axes, and the ribs runners for small sledges drawn by dogs. The hoofs were boiled to make a glue for fastening the feathers and heads on their arrows, the hair used to stuff cushions, and later saddles, strands of the long black beard to ornament articles of wearing-apparel and implements of war, such as shields and quivers. The sinews lying along the back gave them thread and bowstrings, and backed their bows. The horns furnished spoons and ladles, and ornamented their war-bonnets. Water-buckets were made from the lining of the paunch. The skin of the hind leg cut off above the pastern, and again a short distance above the hock, was once used for a moccasin or boot. Fly-brushes were made from the skin of the tail dried on sticks. Knife-sheaths, quivers, bow-cases, gun-covers, saddlecloths, and a hundred other useful and necessary articles, all were furnished by the buffalo.

The Indians killed some smaller game, as elk, deer, and antelope, but for food their dependence was on the buffalo. But before the coming of the whites their knives and arrowheads were merely sharpened stones, weapons which would be inefficient against such great, thick-skinned beasts. Even under the most favorable circumstances, with these primitive implements, they could not kill food in quantities sufficient to supply their needs. There must be some means of taking the buffalo in considerable numbers. Such wholesale capture was accomplished by means of traps or surrounds, which all depended for success on one characteristic of the animal, its curiosity.

The Blackfeet, Plains Crees, Gros Ventres of the Prairie, Sarcees, some bands of the Dakotas, Snakes, Crows, and some others, drove the herds of buffalo into pens from above, or over high cliffs, where the fall killed or crippled a large majority of the herd. The Cheyennes and Arapahoes drove them into pens on level ground; the Blackfeet, Aricaras, Mandans, Gros Ventres of the Village, Pawnees, Omahas, Otoes, and others, surrounded the herds in great circles on the prairie, and then, frightening them so that they started running, kept them from breaking through the line of men, and made them race round and round in a circle, until they were so exhausted that they could not run away, and were easily killed.

These primitive modes of slaughter have been described by earlier writers, and frequently quoted in recent years; yet, in all that has been written on this subject, I fail to find a single account which gives at all a true notion of the methods employed, or the means by which the buffalo were brought into the inclosures. Eyewitnesses have been careless observers, and have taken many things for granted. My understanding of this matter is derived from men who from childhood have been familiar with these things, and from them, during years of close association, I have again and again heard the story of these old hunting methods.

The Blackfoot trap was called the *piskun*. It was an inclosure, one side of which was formed by the vertical wall of a cut bank, the others being built of rocks, logs, poles, and brush six or eight feet high. It was not necessary that these walls should be very strong, but they had to be tight, so that the buffalo could not see through them. From a point on the cut bank above this inclosure, in two diverging lines stretching far out into the prairie, piles of rock were heaped up at short intervals, or bushes were stuck in the ground, forming the wings of a V-shaped chute, which would guide any animals running down the chute to its angle above the piskun. When a herd of buffalo were feeding near at hand, the people prepared for the hunt, in which almost the whole camp took part. It is commonly stated that the buffalo were driven into the piskun by mounted men, but this was not the case. They were not driven, but led, and they were led by an appeal to their curiosity. The man who brought them was usually the possessor of a "buffalo rock," a talisman which was believed to give him greater power to call the buffalo than was had by others. The previous night was spent by this man in praying for success in the enterprise of the morrow. The help of the Sun, *Napi*, and all Above People was asked for, and sweet-grass was burned to them. Early in the morning, without eating or drinking, the man started away from the camp and went up on the prairie. Before he left the lodge, he told his wives that they must not go out, or even look out, of the lodge during his absence. They should stay there, and pray to the Sun for his success, and burn sweet-grass until he returned. When he left the camp and went up on to the prairie toward the buffalo, all the people followed him, and distributed themselves along the wings of the chute, hiding behind the piles of rock or brush. The caller sometimes wore a robe and a bull's-head bonnet, or at times was naked. When he had approached close to the buffalo, he endeavored to attract their attention by moving about, wheeling round and round, and alternately appearing and disappearing. The feeding buffalo soon began to raise their heads and stare at him, and presently the nearest ones would walk toward him to discover what this strange creature might be, and the others would follow. As they began to approach, the man withdrew toward the entrance of the chute. If the buffalo began to trot, he increased his speed, and before very long he had the herd well within the wings. As soon as they had passed the first piles of rock, behind which some of the people were concealed, the Indians sprang into view, and by yelling and waving robes frightened the hindmost of the buffalo, which then began to run down the chute. As they passed along, more and more people showed themselves and added to their terror, and in a very short time the herd was in a headlong stampede, guided toward the angle above the piskun by the piles of rock on either side.

About the walls of the piskun, now full of buffalo, were distributed the women and children of the camp, who, leaning over the inclosure, waving their arms and calling out, did all they could to frighten the penned-in animals, and to keep them from pushing against the walls or trying to jump or climb over them. As a rule the buffalo raced round within the inclosure, and the men shot them down as they passed, until all were killed. After this the people all entered the piskun and cut up the dead, transporting the meat to camp. The skulls, bones, and less perishable offal were removed from the inclosure, and the wolves, coyotes, foxes, and badgers devoured what was left.

It occasionally happened that something occurred to turn the buffalo, so that they passed through the guiding arms and escaped. Usually they went on straight to the angle and jumped over the cliff into the inclosure below. In winter, when snow was on the ground, their straight course was made additionally certain by placing on, or just above, the snow a line of buffalo-chips leading from the angle of the V, midway between its arms, out on to the prairie. These dark objects, only twenty or thirty feet apart, were easily seen against the white snow, and the buffalo always followed them, no doubt thinking this a trail where another herd had passed.

By the *Siksikau* tribe of the Blackfoot nation and the Plains Crees, the piskun was built in a somewhat different way, but the methods employed were similar. With these people, who inhabited a flat country, the inclosure was built of logs and near a timbered stream. Its circular wall was complete; that is, there was no opening or gateway in it, but at one point this wall, elsewhere eight feet high, was cut away so that its height was only four feet. From this point a bridge or causeway of logs, covered with dirt, sloped by a gradual descent down to the level of the prairie. This bridge was fenced on either side with logs, and the arms of the V came together at the point where the bridge reached the ground. The buffalo were driven down the chute as before, ran up on this bridge, and were forced to leap into the pen. As soon as all had entered, Indians who had been concealed nearby ran up and put poles across the opening through which the buffalo had passed, and over these poles hung robes so as entirely to conceal the outer world. Then the butchering of the animals took place.

Further to the south, out on the prairie, where timber and rocks and brush were not obtainable for making traps like these, simpler but less effective methods were adopted. The people would go out on the prairie and conceal themselves in a great circle, open on one side. Then some man would approach the buffalo, and decoy them into the circle. Men would now show themselves at different points and start the buffalo running in a circle, yelling and waving robes to keep them from approaching or trying to break through the ring of men. This had to be done with great judgment, however; for often if the herd got started in one direction it was impossible to turn it, and it would rush through the ring and none would be secured. Sometimes, if a herd was found in a favorable position, and there was no wind, a large camp of people would set up their lodges all about the buffalo, in which case the chances of success in the surround were greatly increased.

The tribes which used the piskun also practised driving the buffalo over high, rough cliffs, where the fall crippled or killed most of the animals which went over. In such situations, no inclosure was built at the foot of the precipice.

In the later days of the piskun in the north, the man who brought the buffalo often went to them on horseback, riding a white horse. He would ride backward and forward before them, zigzagging this way and that, and after a little they would follow him. He never attempted to drive, but always led them. The driving began only after the herd had passed the outer rock piles, and the people had begun to rise up and frighten them.

This method of securing meat has been practised in Montana within thirty years, and even more recently among the Plains Crees of the north. I have seen the remains of old piskuns, and the guiding wings of the chute, and have talked with many men who have taken part in such killings.

All this had to do, of course, with the primitive methods of buffalo killing. As soon as horses became abundant, and sheet-iron arrowheads and, later, guns were secured by the Indians, these old practices began to give way to the more exciting pursuit of running buffalo and of surrounding them on horseback. Of this modern method, as practised twenty years ago, and exclusively with the bow and arrow, I have already written at some length in another place.

To the white travelers on the plains in early days the buffalo furnished support and sustenance. Their abundance made fresh meat easily obtainable, and the early travelers usually carried with them bundles of dried meat, or sacks of pemmican, food made from the flesh of the buffalo, that contained a great deal of nutriment in very small bulk. Robes were used for bedding, and in winter buffalo moccasins were worn for warmth, the hair side within. Coats of buffalo-skin are the warmest covering known, the only garment which will present an effective barrier to the bitter blasts that sweep over the plains of the Northwest.

Perhaps as useful to early travelers as any product of the buffalo, was the "buffalo chip," or dried dung. This, being composed of comminuted woody fiber of the grass, made an excellent fuel, and in many parts of the treeless plains was the only substance which could be used to cook with.

The dismal story of the extermination of the buffalo for its hides has been so often told, that I may be spared the sickening details of the butchery which was carried on from the Mexican to the British boundary line in the struggle to obtain a few dollars by a most ignoble means. As soon as railroads penetrated the buffalo country, a market was opened for the hides. Men too lazy to work were not too lazy to hunt, and a good hunter could kill in the early days from thirty to seventy-five buffalo a day, the hides of which were worth from $1.50 to $4 each. This seemed an easy way to make money, and the market for hides was unlimited. Up to this time the trade in robes had been mainly confined to those dressed by the Indians, and these were for the most part taken from cows. The coming of the railroad made hides of all sorts marketable, and even those taken from naked old bulls found a sale at some price. The butchery of buffalo was now something stupendous. Thousands of hunters followed millions of buffalo and destroyed them wherever found and at all seasons of the year. They pursued them during the day, and at night camped at the watering-places, and built lines of fires along the streams, to drive the buffalo back so that they could not drink. It took less than six years to destroy all the buffalo in Kansas, Nebraska, Indian Territory, and northern Texas. The few that were left of the southern herd retreated to the waterless plains of Texas, and there for a while had a brief respite. Even here the hunters followed them, but as the animals were few and the territory in which they ranged vast, they held out here for some years. It was in this country, and against the last survivors of this southern herd, that "Buffalo Jones" made his successful trips to capture calves.

The extirpation of the northern herd was longer delayed. No very terrible slaughter occurred until the completion of the Northern Pacific Railroad; then, however, the same scenes of butchery were enacted. Buffalo were shot down by tens of thousands, their hides stripped off, and the meat left to the wolves. The result of the crusade was soon seen, and the last buffalo were killed in the Northwest near the boundary line in 1883, and that year may be said to have finished up the species, though some few were killed in 1884 to 1885.

After the slaughter had been begun, but years before it had been accomplished, the subject was brought to the attention of Congress, and legislation looking to the preservation of the species was urged upon that body. Little general interest was taken in the subject, but in 1874, after much discussion, Congress did pass an act providing for the protection of the buffalo. The bill, however, was never signed by the President.

During the last days of the buffalo, a remarkable change took place in its form, and this change is worthy of consideration by naturalists, for it is an example of specialization—of development in one particular direction—which was due to a change in the environment of the species, and is interesting because it was brought about in a very few years, and indicates how rapidly, under favoring conditions, such specialization may sometimes take place.

This change was noticed and commented on by hunters who followed the northern buffalo, as well as by those who assisted in the extermination of the southern herd. The southern hunters, however, averred that the "regular" buffalo had disappeared—gone off somewhere—and that their place had been taken by what they called the southern buffalo, a race said to have come up from Mexico, and characterized by longer legs and a longer, lighter body than the buffalo of earlier years, and which was also peculiar in that the animals never became fat. Intelligent hunters of the northern herd, however, recognized the true state of the case, which was that the buffalo, during the last years of their existence, were so constantly pursued and driven from place to place that they never had time to lay on fat as in earlier years, and that, as a consequence of this continual running, the animal's form changed, and instead of a fat, short-backed, short-legged animal, it became a long-legged, light-bodied beast, formed for running.

This specialization in the direction of speed at first proceeded very slowly, but at last, as the dangers to which the animals were subjected became more and more pressing, it took place rapidly, and as a consequence the last buffalo killed on the plains were extremely long-legged and rangy, and were very different in appearance—as they were in their habits—from the animals of twenty years ago.

Buffalo running was not a sport that required much skill, yet it was not without its dangers. Occasionally a man was killed by the buffalo, but deaths from falls and from bursting guns were more common. Many curious stories of such accidents are told by the few surviving old-timers whose memory goes back fifty years, to the time when flint-lock guns were in use. A mere fall from a horse is lightly regarded by the practised rider; the danger to be feared is that in such a fall the horse may roll on the man and crush him. Even more serious accidents occurred when a man fell upon some part of his equipment, which was driven through his body. Hunters have fallen in such a way that their whipstocks, arrows, bows, and even guns, have been driven through their bodies. The old flint-lock guns, or "fukes," which were loaded on the run, with powder poured in from the horn by guess, and a ball from the mouth, used frequently to burst, causing the loss of hands, arms, and even lives.

While most of the deaths which occurred in the chase resulted from causes other than the resistance of the buffalo, these did occasionally kill a man. A curious accident happened in a camp of Red River half-breeds in the early seventies. The son of an Iroquois half-breed, about twenty years old, went out one day with the rest of the camp to run buffalo. At night he did not return, and the next day all the men went out to search for him. They found the horse and the arms, but could not find the man, and could not imagine what had become of him. About a year later, as the half-breeds were hunting in another part of the country, a cow was seen which had something unusual on her head. They chased and killed her, and found that she had on her head the pelvis of a man, one of the horns having pierced the thin part of the bone, which was wedged on so tightly that they could hardly get it off. Much of the hair on the head, neck, and shoulders of the cow was worn off short, and on the side on which the bone was, down on the neck and shoulders, the hair was short, black, and looked new, as if it had been worn entirely off the skin, and was just beginning to grow out again. It is supposed that this bone was part of the missing young man, who had been hooked by the cow, and carried about on her head until his body fell to pieces.

My old and valued friend Charles Reynolds, for years chief of scouts at Fort Lincoln, Dakota, and who was killed by the Sioux in the Custer fight in 1876, told me of the death of a hunting partner of his, which shows how dangerous even a dying buffalo may be. The two men had started from the railroad to go south and bring in a load of meat. On finding a bunch of buffalo, they shot down by stalking what they required, and then on foot went up to the animals to skin them. One cow, lying on her side, was still moving a little convulsively, but dying. The man approached her as if about to cut her throat, but when he was within a few feet of her head, she sprang to her feet, rushed at him, struck him in the chest with her horns, and then fell dead. Charley ran up to his partner, and to his horror saw that the cow's horn had ripped him up from the belly to the throat, so that he could see the heart still expanding and contracting.

Charley buried his partner there, and returning to the town, told his story. He was at once arrested on the charge that he had murdered his companion, and was obliged to return to the place and to assist in digging up the body to satisfy the suspicious officials of the truth of his statements.

In the early days, when the game was plenty, buffalo-running was exhilarating sport. Given a good horse, the only other requisite to success was the ability to remain on his back till the end of the chase. No greater degree of skill was needed than this, and yet the quick motion of the horse, the rough ground to be traversed, and the feeling that there was something ahead that must be overtaken and stopped, made the ride attractive. There was the very slightest spice of danger; for while no one anticipated a serious accident, it was always possible that one's horse might step into a badger-hole, in which case his rider would get a fall that would make his bones ache.

The most exciting, and by far the most interesting, hunts in which I ever took part were those with the Indians of the plains. They were conducted almost noiselessly, and no ring of rifle-shot broke the stillness of the air, nor puff of smoke rose toward the still, gray autumn sky. The consummate grace and skill of the naked Indians, and the speed and quickness of their splendid ponies, were well displayed in such chases as these. More than one instance is recorded where an Indian sent an arrow entirely through the bodies of two buffalo. Sometimes such a hunt was signalized by some feat of daring bravado that, save in the seeing, was scarcely credible, as when the Cheyenne Big Ribs rode his horse close up to the side of a huge bull, and, springing on his back, rode the savage beast for some distance, and then with his knife gave him the death-stroke. Or a man might find himself in a position of comical danger, as did "The Trader" who was thrown from his horse on to the horns of a bull without being injured. One of the horns passed under his belt and supported him, and at the same time prevented the bull from tossing him. In this way he was carried for some distance on the animal's head, when the belt gave way and he fell to the ground unhurt, while the bull ran on. There were occasions when buffalo or horses fell in front of horsemen riding at full run, and when a fall was avoided only by leaping one's horse over the fallen animal. In the buffalo chase of old days it was well for a man to keep his wits about him; for, though he might run buffalo a thousand times without accident, the moment might come when only instant action would save him his life, or at least an ugly hurt.

In the early days of the first Pacific Railroad, and before the herds had been driven back from the track, singular hunting-parties were sometimes seen on the buffalo range. These hunters were capitalists connected with the newly constructed road, and some of them now for the first time bestrode a horse, while few had ever used firearms. On such a hunt, one well-known railroad director, eager to kill a buffalo, declined to trust himself on horseback, preferring to bounce over the rough prairie in an ambulance driven by an alarmed soldier, who gave less attention to the mules he was guiding than to the loaded and cocked pistol which his excited passenger was brandishing. These were amusing excursions, where a merry party of pleasant officers from a frontier post, and their guests, a jolly crowd of merchants, brokers, and railroad men from the East, started out to have a buffalo-hunt. With them went the post guide and a scout or two, an escort of soldiers, and the great blue army-wagons, under whose white tilts were piled all the comforts that the post could furnish—unlimited food and drink, and many sacks of forage for the animals. Here all was mirth and jest and good-fellowship, and, except that canvas covered them while they slept, the hunters lived in as much comfort as when at home. The killing of buffalo was to them only an excuse for their jolly outing amid novel scenes.

It was on the plains of Montana, in the days when buffalo were still abundant, that I had one of my last buffalo-hunts—a hunt with a serious purpose. A company of fifty or more men, who for weeks had been living on bacon and beans, longed for the "boss ribs" of fat cow, and when we struck the buffalo range two of us were deputed to kill some meat. My companion was an old prairie-man of great experience, and I myself was not altogether new to the West, for I had hunted in many territories, and had more than once been "jumped" by unfriendly Indians. Our horses were not buffalo-runners, yet we felt a certain confidence that if we could find a bunch and get a good start on them, we would bring in the desired meat. The troops would march during the day, for the commanding officer had no notion of waiting in camp merely for fresh meat, and we were to go out, hunt, and overtake the command at their night's camp.

The next day after we had reached the buffalo range, we started out long before the eastern sky was gray, and were soon riding off over the chilly prairie. The trail which the command was to follow ran a little north of east, and we kept to the south and away from it, believing that in this direction we would find the game, and that if we started them they would run north or northwest—against the wind, so that we could kill them near the trail. Until some time after the sun had risen, we saw nothing larger than antelope; but at length, from the top of a high hill, we could see, far away to the east, dark dots on the prairie, which we knew could only be buffalo. They were undisturbed too; for, though we watched them for some time, we could detect no motion in their ranks.

It took us nearly two hours to reach the low, broken buttes on the north side of which the buffalo were; and, riding up on the easternmost of these, we tried to locate our game more exactly. It was important to get as close as possible before starting them, so that our first rush might carry us into the midst of them. Knowing the capabilities of our horses, which were thin from long travel, we felt sure that if the buffalo should take the alarm before we were close to them, we could not overtake the cows and young animals, which always run in the van, and should have to content ourselves with old bulls. On the other hand, if we could dash in among them during the first few hundred yards of the race, we should be able to keep up with and select the fattest animals in the herd.

When we reached a point just below the crest of the hill, I stopped and waited, while my companion rode on. Just before he got to the top he too halted, then took off his hat and peered over the ridge, examining so much of the prairie beyond as was now visible to him. His inspection was careful and thorough, and when he had made sure that nothing was in sight, his horse took a step or two forward and then stopped again, and the rider scanned every foot of country before him. The horse, trained as the real hunter's horse is always trained, understood what was required of him, and with pricked ears examined the prairie beyond with as much interest as did his rider. When the calf of Charley's right leg pressed the horse's side, two or three steps more were taken, and then a lifting of the bridle-hand caused another halt.

At length I saw my companion slowly bend forward over his horse's neck, turn, and ride back to me. He had seen the backs of two buffalo lying on the edge of a little flat hardly a quarter of a mile from where we stood. The others of the band must be still nearer to us. By riding along the lowest part of the sag which separated the two buttes, and then down a little ravine, it seemed probable that we could come within a few yards of the buffalo unobserved. Our preparations did not take long. The saddle cinches were loosened, blankets arranged, saddles put in their proper places and tightly cinched again. Cartridges were brought round to the front and right of the belt, where they would be convenient for reloading. Our coats, tied behind the saddle, were looked to, the strings which held them being tightened and securely retied. All this was not lost on our horses, which understood as well as we did what was coming. We skirted the butte, rode through the low sag and down into the little ravine, which soon grew deeper, so that our heads were below the range of vision of almost anything on the butte. Passing the mouth of the little side ravine, however, there came into full view a huge bull, lying well up on the hillside. Luckily his back was toward us, and, each bending low over his horse's neck, we rode on, and in a moment were hidden by the side of the ravine. Two or three minutes more, and we came to another side ravine, which was wide and commanded a view of the flat. We stopped before reaching this, and a peep showed that we were within a few yards of two old cows, a young heifer, and a yearling, all of them to the north of us. Beyond, we could see the backs of others, all lying down.

We jumped on our horses again, and setting the spurs well in, galloped up the ravine and up on the flat; and as we came into view, the nearest buffalo, as if propelled by a huge spring, were on their feet, and, with a second's pause to look, dashed away to the north. Scattered over the flat were fifty or seventy-five buffalo, all of which, by the time we had glanced over the field, were off, with heads bending low to the ground, and short, spiky tails stretched out behind. We were up even with the last of the cows, and our horses were running easily and seemed to have plenty of reserve power. Charley, who was a little ahead of me, called back: "They will cross the trail about a mile north of here. Kill a couple when we get to it." I nodded, and we went on. The herd raced forward over the rolling hills, and in what seemed a very short time we rushed down a long slope on to a wide flat, in which was a prairie-dog town of considerable extent. We were on the very heels of the herd, and in a cloud of dust kicked up by their rapid flight. To see the ground ahead was impossible. We could only trust to our horses and our good luck to save us from falling. Our animals were doing better than we had supposed they could, and were going well and under a pull. I felt that a touch of the spurs and a little riding would bring us up even with the leaders of the buffalo. The pace had already proved too much for several bulls, which had turned off to one side and been passed by. As we flew across the flat, I saw far off a dark line and two white objects, which I knew must be our command. I called to my comrade, and, questioning by the sign, pointed at the buffalo. He nodded, and in a moment we had given free rein to our horses and were up among the herd. During the ride I had two or three times selected my game, but the individuals of the band changed positions so constantly that I could not keep track of them. Now, however, I picked out a fat two-year-old bull; but as I drew up to him he ran faster than before, and rapidly made his way toward the head of the band. I was resolved that he should not escape, and so, though I was still fifteen or twenty yards in the rear, fired. At the shot he fell heels overhead directly across a cow which was running by his side and a little behind him. I saw her turn a somersault, and almost at the same instant heard Charley shoot twice in quick succession, and saw two buffalo fall. I fired at a fat young cow that I had pushed my pony up close to. At the shot she whirled, my horse did the same, and she chased me as hard as she could go for seventy-five yards, while I did some exceedingly vigorous spurring, for she was close behind me all the time. To do my horse justice, I think that he would have run as fast as he could, even without the spurs, for he appreciated the situation. At no time was there any immediate danger that the cow would overtake us; if there had been, I should have dodged her. Presently the cow stopped, and stood there very sick. When I rode back, I did not find it easy to get my horse near her; but another shot was not needed, and while I sat looking at her she fell over dead. The three buffalo first killed had fallen within a hundred yards of the trail where the wagons afterward passed, and my cow was but little farther away. The command soon came up, the soldiers did the butchering, and before long we were on the march again across the parched plain.

Of the millions of buffalo which even in our own time ranged the plains in freedom, none now remain. From the prairies which they used to darken, the wild herds, down to the last straggling bull, have disappeared. In the Yellowstone National Park, protected from destruction by United States troops, are the only wild buffalo which exist within the borders of the United States. These are mountain buffalo, and, from their habit of living in the thick timber and on the rough mountainsides, they are only now and then seen by visitors to the park. It is impossible to say just how many there are, but from the best information that I can get, based on the estimates of reliable and conservative men, I conclude that the number was not less than four hundred in the winter of 1891–92. Each winter or spring the government scout employed in the park sees one or more herds of these buffalo, and as such herds are usually made up in part of young animals and have calves with them, it is fair to assume that they are steadily, if slowly, increasing. The report of a trip made in January, 1892, speaks of four herds seen in the Hayden Valley, which numbered respectively 78, 50, 110, and 15. Besides these, a number of scattering groups were seen at a distance, which would bring the number up to three hundred.

In the far northwest, in the Peace River district, there may still be found a few wood buffalo. They are seldom killed, and the estimate of their numbers varies from five hundred to fifteen hundred. This cannot be other than the merest guess, since they are scattered over many thousand square miles of territory which is without inhabitants, and for the most part unexplored.

On the great plains is still found the buffalo skull half buried in the soil and crumbling to decay. The deep trails once trodden by the marching hosts are grass-grown now, and fast filling up. When these most enduring relics of a vanished race shall have passed away, there will be found, in all the limitless domain once darkened by their feeding herds, not one trace of the American buffalo.

CHAPTER 13

Red Letter Days in British Columbia

by Lt. Townsend Whelen

TOWNSEND WHELEN (1877–1961) WAS A HUNTER, SOLDIER, writer, outdoorsman, and rifleman. Whelen was a colonel in the U.S. Army, and a prolific writer on guns and hunting, writing over two thousand magazine articles in his career. He was a contributing editor to *Sports Afield, American Rifleman, Field & Stream, Outdoor Life, Guns & Ammo*, and other magazines.

*   *   *

In the month of July, 1901, my partner, Bill Andrews, and I were at a small Hudson Bay post in the northern part of British Columbia, outfitting for a long hunting and exploring trip in the wild country to the North. The official map showed this country as "unexplored," with one or two rivers shown by dotted lines. This map was the drawing card which had brought us thousands of miles by rail, stage, and pack train to this out-of-the-way spot. By the big stove in the living room of the factor's house we listened to weird tales of this north country, of its enormous mountains and glaciers, its rivers and lakes and of the quantities of game and fish. The factor told us of three men who had tried to get through there in the Klondike rush several years before and had not been heard from yet. The trappers and Siwashes could tell us of trails which ran up either side of the Scumscum, the river on which the post stood, but no one knew what lay between that and the Yukon to the north.

We spent two days here outfitting and on the morning of the third said goodbye to the assembled population and started with our pack train up the east bank of the Scumscum. We were starting out to live and travel in an unknown wilderness for over six months, and our outfit may perhaps interest my readers: We had two saddle horses, four pack horses and a dog. A small tent formed one pack cover. We had ten heavy army blankets, which we used for saddle blankets while traveling, they being kept clean by using canvas sweat pads under them. We were able to pack 150 pounds of grub on each horse, divided up as nearly as I can remember as follows: One hundred and fifty pounds flour, 50 pounds sugar, 30 pounds beans, 10 pounds rice, 10 pounds dried apples, 20 pounds prunes, 30 pounds corn meal, 20 pounds oatmeal, 30 pounds potatoes, 10 pounds onions, 50 pounds bacon, 25 pounds salt, 1 pound pepper, 6 cans baking powder, 10 pounds soap, 10 pounds tobacco, 10 pounds tea, and a few little incidentals weighing probably 10 pounds. We took two extra sets of shoes for each horse, with tools for shoeing, 2 axes, 25 boxes of wax matches, a large can of gun oil, canton flannel for gun rags, 2 cleaning rods, a change of underclothes, 6 pairs of socks and 6 moccasins each, with buckskin for resoling, toilet articles, 100 yards of fishing line, 2 dozen fish hooks, an oil stove, awl, file, screw-driver, needles and thread, etc.

For cooking utensils we had 2 frying pans, 3 kettles to nest, 2 tin cups, 3 tin plates and a gold pan. We took 300 cartridges for each of our rifles. Bill carried a .38–55 Winchester, model '94, and I had my old .40–72 Winchester, model '95, which had proved too reliable to relinquish for a high-power small bore. Both rifles were equipped with Lyman sights and carefully sighted. As a precaution we each took along extra front sights, firing pins and main-springs, but did not have a chance to use them. I loaded the ammunition for both rifles myself, with black powder, smokeless priming, and lead bullets. Both rifles proved equal to every emergency.

Where the post stood the mountains were low and covered for the most part with sage brush, with here and there a grove of pines or quaking aspen. As our pack train wound its way up the narrow trail above the riverbank we saw many Siwashes spearing salmon, a very familiar sight in that country. These gradually became fewer and fewer, then we passed a miner's cabin and a Siwash village with its little log huts and its hay fields, from which grass is cut for the winter consumption of the horses. Gradually all signs of civilization disappeared, the mountains rose higher and higher, the valley became a canon, and the roar of the river increased, until finally the narrowing trail wound around an outrageous corner with the river a thousand feet below, and looming up in front of us appeared a range of snow-capped mountains, and thus at last we were in the haven where we would be.

That night we camped on one of the little pine-covered benches above the canon. My, but it was good to get the smell of that everlasting sage out of our nostrils, and to take long whiffs of the balsam-ladened air! Sunset comes very late at this latitude in July, and it was an easy matter to wander up a little draw at nine in the evening and shoot the heads of three grouse. After supper it was mighty good to lie and smoke and listen to the tinkle of the horse bells as they fed on the luscious mountain grass. We were old campmates, Bill and I, and it took us back to many trips we had had before, which were, however, to be surpassed many times by this one. I can well remember how as a boy, when I first took to woods loafing, I used to brood over a little work which we all know so well, entitled, "Woodcraft," by that grand old man, "Nessmuk," and particularly that part where he relates about his eight-day tramp through the then virgin wilderness of Michigan. But here we were, starting out on a trip which was to take over half a year, during which time we were destined to cover

over 1,500 miles of unexplored mountains, without the sight of a human face or an axe mark other than our own.

The next day after about an hour's travel, we passed the winter cabin of an old trapper, now deserted, but with the frames for stretching bear skins and boards for marten pelts lying around—betokening the owner's occupation. The dirt roof was entirely covered with the horns of deer and mountain sheep, and we longed to close our jaws on some good red venison. Here the man-made trails came to an end, and henceforth we used the game trails entirely. These intersect the country in every direction, being made by the deer, sheep and caribou in their migrations between the high and low altitudes. In some places they were hardly discernible, while in others we followed them for days, when they were as plainly marked as the bridle paths in a city park. A little further on we saw a whole family of goats sunning themselves on a high bluff across the river, and that night we dined on the ribs of a fat little spike buck which I shot in the park where we pitched our tent.

To chronicle all the events which occurred on that glorious trip would, I fear, tire my readers, so I will choose from the rich store certain ones which have made red-letter days in our lives. I can recollect but four days when we were unable to kill enough game or catch enough fish to keep the table well supplied, and as luck would have it, those four days came together, and we nearly starved. We had been camped for about a week in a broad wooded valley, having a glorious loaf after a hard struggle across a mountain pass, and were living on trout from a little stream alongside camp, and grouse which were in the pine woods by the thousands. Tiring of this diet we decided to take a little side trip and get a deer or two, taking only our three fattest horses and leaving the others behind to fatten up on the long grass in the valley, for they had become very poor owing to a week's work high up above timber line. The big game here was all high up in the mountains to escape the heat of the valley. So we started one morning, taking only a little tea, rice, three bannocks, our bedding and rifles, thinking that we would enjoy living on meat straight for a couple of days. We had along with us a black mongrel hound named Lion, belonging to Bill. He was a fine dog on grouse but prone to chase a deer once in a while.

About eight miles up the valley could be seen a high mountain of green serpentine rock and for many days we had been speculating on the many fine bucks which certainly lay in the little ravines around the base, so we chose this for our goal. We made the top of the mountain about three in the afternoon, and gazing down on the opposite side we saw a little lake with good horse feed around it and determined to camp there. About halfway down we jumped a doe and as it stood on a little hummock Bill blazed away at it and undershot. This was too much for Lion, the hound, and he broke after the deer, making the mountainside ring with his baying for half an hour. Well, we hunted all the next day, and the next, and never saw a hair. That dog had chased the deer all out of the country with his barking.

By this time our little grubstake of rice, bannocks and tea was exhausted, and, to make things worse, on the third night we had a terrific hailstorm, the stones covering the ground three inches deep. Breakfast the next morning consisted of tea alone and we felt pretty glum as we started out, determining that if we did not find game that day we would pull up stakes for our big camp in the valley. About one o'clock I struck a fresh deer trail and had not followed it long before three or four others joined it, all traveling on a game trail which led up a valley. This valley headed up about six miles from our camp in three little ravines, each about four miles long. When I got to the junction of these ravines it was getting dark and I had to make for camp. Bill was there before me and had the fire going and some tea brewing, but nothing else. He had traveled about twenty miles that day and had not seen a thing. I can still see the disgusted look on his face when he found I had killed nothing. We drank our tea in silence, drew our belts tighter and went to bed.

The next morning we saddled up our horses and pulled out. We had not tasted food for about sixty hours and were feeling very faint and weak. I can remember what an effort it was to get into the saddle and how sick and weak I felt when old Baldy, my saddle horse, broke into a trot. Our way back led near the spot where I had left the deer trail the night before, and we determined to ride that way hoping that perhaps we might get a shot at them. Bill came first, then Loco, the pack horse, and I brought up the rear. As we were crossing one of the little ravines at the head of the main valley Loco bolted and Bill took after him to drive him back into the trail. I sat on my horse idly watching the race, when suddenly I saw a mouse-colored flash and then another and heard the thump, thump of cloven feet. Almost instantly the whole ravine seemed to be alive with deer. They were running in every direction. I leaped from my horse and cut loose at the nearest, which happened to be a doe. She fell over a log and I could see her tail waving in little circles and knew I had her. Then I turned on a big buck on the other side of the ravine and at the second shot he stumbled and rolled into the little stream. I heard Bill shooting off to the left and yelled to him that we had enough, and he soon joined me, saying he had a spike buck down. It was the work of but a few minutes to dress the deer and soon we had a little fire going and the three livers hanging in little strips around it. Right here we three, that is, Bill, the dog and myself, disposed of a liver apiece, and my! how easily and quickly it went—the first meat in over a week. Late that night we made our horse camp in the lower valley, having to walk all the way as our horses packed the meat. The next day was consumed entirely with jerking meat, cooking and eating. We consumed half the spike buck that day. When men do work such as we were doing their appetites are enormous, even without a fast of four days to sharpen them up.

One night I well remember after a particularly hard day with the pack train through a succession of windfalls. We killed a porcupine just before camping and made it into a stew with rice, dough balls, onions and thick gravy, seasoned with curry. It filled the kettle to within an inch of the top and we ate the whole without stopping, whereat Bill remarked that it was enough for a whole boarding-house. According to the catalogue of Abercrombie and Fitch that kettle held eight quarts.

We made it the rule while our horses were in condition, to travel four days in the week, hunt two and rest one. Let me chronicle a day of traveling; it may interest some of you who have never traveled with a pack train. Arising at the first streak of dawn, one man cooked the breakfast while the other drove in the horses. These were allowed to graze free at every camping place, each horse having a cow bell around its neck, only Loco being hobbled, for he had a fashion of wandering off on an exploring expedition of his own and leading all the other horses with him. The horses were liable to be anywhere within two miles of camp, and it was necessary to get behind them to drive them in. Four miles over these mountains would be considered a pretty good day's work in the East. Out here it merely gave one an appetite for his breakfast. If you get behind a pack of well-trained horses they will usually walk right straight to camp, but on occasions I have walked, thrown stones and cussed from seven until twelve before I managed to get them in. Sometimes a bear will run off a pack of horses. This happened to us once and it took two days to track them to the head of a canon, fifteen miles off, and then we had to break Loco all over again.

Breakfast and packing together would take an hour, so we seldom got started before seven o'clock. One of us rode first to pick out the trail, then followed the four pack horses and the man in the rear, whose duty it was to keep them in the trail and going along. Some days the trail was fine, running along the grassy south hillsides with fine views of the snowcapped ranges, rivers, lakes and glaciers; and on others it was one continual struggle over fallen logs, boulders, through ice-cold rivers, swifter than the Niagara rapids, and around bluffs so high that we could scarcely distinguish the outlines of the trees below. Suppose for a minute that you have the job of keeping the horses in the trail. You ride behind the last horse, lazily watching the train. You do not hurry them as they stop for an instant to catch at a whiff of bunch grass beside the trail. Two miles an hour is all the speed you can hope to make. Suddenly one horse will leave the trail enticed by some particularly green grass a little to one side, and leaning over in your saddle you pick up a stone and hurl it at the delinquent, and he falls into line again. Then everything goes well until suddenly one of the pack horses breaks off on a faint side trail going for all he is worth. You dig in your spurs and follow him down the mountain side over rocks and down timber until he comes to a stop half a mile below in a thicket of quaking aspen. You extricate him and drive him back. The next thing you know one of the horses starts to buck and you notice that his pack is turning; then everything starts at once. The pack slides between the horse's legs, he bucks all the harder, the frying pan comes loose, a side pack comes off and the other horses fly in every direction. Perhaps in an hour you have corralled the horses, repacked the cause of your troubles and are hitting the trail again. In another day's travel the trail may lead over down timber and big boulders and for eight solid hours you are whipping the horses to make them jump the obstructions, while your companion is pulling at the halters.

Rustling with a pack train is a soul-trying occupation. Where possible we always aimed to go into camp about three in the afternoon. Then the horses got a good feed before dark—they will not feed well at night—and we had plenty of time to make a comfortable camp and get a good supper. We seldom pitched our tent on these one-night camps unless the weather looked doubtful, preferring to make a bed of pine boughs near the fire. The blankets were laid on top of a couple of pack sheets and the tent overall.

For several days we had been traveling thus, looking for a pass across a long snow-capped mountain range which barred our way to the north. Finally, we found a pass between two large peaks where we thought we could get through, so we started up. When we got up to timberline the wind was blowing so hard that we could not sit on our horses. It would take up large stones the size of one's fist and hurl them down the mountain side. It swept by us cracking and roaring like a battery of rapid-fire guns. To cross was impossible, so we backtracked a mile to a spot where a little creek crossed the trail, made camp and waited. It was three days before the wind went down enough to allow us to cross.

The mountain sheep had made a broad trail through the pass and it was easy to follow, being mostly over shale rock. That afternoon, descending the other side of the range, we camped just below timber line by a little lake of the most perfect emerald hue I have ever seen. The lake was about a mile long. At its head a large glacier extended way up towards the peaks. On the east was a wall of bright red rock, a thousand feet high, while to the west the hillside was covered with dwarf pine trees, some of them being not over a foot high and full-grown at that. Below our camp the little stream, the outlet of the lake, bounded down the hillside in a succession of waterfalls. A more beautiful picture I have yet to see. We stayed up late that night watching it in the light of the full moon and thanked our lucky stars that we were alive. It was very cold; we put on all the clothes we owned and turned in under seven blankets. The heavens seemed mighty near, indeed, and the stars crackled and almost exploded with the still silver mountains sparkling all around. We could hear the roar of the waterfalls below us and the bells of the horses on the hillside above. Our noses were very cold. Far off a coyote howled and so we went to sleep—and instantly it was morning.

I arose and washed in the lake. It was my turn to cook, but first of all I got my telescope and looked around for signs of game. Turning the glass to the top of the wooded hillside, I saw something white moving, and getting a steady position, I made it out to be the rump of a mountain sheep. Looking carefully I picked out four others. Then I called Bill. The sheep were mine by right of discovery, so we traded the cook detail and I took my rifle and belt, stripped to trousers, moccasins and shirt, and started out, going swiftly at first to warm up in the keen mountain air. I kept straight up the hillside until I got to the top and then started along the ridge toward the sheep. As I crossed a little rise I caught sight of them five hundred yards ahead, the band numbering about fifty. Some were feeding, others were bedded down in some shale. From here on it was all stalking, mostly crawling through the small trees and bushes which were hardly knee-high. Finally, getting within one hundred and fifty yards, I got a good, steady prone position between the bushes, and picking out the largest ram, I got the white Lyman sight nicely centered behind his shoulder and very carefully and gradually I pressed the trigger. The instant the gun went off I knew he was mine, for I could call the shot exactly. Instantly the sheep were on the move. They seemed to double up, bunch and then vanish. It was done so quickly that I doubt if I could have gotten in another shot even if I had wished it. The ram I had fired at was knocked completely off its feet, but picked himself up instantly and started off with the others; but after he had run about a hundred yards I saw his head drop and turning half a dozen somersaults, he rolled down the hill and I knew I had made a heart shot. His horns measured 161/2 inches at the base, and the nose contained an enormous bump, probably caused in one of his fights for the supremacy of the herd.

I dressed the ram and then went for the horses. Bill, by this time, had everything packed up, so after going up the hill and loading the sheep on my saddle horse, we started down the range for a region where it was warmer and less strenuous and where the horse feed was better. That night we had mountain sheep ribs—the best meat that ever passed a human's mouth—and I had a head worth bringing home. A 161/2-inch head is very rare in these days. I believe the record head measured about 19 inches. I remember distinctly, however, on another hunt in the Lillooet district of British Columbia, finding in the long grass of a valley the half-decayed head of an enormous ram. I measured the pith of the skull where the horn had been and it recorded 18 inches. The horn itself must have been at least 21 inches. The ram probably died of old age or was unable to get out of the high altitude when the snow came.

We journeyed on and on, having a glorious time in the freedom of the mountains. We were traveling in a circle, the diameter of which was about three hundred miles. One day we struck an enormous glacier and had to bend way off to the right to avoid it. For days as we travelled that glacier kept us company. It had its origin way up in a mass of peaks and perpetual snow, being fed from a dozen valleys. At least six moraines could be distinctly seen on its surface, and the air in its vicinity was decidedly cool. Where we first struck it it was probably six miles wide and I believe it was not a bit less than fifty miles long. We named it Chilco glacier, because it undoubtedly drained into a large lake of that name near the coast. At this point we were not over two hundred miles from the Pacific Ocean.

As the leaves on the aspen trees started to turn we gradually edged around and headed toward our starting point, going by another route, however, trusting to luck and the careful map we had been making to bring us out somewhere on the Scumscum river above the post. The days were getting short now and the nights very cold. We had to travel during almost all the daylight and our horses started to get poor. The shoes we had taken for them were used up by this time and we had to avoid as much as possible the rocky country. We travelled fast for a month until we struck the headwaters of the Scumscum; then knowing that we were practically safe from being snowed up in the mountain we made a permanent camp on a hillside where the horse feed was good and started to hunt and tramp to our hearts' delight, while our horses filled up on the grass. We never killed any more game than we could use, which was about one animal every ten days. In this climate meat will keep for a month if protected from flies in the daytime and exposed to the night air after dark.

We were very proud of our permanent camp. The tent was pitched under a large pine tree in a thicket of willows and quaking aspen. All around it was built a windbreak of logs and pine boughs, leaving in front a yard, in the center of which was our campfire. The windbreak went up six feet high and when a fire was going in front of the tent we were as warm as though in a cabin, no matter how hard the wind blew. Close beside the tent was a little spring, and a half a mile away was a lake full of trout from fifteen pounds down. We spent three days laying in a supply of firewood. Altogether it was the best camp I ever slept in. The hunting within tramping distance was splendid. We rarely hunted together, each preferring to go his own way. When we did not need meat we hunted varmints, and I brought in quite a number of prime coyote pelts and one wolf. One evening Bill staggered into camp with a big mountain lion over his shoulders. He just happened to run across it in a little pine thicket. That was the only one we saw on the whole trip, although their tracks were everywhere and we frequently heard their mutterings in the still evenings. The porcupines at this camp were unusually numerous. They would frequently get inside our wind break and had a great propensity for eating our soap. Lion, the hound, would not bother them; he had learned his lesson well. When they came around he would get an expression on his face as much as to say, "You give me a pain."

The nights were now very cold. It froze every night and we bedded ourselves down with lots of skins and used enormous logs on the fire so that it would keep going all night. We shot some marmots and made ourselves fur caps and gloves and patched up our outer garments with buckskin. And still the snow did not come.

One day while out hunting I saw a big goat on a bluff off to my right and determined to try to get him for his head, which appeared through my telescope to be an unusually good one. He was about half a mile off when I first spied him and the bluff extended several miles to the southwest like a great wall shutting off the view in that direction. I worked up to the foot of the bluffs and then along; climbing up several hundred feet I struck a shelf which appeared to run along the face at about the height I had seen the goat. It was ticklish work, for the shelf was covered with slide rock which I had to avoid disturbing, and then, too, in places it dwindled to a ledge barely three feet wide with about five hundred feet of nothing underneath. After about four hundred yards of this work I heard a rock fall above me and looking up saw the billy leaning over an outrageous corner looking at me. Aiming as nearly as I could straight up I let drive at the middle of the white mass. There was a grunt, a scramble and a lot of rocks, and then down came the goat, striking in between the cliff and a big boulder and not two feet from me. I fairly shivered for fear he would jump up and butt me off the ledge, but he only gave one quiver and lay still. The 330-grain bullet entering the stomach, had broken the spine and killed instantly. He was an old grandfather and had a splendid head, which I now treasure very highly. I took the head, skin, fat and some of the meat back to camp that night, having to pack it off the bluff in sections. The fat rendered out into three gold-pans full of lard. Goat-fat is excellent for frying and all through the trip it was a great saving on our bacon.

Then one night the snow came. We heard it gently tapping on the tent, and by morning there was three inches in our yard. The time had come only too soon to pull out, which we did about ten o'clock, bidding good-bye to our permanent camp with its comfortable windbreak, its fireplace, table and chairs. Below us the river ran through a canon and we had to cross quite a high mountain range to get through. As we ascended the snow got deeper and deeper. It was almost two feet deep on a level on top of the range. We had to go down a very steep hog-back, and here had trouble in plenty. The horses' feet balled up with snow and they were continually sliding. A pack horse slid down on top of my saddle horse and started him. I was on foot in front and they knocked me down and the three of us slid until stopped by a fallen tree. Such a mess I never saw. One horse was on top of another. The pack was loose and frozen ropes tangled up with everything. It took us half an hour to straighten up the mess and the frozen lash ropes cut our hands frightfully. My ankle had become slightly strained in the mix-up and for several days I suffered agonies with it. There was no stopping—we had to hit the trail hard or get snowed in. One day we stopped to hunt. Bill went out while I nursed my leg. He brought in a fine seven-point buck.

Speaking of the hunt he said: "I jumped the buck in a flat of down timber. He was going like mad about a hundred yards off when I first spied him. I threw up the old rifle and blazed away five times before he tumbled. Each time I pulled I was conscious that the sights looked just like that trademark of the Lyman sight showing the running deer and the sight. When I went over to look at the buck I had a nice little bunch of five shots right behind the shoulder. Those Lyman sights are surely the sights for a hunting rifle." Bill was one of the best shots on game I ever saw. One day I saw him cut the heads off of three grouse in trees while he sat in the saddle with his horse walking up hill. Both our rifles did mighty good work. The more I use a rifle the more I become convinced of the truth of the saying, "Beware of the man with one gun." Get a good rifle to suit you exactly. Fix the trigger pull and sights exactly as you wish them and then stick to that gun as long as it will shoot accurately and you will make few misses in the field.

Only too soon we drove our packtrain into the post. As we rode up two men were building a shack. One of them dropped a board and we nearly jumped out of our skins at the terrific noise. My! how loud everything sounded to our ears, accustomed only to the stillness of those grand mountains. We stayed at the post three days, disposing of our horses and boxing up our heads and skins, and then pulled out for civilization. Never again will such experiences come to us. The day of the wilderness hunter has gone for good. And so the hunt of our lives came to an end.

Leopards and Rhinos

by Carl Akeley

INTRODUCED EARLIER IN THIS BOOK, THE AUTHOR OF *BRIGHTEST Africa* is back with another story of hunting in Africa in the days when pioneering hunters like Akeley were the first to report on experiences in the game fields untouched by white hunters. Even in lands teeming with game, Akeley faced dangers that threatened a savage end to his adventures.

* * *

There is a general belief firmly fixed in the popular mind by constant repetition that the ostrich is a very stupid bird. A man might well expect easy hunting of a bird that tried to hide by the traditional method of sticking its head in the sand. But I found that the ostrich, like other African animals, did not always realize its obligation to tradition or abide by the rules set down for its behaviour. I went a long way into the waterless desert of Somaliland after ostriches. We were just across the Haud and were camped in a "tug" or dry stream bed whereby digging we could get water for our sixty men and the camels. During two days of hunting in the dry bush of this desert I had seen many ostriches, but none of them had put its head into the ground and left its big black-and-white plumed body for me to shoot at. On the contrary, in this my first experience with them I found them exceedingly wary. They kept their bodies hidden behind the bush. Only their heads were exposed, each head only about large enough to carry a pair of very keen eyes and much too small to serve as a target at the distance that they maintained. As a result of being continually outwitted by them for two days I began to think ill of the man who originally started the story about their stupidity.

With the difficulties of the chase firmly in mind I set out early on the third day to see if I could get a specimen. Concluding that the smaller the party the better the opportunity, I took only a mule and my pony boy. When only a half mile from camp I met an old hyena who was loafing along after a night out. He looked like a good specimen, but after I shot him, one look at his dead carcass was enough to satisfy me that he was not as desirable as I had thought, for his skin was badly diseased. I had very good reason to think of this very hard later in the day. A little farther along I shot a good wart hog for our scientific collection. Leaving the specimen where it lay, I marked the spot and continued in search of the plume-bearers.

Soon after this I climbed to the top of a termite hill about eight feet high to look the country over with field glasses. As I held the glasses to my eyes while adjusting the focus, I suddenly realized that the letter S that I was focussing on was the head and neck of an ostrich and that there was a second letter S beside it. The birds remained perfectly motionless watching and I did likewise, locating their position meanwhile by the termite hills which were nearly in line between us. Suddenly the heads ducked and disappeared behind the bush. I dropped from my perch and ran rapidly to where they had been, but found only their trail in the sand.

When I had given up tracking them and was about to start farther afield I came into an opening in the bush that was about thirty yards wide and two hundred yards long. Near the centre of the opening was a dense green bush a dozen feet in diameter.

A beautiful cock ostrich broke into the clearing at full speed just below the bush and as I raised my rifle he disappeared behind the bush. I held ready to catch him as he passed out from behind it on the other side, where there was fifteen or twenty yards of clear ground before he would reach cover again. I stood there ready with my gun up until I felt foolish. Then I ran quickly to the bush expecting to find him just on the other side. He was nowhere in sight, but his trail told the story. As he had come into the open he had seen me and when behind the bush he had stopped short, as indicated by a great hole and swirl of sand where he had caught himself by one foot, had turned at right angles and run straight away the length of the clearing, keeping the bush between himself and his enemy. I have not known many animals to do a more clever thing than this. I got one shot at him later—putting my sights at three hundred yards—but the bullet struck in the sand between his legs.

We returned to camp later in the afternoon and after a little rest and refreshment I started out again with only the pony boy and carrying the necessary tools to get the head of the wart hog that I had shot in the morning. We had no difficulty in finding the place where I had shot him, but there was nothing to be seen of the pig. The place was strewn with vulture features, but surely vultures could not make away with the head. A crash in the bushes at one side led me in a hurry in that direction and a little later I saw my pig's head in the mouth of a hyena travelling up the slope of a ridge out of range. That meant that my wart hog specimen was lost, and, having got no ostriches, I felt it was a pretty poor day.

The sun was setting, and with little to console us the pony boy and I started for camp. As we came near to the place where I had shot the diseased hyena in the morning, it occurred to me that perhaps there might be another hyena about the carcass, and feeling a bit "sore" at the tribe for stealing my wart hog, I thought I might pay off the score by getting a good specimen of a hyena for the collections. The pony boy led me to the spot, but the dead hyena was nowhere in sight. There was the blood where he had fallen, and in the dusk we could make out a trail in the sand where he had been dragged away.

Advancing a few steps, a slight sound attracted my attention, and glancing to one side I got a glimpse of a shadowy form going behind a bush. I then did a very foolish thing. Without a sight of what I was shooting at, I shot hastily into the bush. The snarl of a leopard told me what kind of a customer I was taking chances with. A leopard is a cat and has all the qualities that gave rise to the "nine lives" legend. To kill him you have got to kill him clear to the tip of his tail. Added to that, a leopard, unlike a lion, is vindictive. A wounded leopard will fight to a finish practically every time, no matter how many chances it has to escape. Once aroused, its determination is fixed on fight, and if a leopard ever gets hold, it claws and bites until its victim is in shreds. All this was in my mind, and I began looking about for the best way out of it, for I had no desire to try conclusions with a possibly wounded leopard when it was so late in the day that I could not see the sights of my rifle. My intention was to leave it until morning and if it had been wounded, there might then be a chance of finding it. I turned to the left to cross to the opposite bank of a deep, narrow *tug* and when there I found that I was on an island where the *tug* forked, and by going along a short distance to the point of the island I would be in position to see behind the bush where the leopard had stopped. But what I had started the leopard was intent on finishing. While peering about I detected the beast crossing the *tug* about twenty yards above me. I again began shooting, although I could not see to aim. However, I could see where the bullets struck as the sand spurted up beyond the leopard. The first two shots went above her, but the third scored. The leopard stopped and I thought she was killed. The pony boy broke into a song of triumph which was promptly cut short by another song such as only a thoroughly angry leopard is capable of making as it charges. For just a flash I was paralyzed with fear, then came power for action. I worked the bolt of my rifle and became conscious that the magazine was empty. At the same instant I realized that a solid point cartridge rested in the palm of my left hand, one that I had intended, as I came up to the dead hyena, to replace with a soft nose. If I could but escape the leopard until I could get the cartridge into the chamber!

As she came up the bank on one side of the point of the island, I dropped down the other side and ran about to the point from which she had charged, by which time the cartridge was in place, and I wheeled—to face the leopard in mid-air. The rifle was knocked flying and in its place was eighty pounds of frantic cat. Her intention was to sink her teeth into my throat and with this grip and her forepaws hang to me while with her hind claws she dug out my stomach, for this pleasant practice is the way of leopards. However, happily for me, she missed her aim. Instead of getting my throat she was to one side. She struck me high in the chest and caught my upper right arm with her mouth. This not only saved my throat but left her hind legs hanging clear where they could not reach my stomach. With my left hand I caught her throat and tried to wrench my right arm free, but I couldn't do it except little by little. When I got grip enough on her throat to loosen her hold just a little she would catch my arm again an inch or two lower down. In this way I drew the full length of the arm through her mouth inch by inch. I was conscious of no pain, only of the sound of the crushing of tense muscles and the choking, snarling grunts of the beast. As I pushed her farther and farther down my arm I bent over, and finally when it was almost freed I fell to the ground, the leopard underneath me, my right hand in her mouth, my left hand clutching her throat, my knees on her lungs, my elbows in her armpits spreading her front legs apart so that the frantic clawing did nothing more than tear my shirt. Her body was twisted in an effort to get hold of the ground to turn herself, but the loose sand offered no hold. For a moment there was no change in our positions, and then for the first time I began to think and hope I had a chance to win this curious fight. Up to that time it had been simply a good fight in which I expected to lose, but now if I could keep my advantage perhaps the pony boy would come with a knife. I called, but to no effect. I still held her and continued to shove the hand down her throat so hard she could not close her mouth and with the other I gripped her throat in a strangle hold. Then I surged down on her with my knees. To my surprise I felt a rib go. I did it again. I felt her relax, a sort of letting go, although she was still struggling. At the same time I felt myself weakening similarly, and then it became a question as to which would give up first. Little by little her struggling ceased. My strength had outlasted hers.

After what seemed an interminable passage of time I let go and tried to stand, calling to the pony boy that it was finished. He now screwed up his courage sufficiently to approach. Then the leopard began to gasp, and I saw that she might recover; so I asked the boy for his knife. He had thrown it away in his fear, but quickly found it, and I at last made certain that the beast was dead. As I looked at her later I came to the conclusion that what had saved me was the first shot I had fired when she went into the bush. It had hit her right hind foot. I think it was this broken foot which threw out the aim of her spring and made her get my arm instead of my throat. With the excitement of the battle still on me I did not realize how badly used up I was. I tried to shoulder the leopard to carry it to camp, but was very soon satisfied to confine my efforts to getting myself to camp.

When I came inside the *zareba*, my companions were at dinner before one of the tents. They had heard the shots and had speculated on the probabilities. They had decided that I was in a mix-up with a lion or with natives, but that I would have the enemy or the enemy would have me before they could get to me; so they had continued their dinner. The fatalistic spirit of the country had prevailed. When I came within their range of vision, however, my appearance was quite sufficient to arrest attention, for my clothes were all ripped, my arm was chewed into an unpleasant sight, and there was blood and dirt all over me. Moreover, my demands for all the antiseptics in camp gave them something to do, for nothing was keener in my mind than that the leopard had been feeding on the diseased hyena that I had shot in the morning. To the practical certainty of blood poisoning from any leopard bite not quickly treated was added the certainty that this leopard's mouth was particularly foul with disease. While my companions were getting the surgical appliances ready, my boys were stripping me and dousing me with cold water. That done, the antiseptic was pumped into every one of the innumerable tooth wounds until my arm was so full of the liquid that an injection in one drove it out of another. During the process I nearly regretted that the leopard had not won. But it was applied so quickly and so thoroughly that it was a complete case.

Later in the evening they brought the leopard in and laid it beside my cot. Her right hind foot showed where the first shot had hit her. The only other bullet that struck her was the last before she charged and that had creased her just under the skin on the back of the neck, from the shock of which she had instantly recovered.

This encounter took place fairly soon after our arrival on my first trip to Africa. I have seen a lot of leopards since and occasionally killed one, but I have taken pains never to attempt it at such close quarters again. In spite of their fighting qualities I have never got to like or respect leopards very much. This is not because of my misadventure; I was hurt much worse by an elephant, but I have great respect and admiration for elephants. I think it is because the leopard has always seemed to me a sneaking kind of animal, and also perhaps because he will eat carrion even down to a dead and diseased hyena. A day or two before my experience with the leopard someone else had shot a hyena near our camp and had left him over night. The next morning the dead hyena was lodged fifteen feet from the ground in the crotch of a tree at some distance from where he was killed. A leopard, very possibly my enemy, had dragged him along the ground and up the tree and placed him there for future use. While such activities cannot increase one's respect for the taste of leopards, they do give convincing evidence of the leopard's strength, for the hyena weighed at least as much as the leopard.

The leopard, like the elephant, is at home in every kind of country in East Africa—on the plains, among the rocky hills, among the bamboo, and in the forest all the way up to timber line on the equatorial mountains. Unlike the lion, the leopard is a solitary beast. Except for a mother with young, I have never seen as many as two leopards together. It is my belief that like the lion they do their hunting at night almost exclusively, and I am quite sure that this is their general habit despite the fact that the only unmistakable evidence of day hunting I ever saw myself in Africa was done by a leopard. I was out one day in some tall grass and came upon the body of a small antelope. As I came up I heard an animal retreat and I thought I recognized a leopard's snarl. The antelope was still warm. It had evidently just been killed and the tracks around it were those of a leopard.

One of the leopard's chief sources of food supply consists of monkeys and baboons. I remember a certain camp we had near the bottom of a cliff. Out of this cliff grew a number of fig trees in which the baboons were accustomed to sleep fairly well out of reach of the leopards. They were, however, not completely immune, and we could hear the leopards at the top of the cliff almost every night, and once in a while the remnants of a baboon testified to the success of the leopard's night prowling. Besides monkeys and baboons, leopards seem inordinately fond of dogs. A pack of dogs like Paul Rainey's can make short work of a leopard, but on the other hand a leopard can make short work of a single dog and seemingly takes great pleasure in doing so. One night in a shack in Nyiri, a settler sat talking to his neighbour, while his dog slept under the table. Suddenly, and quite unannounced, a leopard slipped in through the open door. Confusion reigned supreme for a moment and then the men found themselves on the table. The leopard was under the table killing the dog and somehow in the excitement the door had been closed. One after the other the men fled out of the window, leaving the dog to his fate. A traveller had a similar but more painful experience with a leopard at the Dak Bungalow at Voi. Voi is a station on the Uganda Railroad where there was, and I suppose still is, a railroad hotel of a rather primitive kind known as the Dak Bungalow. One night a man was sleeping in one of the Bungalow rooms and, hearing a commotion outside, he started out to see what it was. As he passed through the open doorway on to the porch he was attacked by the leopard that had evidently come stalking his dogs.

Leopards are not particularly afraid of man. I never knew one to attack a man unprovoked except when caught at such close quarters as the case at Voi, but they prowl around man's habitation without compunction. I had a camp in Somaliland once where the tents were surrounded by two thorn thickets—the inner and outer zareba. A leopard came in one night, killed a sheep, dragged it under the very fly of my tent on the way out, jumped the zareba, and got away. Fifteen years ago, when Nairobi was a very small place, the daughter of one of the government officers went into her room one evening to dress. As she opened the door she heard a noise and looking she noticed the end of a leopard's tail sticking out from under the bed with the tip gently moving from side to side. With great presence of mind the young lady quietly went out and closed the door. Nairobi had many possibilities of thrills in those days. It was about the same time that a gentleman hurrying from town up to the Government House one evening met a lion in the middle of the street to the embarrassment of both parties.

But it is stupidity, not duty, that keeps the rhino from reasoning. He is the stupidest old fellow in Africa. I know that many experienced hunters likewise consider him one of the most dangerous animals in Africa. I can't quite agree with this. Of course, if he runs over you not only is it dangerous, but it is also likely to be fatal. It is also true that as soon as he smells man he is likely to start charging around in a most terrifying manner, but the rhino is never cunning like the elephant, nor is his charge accurate like that of a lion, nor is the rhino vindictive like the buffalo or the leopard. Most men's estimates of the relative dangers of African animals are based upon their own experiences. The animals that have mauled them worst or scared them worst they hold most dangerous. I have been mauled by an elephant, chewed by a leopard, and scared half to death a dozen times by lions, so that I have the very firmest convictions about the dangers of these animals. On the other hand, I have twice been caught by rhinos in positions where an elephant, a lion, or a leopard would have had me in no time, and both times the rhinos left me unmolested.

When I first went to Africa I had the same experience as everyone else. Rhinos getting wind of me would charge me and to save myself I'd shoot. I suppose I had stood off twenty of these charges with my rifle before I discovered that if I did not shoot it would not necessarily be fatal. I discovered the fact, of course, quite by accident. I was going along the bank of the Tana River one day with my camera. My gun boys were some distance behind so as not to disturb any animal that might afford a picture. Suddenly I was set all a-quiver by the threshings and snortings of a rhino coming through the bushes in my direction. I very hastily took stock of the situation. There was nothing to climb. Between me and the thicket from which the rhino was coming was about twenty-five feet of open space. Behind me was a 30-foot drop to the crocodile-infested waters of the Tana. The only hope I saw was a bush overhanging the brink which looked as if it might or might not hold me if I swung out on it. I decided to try the bush and let the rhino land in the river, trusting to luck that I wouldn't join him there. The bushes were thrust aside and he came full tilt into the opening where he could see me. Everything was set for the final act. He suddenly stopped with a snort. His head drooped.

His eyes almost closed. He looked as if he were going to sleep. The terrible beast had become absolutely ludicrous. While this was going on I felt a poke in my back. I reached behind and took my rifle from the gun boy who had come up with equal celerity and bravery. I drew a bead on the old fellow but I could not shoot. A stupider or more ludicrous looking object I never saw. I began talking to him, but it did not rouse him from his lethargy. There he stood, half asleep and totally oblivious, while I, with the gun half aimed, talked to him about his ugly self. About this time my porters came into hearing on a path behind the rhino. He pricked up his ears and blundered off in that direction. I heard the loads dropping as the porters made for the trees. The rhino charged through the *safari* and off into the bush.

At another time, somewhat later, three of them charged me when I was sitting down and unarmed. I couldn't rise in time to get away or reach a gun, so I merely continued to sit. This time they didn't stop and doze, but they went by on both sides ten or fifteen feet away. Such a charge was much more pleasing to me and apparently quite as satisfactory to them as one in which they were successful in their attack. These experiences have led me to think that in his blundering charges the rhino has no clear objective, as a lion has, for instance. Even his blundering charge is dangerous, of course, if you are in the way, but I firmly believe that the rhino is too stupid to be either accurate in his objective, fixed in his purpose, or vindictive in his intentions.

This does not mean that a lot of people have not been killed by rhinos. They have; but I do believe that compared with other African animals the danger of the rhino is generally exaggerated. When he smells something he comes toward the scent until he sees what it is. As he can't see very far, no man with a gun is likely to let him come within seeing distance without shooting. So the stupid old beast goes charging around hoping to see the source of what he smells and in addition to getting himself shot has made a reputation for savagery. In fact, he has blundered around and been shot so much that old rhinos with big horns are growing scarce.

I remember coming up over the top of a little rise one day and seeing across the plain an old rhino standing motionless in the shade of a solitary acacia about two hundred yards away. The usual tick birds sat on his back. It was a typical rhino pose. As I stood looking for more entertainment, a second rhino came mouching along between me and number one. Number one evidently heard him. The birds flew off his back, he pricked up his ears, and broke into a charge toward number two. Number two reciprocated. Their direction was good and they had attained full speed. I longed for a camera to photograph the collision. But the camera would have done me no good. The collision did not happen. When about twenty feet from each other they stopped dead, snorted, and turned around, number one returning to doze under his tree and number two continuing the journey which had been interrupted. I suppose that rhinos have acquired the habit of charging whenever they smell anything because until the white man came along they could investigate in this peculiar manner with impunity. Everything but an elephant or another rhino would get out of the way of one of these investigating rushes, and of course an elephant or another rhino is big enough for even the rhino's poor eyes to see before he gets into trouble.

The coming of the white man with the rifle upset all this, but the rhino has learned less about protecting himself from man than the other animals. Man went even further in breaking the rules of rhino existence. The railroad was an even worse affront than the rifle. The rhino furnished some of the comedy of the invasion of the game country by the Uganda Railway. In the early days of that road a friend of mine was on the train one day when a rhino charged it. The train was standing still out in the middle of the plain. An old rhino, either hearing it or smelling man, set out on the customary charge. The train didn't move and he didn't swerve.

He hit the running board of one car at full speed. There was a terrific jolt. My friend rushed to the platform. As he reached it the rhino was getting up off his knees. He seemed a little groggy but he trotted off, conscious, perhaps, that railroad trains cannot be routed by the rhino's traditional method of attack.

The Forest and the Steppe

by Ivan Turgenev

THE STORIES IN IVAN TURGENEV'S *A HUNTER'S SKETCHES* WERE written and published in installments between 1847 and 1851. [In some translations, the book is called *A Sportsman's Sketches*.] The complete book of twenty-two sketches was published in 1852, and twenty years later three additional chapters were added. Turgenev's fervent passion toward nature and the Russian countryside are evident throughout the book but reach a peak of atmosphere and beautiful descriptions in this piece, the book's final chapter. Ernest Hemingway was responsible for bringing *A Hunter's Sketches* to the attention of many readers by his occasional mentions of the book as a personal reading favorite.

* * *

The reader is, very likely, already weary of my sketches; I hasten to reassure him by promising to confine myself to the fragments already printed; but I cannot refrain from saying a few words at parting about a hunter's life.

Hunting with a dog and a gun is delightful in itself, *für sich*, as they used to say in old days; but let us suppose you were not born a hunter, but are fond of nature and freedom all the same; you cannot then help envying us hunters. . . . Listen.

Do you know, for instance, the delight of setting off before daybreak in spring? You come out on to the steps.... In the dark-grey sky stars are twinkling here and there; a damp breeze in faint gusts flies to meet you now and then; there is heard the secret, vague whispering of the night; the trees faintly rustle, wrapt in darkness. And now they put a rug in the cart, and lay a box with the samovar at your feet. The trace-horses move restlessly, snort, and daintily paw the ground; a couple of white geese, only just awake, waddle slowly and silently across the road. On the other side of the hedge, in the garden, the watchman is snoring peacefully; every sound seems to stand still in the frozen air—suspended, not moving. You take your seat; the horses start at once; the cart rolls off with a loud rumble. You ride—ride past the church, downhill to the right, across the dyke.... The pond is just beginning to be covered with mist. You are rather chilly; you cover your face with the collar of your fur cloak; you doze. The horses' hoofs splash sonorously through the puddles; the coachman begins to whistle. But by now you have driven over four versts ... the rim of the sky flushes crimson; the jackdaws are heard, fluttering clumsily in the birch-trees; sparrows are twittering about the dark hayricks. The air is clearer, the road more distinct, the sky brightens, the clouds look whiter, and the fields look greener. In the huts there is the red light of flaming chips; from behind gates comes the sound of sleepy voices. And meanwhile the glow of dawn is beginning; already streaks of gold are stretching across the sky; mists are gathering in clouds over the ravines; the larks are singing musically; the breeze that ushers in the dawn is blowing; and slowly the purple sun floats upward. There is a perfect flood of light; your heart is fluttering like a bird. Everything is fresh, gay, delightful! One can see a long way all round. That way, beyond the copse, a village; there, further, another, with a white church, and there a birch-wood on the hill; behind it the marsh, for which you are bound ... Quicker, horses, quicker! Forward at a good trot! ... There are three versts to go—not more. The sun mounts swiftly higher; the sky is clear. It will be a glorious day. A herd of cattle comes straggling from the village to meet you. You go up the hill. . . . What a view! the river winds for ten versts, dimly blue through the mist; beyond it meadows of watery green; beyond the meadows sloping hills; in the distance the plovers are wheeling with loud cries above the marsh; through the moist brilliance suffused in the air the distance stands out clearly . . . not as in the summer. How freely one drinks in the air, how quickly the limbs move, how strong is the whole man, clasped in the fresh breath of spring! . . .

And a summer morning—a morning in July! Who but the hunter knows how soothing it is to wander at daybreak among the underwoods? The print of your feet lies in a green line on the grass, white with dew. You part the drenched bushes; you are met by a rush of the warm fragrance stored up in the night; the air is saturated with the fresh bitterness of wormwood, the honey sweetness of buckwheat and clover; in the distance an oak wood stands like a wall, and glows and glistens in the sun; it is still fresh, but already the approach of heat is felt. The head is faint and dizzy from the excess of sweet scents. The copse stretches on endlessly. Only in places there are yellow glimpses in the distance of ripening rye, and narrow streaks of red buckwheat. Then there is the creak of cartwheels; a peasant makes his way among the bushes at a walking pace, and sets his horse in the shade before the heat of the day. You greet him, and turn away; the musical swish of the scythe is heard behind you. The sun rises higher and higher. The grass is speedily dry. And now it is quite sultry. One hour passes, another. . . . The sky grows dark over the horizon; the still air is baked with prickly heat. "Where can one get a drink here, brother?" you inquire of the mower. "Yonder, in the ravine's a well." Through the thick hazel bushes, tangled by the clinging grass, you drop down to the bottom of the ravine. Right under the cliff a little spring is hidden; an oak bush greedily spreads out its twigs like great fingers over the water; great silvery bubbles rise trembling from the bottom, covered with fine velvety moss. You fling yourself on the ground, you drink, but you are too lazy to stir. You are in the shade, you drink in the damp fragrance, you take your ease, while the bushes face you, glowing and, as it were, turning yellow in the sun. But what is that? There is a sudden flying gust of wind; the air is astir all about you: was not that thunder? Is it the heat thickening? Is a storm coming on? . . . And now there is a faint flash of lightning. Yes, there will be a storm! The sun is still blazing; you can still go on hunting. But the storm-cloud grows; its front edge, drawn out like a long sleeve, bends over into an arch. Make haste! Over there you think you catch sight of a haybarn . . . make haste! . . . You run there, go in. . . . What rain! What flashes of lightning! The water drips in through some hole in the thatch-roof on to the sweet-smelling hay. But now the sun is shining bright again. The storm is over; you come out. My God, the joyous sparkle of everything! The fresh, limpid air, the scent of raspberries and mushrooms! And then the evening comes on. There is the blaze of fire glowing and covering half the sky. The sun sets; the air near you has a peculiar transparency as of crystal; over the distance lies a soft, warm-looking haze; with the dew a crimson light is shed on the fields, lately plunged in floods of limpid gold; from trees and bushes and high stacks of hay run long shadows. The sun has set; a star gleams and quivers in the fiery sea of the sunset; and now it pales; the sky grows blue; the separate shadows vanish; the air is plunged in darkness. It is time to turn homewards to the village, to the hut, where you will stay the night. Shouldering your gun, you move briskly, in spite of fatigue. Meanwhile, the night comes on: now you cannot see twenty paces from you; the dogs show faintly white in the dark. Over there, above the black bushes, there is a vague brightness on the horizon. What is it?—a fire? . . . No, it is the moon rising. And away below, to the right, the village lights are twinkling already. And here at last is your hut. Through the tiny window you see a table, with a white cloth, a candle burning, supper. . . .

Another time you order the racing droshky to be got out, and set off to the forest to shoot woodcock. It is pleasant making your way along the narrow path between two high walls of rye. The ears softly strike you in the face; the corn-flowers cling round your legs; the quails call around; the horse moves along at a lazy trot. And here is the forest, all shade and silence. Graceful aspens rustle high above you; the long hanging branches of the birches scarcely stir; a mighty oak stands like a champion beside a lovely lime-tree. You go along the green path, streaked with shade; great yellow flies stay suspended, motionless, in the sunny air, and suddenly dart away; midges hover in a cloud, bright in the shade, dark in the sun; the birds are singing peacefully; the golden little voice of the warbler sings of innocent, babbling joyousness, in sweet accord with the scent of the lilies of the valley. Further, further, deeper into the forest ... the forest grows more dense. ... An unutterable stillness falls upon the soul within; without, too, all is still and dreamy. But now a wind has sprung up, and the tree-tops are booming like falling waves. Here and there, through last year's brown leaves, grow tall grasses; mushrooms stand apart under their wide-brimmed hats. All at once a hare skips out; the dog scurries after it with a resounding bark. ...

And how fair is this same forest in late autumn, when the snipe are on the wing! They do not keep in the heart of the forest; one must look for them along the outskirts. There is no wind, and no sun, no light, no shade, no movement, no sound; the autumn perfume, like the perfume of wine, is diffused in the soft air; a delicate haze hangs over the yellow fields in the distance. The still sky is a peacefully untroubled white through the bare brown branches; in parts, on the limes, hang the last golden leaves. The damp earth is elastic under your feet; the high dry blades of grass do not stir; long threads lie shining on the blanched turf, white with dew. You breathe tranquilly; but there is a strange tremor in the soul. You walk along the forest's edge, look after your dog, and meanwhile loved forms, loved faces, dead and living, come to your mind; long, long slumbering impressions unexpectedly awaken; the fancy darts off and soars like a bird; and all moves so clearly and stands out before your eyes. The heart at one time throbs and beats, plunging passionately forward; at another it is drowned beyond recall in memories. Your whole life, as it were, unrolls lightly and rapidly before you; a man at such times possesses all his past, all his feelings and his powers—all his soul; and there is nothing around to hinder him—no sun, no wind, no sound. . . .

And a clear, rather cold autumn day, with a frost in the morning, when the birch, all golden like some tree in a fairy-tale, stands out picturesquely against the pale-blue sky; when the sun, standing low in the sky, does not warm, but shines more brightly than in summer; the small aspen copse is all a-sparkle through and through, as though it were glad and at ease in its nakedness; the hoar-frost is still white at the bottom of the hollows; while a fresh wind softly stirs up and drives before it the falling, crumpled leaves; when blue ripples whisk gladly along the river, lifting rhythmically the scattered geese and ducks; in the distance the mill creaks, half hidden by the willows; and with changing colours in the clear air the pigeons wheel in swift circles above it.

Sweet, too, are dull days in summer, though the hunters do not like them. On such days one can't shoot the bird that flutters up from under your very feet and vanishes at once in the whitish dark of the hanging fog. But how peaceful, how unutterably peaceful it is everywhere! Everything is awake, and everything is hushed. You pass by a tree: it does not stir a leaf; it is musing in repose. Through the thin steamy mist, evenly diffused in the air, there is a long streak of black before you. You take it for a neighbouring copse close at hand; you go up—the copse is transformed into a high row of wormwood in the boundary-ditch. Above you, around you, on all sides—mist. . . . But now a breeze is faintly astir; a patch of pale-blue sky peeps dimly out; through the thinning, as it were, steaming mist, a ray of golden-yellow sunshine breaks out suddenly, flows in a long stream, strikes on the fields and in the copse—and now everything is overcast again. For long this struggle is drawn out, but how unutterably brilliant and magnificent the day becomes when at last light triumphs and the last waves of the warmed mist here unroll and are drawn out over the plains, there wind away and vanish into the deep, softly shining heights.

Again you set off into outlying country, to the steppe. For some ten versts you make your way over cross-roads, and here at last is the highroad. Past endless trains of wagons, past wayside taverns, with the hissing samovar under a shed, wide-open gates and a well, from one hamlet to another; across endless fields, alongside green hempfields, a long, long time you drive. The magpies flutter from willow to willow; peasant women with long rakes in their hands wander in the fields; a man in a threadbare nankin overcoat, with a wicker pannier over his shoulder, trudges along with weary step; a heavy country coach, harnessed with six tall, broken-winded horses, rolls to meet you. The corner of a cushion is sticking out of a window, and on a sack up behind, hanging on to a string, perches a groom in a fur cloak, splashed with mud to his very eyebrows. And here is the little district town with its crooked little wooden houses, its endless fences, its empty stone shops, its old-fashioned bridge over a deep ravine. On, on! ... The steppe country is reached at last. You look from a hill-top; what a view! Round low hills, tilled and sown to their very tops, are seen in broad undulations; ravines, overgrown with bushes, wind coiling among them; small copses are scattered like oblong islands; from village to village run narrow paths; churches stand out white; between willow bushes glimmers a little river, in four places dammed up by dykes; far off, in a field, in a line, an old manor house, with its outhouses, orchard, and threshing-floor, huddles close up to a small pond. But on, on you go. The hills are smaller and ever smaller; there is scarcely a tree to be seen. Here it is at last—the boundless, untrodden steppe!

And on a winter day to walk over the high snowdrifts after hares; to breathe the keen frosty air, while half-closing the eyes involuntarily at the fine blinding sparkle of the soft snow; to admire the emerald sky above the reddish forest! . . . And the first spring day when everything is shining, and breaking up, when across the heavy streams, from the melting snow, there is already the scent of the thawing earth; when on the bare thawed places, under the slanting sunshine, the larks are singing confidingly, and, with glad splash and roar, the torrents roll from ravine to ravine.

But it is time to end. By the way, I have spoken of spring: in spring it is easy to part; in spring even the happy are drawn away to the distance. . . . Farewell, reader! I wish you unbroken prosperity.

Hunting the African Buffalo

by Carl Akeley

OUR STORIES OF PIONEERING AFRICA HUNTING WOULD NOT BE complete without returning to Akley's *Brightest Africa* book for his tale of hunts for the African buffalo. This is big game hunting on the knife-edge of danger.

* * *

The buffalo is different from any other kind of animal in Africa. A lion prefers not to fight a man. He almost never attacks unprovoked, and even when he does attack he is not vindictive. The elephant, like the lion, prefers to be left alone. But he is quicker to attack than the lion and he isn't satisfied merely to knock out his man enemy. Complete destruction is his aim. The buffalo is even quicker than the elephant to take offence at man and he is as keen-sighted, clever, and vindictive as the elephant. As a matter of fact, the domesticated bull is more likely to attack man without provocation than any wild animal I know, and those who wandered on foot around the bulls on our Western prairies in the old cattle days probably experienced the same kind of charges one gets from African buffaloes.

Nevertheless, despite all these qualities, which are almost universally attributed to the African buffalo, I am confident that the buffalo, like the elephant and other wild animals, has no instinctive enmity to man. That enmity, I am sure, is acquired by experience. I had an experience on the Aberdare Plateau with a band of elephants that had seen little or nothing of man, and until they learned about men from me they paid no more attention to me than if I had been an antelope. But after I had shot one or two as specimens, they acquired the traditional elephant attitude. I had a curiously similar experience with buffaloes.

It happened in this way. Mrs. Akeley, Cuninghame, the famous hunter, and I had been trying for some time, but with little luck, to get buffalo specimens for a group for the Field Museum at Chicago.

We had reason to believe that there was a herd of buffaloes living in the triangle made by the junction of the Theba and Tana rivers. As the buffaloes would have to water from one stream or the other, we felt pretty sure of locating them by following down the Theba to the junction and then up the Tana.

From the swamp down the Theba to its junction with the Tana occupied three days in which we saw no fresh signs of buffalo. On the second march up the Tana, as I was travelling ahead of the *safari* at about midday, looking out through an opening in a strip of thorn bush that bordered the river, I saw in the distance a great black mass on the open plain which, on further investigation with the field glasses, I was reasonably certain was a herd of buffaloes. Sending a note back to Cuninghame, who was in charge of the *safari*, suggesting that he make camp at a hill on the banks of the Tana about two miles ahead of my position and await me there, I started off over the plain with my two gun boys. Coming up out of a dry stream-bed that I had used to conceal my approach, I came on to a large herd of eland, and my first fear was that I had mistaken eland for buffaloes.

Going farther on, however, we saw a herd of about five hundred buffaloes lying up in a few scattered thorn trees four or five hundred yards away. At first it seemed an almost impossible situation. There was practically no cover and no means of escape in case the herd detected us and saw fit to charge, and at that time my respect for the buffaloes led me to be extremely cautious. We worked around the herd trying to find some place where a safe approach might be made. Finally, seeing a little band of a dozen buffaloes off at one side on the bank of a ravine which offered splendid protection, we stalked them but, unfortunately, not one in the band was desirable as a specimen. Since this was so, I tried them out, giving them my wind, then going up where they could see me better. I found that they were quite indifferent either to the scent or the sight of man. They finally moved off quietly without alarm. I then knew that this herd, like the Aberdare elephants, had had little or no experience with men, and that there was perhaps less to fear from them than from the traditional buffalo of the sportsman. So going back to the main herd, I crept up boldly to within a hundred yards of them. They saw me, faced about, closely inspecting me, but with no sign of alarm. It was approaching dusk, and in this great black mass it was difficult to pick out a good pair of horns except with the aid of glasses. I carefully located a fine bull and then shot, as I supposed, at the one I had located. As I fired, the animals bolted, first away, then back toward me. They wheeled, ran halfway between the dead animal and me, and passing on about a hundred yards to the right wheeled about again and stood watching me, the bulls in the front, lined up like soldiers, the calves and cows in the background. On coming up to the dead animal, I found, much to my regret, that I had shot a cow and not the bull I had picked out through the glasses.

I returned to camp feeling that now at last, from this herd living apparently in the open, we should have relatively little difficulty in completing our series of specimens. On the following morning, much to our disappointment, our first glimpse of the herd was just as it disappeared in the thorn bush along the bank of the river. We put in nearly a week of hard work to complete the series.

During those seven days of continual hunting, that herd which had been indifferent and unsuspecting at the beginning, like the elephants, became cautious, vigilant, and aggressive. For instance, on one occasion near the close of the week, after having spent the day trying to locate the herd, I suddenly came face to face with them just at the edge of the bush at night on my way back to camp. They were tearing along at a good pace, apparently having been alarmed. I stepped to one side and crouched in the low grass while they passed me in a cloud of dust at twenty-five or thirty yards. Even had I been able to pick out desirable specimens at this time I should have been afraid to shoot for fear of getting into difficulties when they had located my position. I turned and followed them rapidly as they sped away over the hard ground until the noise of their stampede suddenly stopped. I then decided that it was best to get to some point of vantage and await further developments. I climbed an acacia tree that enabled me to look over the top of the bush. Fifty yards ahead I could see about fifty buffaloes lined up in a little open patch looking back on their trail. As I was perched in the tree endeavouring to pick out a desirable animal, I suddenly discovered a lone old bull buffalo coming from the bush almost directly underneath me, sniffing and snuffing this way and that. Very slowly, very cautiously he passed around the tree, then back to the waiting herd, when they all resumed their stampede and made good their escape for the day.

One morning I came in sight of the herd just as it was entering the thorn bush and followed hurriedly on the trail, until just at the edge of the jungle I happened to catch sight of the two black hoofs of an old cow behind the low-hanging foliage. I stopped, expecting a charge. After a few moments I backed slowly away until I reached a tree where I halted to await developments. Stooping down I could see the buffalo's nose and black, beady eyes as she stood motionless. The rest of the herd had gone on out of hearing and I think she was quite alone in her proposed attack. After a few moments, apparently realizing that her plan had failed, she turned about and followed the herd, moving very quietly at first, then breaking into a gallop.

On the following day toward evening we came up again with the herd in the same region. As we first saw them they were too far away for us to choose and shoot with certainty. We managed to crawl to a fair-sized tree midway between us and the herd, and from the deep branches picked out the young herd bull of the group. When we had shot and he had disappeared into the bush, a calf accompanied by its mother gave us a fleeting glimpse of itself, with the result that we added the calf to our series.

The herd disappeared into the bush and after a few minutes we descended from our perch and inspected the calf, then started off in the direction the wounded bull had taken, and found him lying dead just a few yards away.

This completed the series, much to our great joy, for by this time we were thoroughly tired of buffalo-hunting. It had been a long, hard hunt, and our *safari* as well as ourselves were considerably the worse for wear. To shoot a half-dozen buffaloes is a very simple matter and ought to be accomplished almost any day in British East Africa or Uganda, but to select a series of a half dozen that will have the greatest possible scientific value by illustrating the development from babyhood to old age is quite a different matter.

These buffaloes of the Tana country that we found on the plains and in the bush apparently rarely or never go into the swamps, a fact not only confirmed by observation but also indicated by the condition of the hoofs. These are horny, round, and smooth as a result of travelling on the hard and more or less stony ground of the region. But the *tinga-tinga* buffaloes have lived in the swamp for years and spend practically no time on hard ground; hence the hoofs are long, sharp, and unworn as a result of walking always in the soft mud and water. All this despite the fact that these two herds may actually come in contact at the edge of the swamp. Other herds live in forest country but come out into the grasslands to feed at night, always going back into the forest at daybreak.

In Uganda, where buffaloes are recognized as a menace to life and are of no particular value except for food, they are officially treated as vermin and one may shoot as many as he will. Here the herds had increased to an enormous extent and, because of the dense jungles and general inaccessibility of the country, it was rather difficult to hunt them. While elephant-hunting in Uganda we found the buffaloes a decided nuisance, frequently coming on to them unexpectedly while hot on an elephant trail, sometimes having difficulty in getting rid of them, not wishing to shoot or stampede them because of the danger of frightening away the elephants, to say nothing of the constant menace of running into a truculent old bull at very close quarters in dense jungle. The buffaloes actually mingle with the elephants, each quite indifferent to the other excepting that on one occasion we found elephant calves charging into a herd of buffaloes, evidently only in play. They chased about squealing and stampeding the buffaloes, who kept at a safe distance but did not actually take alarm. Occasionally an old cow whose calf was being hard-pressed by the young elephants would turn, apparently with the intention of having it out, but would always bolt before the elephant could actually reach her. Despite the fact that the record head, fifty-four inches in spread, was shot by Mr. Knowles in Uganda, from our general observation the heads in Uganda run smaller than those of British East Africa while the animals are perhaps heavier.

Although in our buffalo-hunting we have never had any actually serious encounters, I fully appreciate that the buffalo deserves his reputation as one of the most dangerous of big-game animals. His eyesight is good, he has keen scent, and is vigilant and vindictive. While the lion is usually satisfied with giving his victim a knock-out blow or bite, the buffalo, when once on the trail of man, will not only persist in his efforts to find him but, when he has once come up with him, will not leave while there is a vestige of life remaining in the victim. In some cases he will not leave while there is a fragment of the man remaining large enough to form a target for a buffalo's stamping hoofs.

A hunter I met once told me of an experience he had with a buffalo which shows in rather a terrible way these characteristics of the animal. He and a companion wounded a buffalo and followed it into the long grass. It was lurking where they did not expect it and with a sudden charge it was upon them before they had a chance to shoot. The buffalo knocked down the man who told me the story and then rushed after his companion. The first victim managed to climb a tree although without his gun. By that time the other man was dead. But the buffalo was not satisfied. For two hours he stamped and tossed the remains while the wounded man in the tree sat helplessly watching. When the buffalo left, my informant told me, the only evidence of his friend was the trampled place on the ground where the tragedy had taken place. There is nothing in Africa more vindictive than this.

There was another case of an old elephant hunter in Uganda who shot a buffalo for meat. The bullet did not kill the animal and it retreated into the thick bush where there were even some good-sized trees. The old hunter followed along a path. Suddenly the buffalo caught him and tossed him. As he went into the air he grasped some branches overhanging the trail. There he hung unable to get up and afraid to drop down while the wild bull beneath him charged back and forth with his long horns ripping at the hunter's legs. Happily the gun boy came up in time to save his master by killing the beast. This hunter was an extraordinary character. He was very successful and yet he was almost stone deaf. How he dared hunt elephants or any other big game without the aid of his hearing I have never been able to conceive, yet he did it and did it well.

One morning Cuninghame, having gone out with some boys to shoot meat for camp, came upon three old buffaloes. He sent a runner back to camp with the news, and Mrs. Akeley and I started out to join him. Halfway from camp we were obliged to make a wide detour to avoid an old rhino and calf, but soon caught up with Cuninghame. He reported, however, that the buffaloes had passed on into some dense bush. We started to follow but suddenly came upon two rhinos. We quickly turned to leeward in order not to disturb them by giving them our wind, for we were not anxious to bring on a general stampede of the game in the neighbourhood. This turn brought us to the windward of the old cow and calf that we had first avoided, with the result that she came charging up, followed by the calf close at her heels, snorting like a locomotive. Cuninghame helped Mrs. Akeley up a convenient tree. He stood at the base of the tree and I at the foot of another where we waited with our guns ready, watching the old cow go tearing past within twenty feet of us.

We continued on the buffalo trail, but the stampede of the rhino had resulted in alarming the buffaloes so that instead of finding them nearby, we were forced to follow them for an hour or more before again coming in sight of them; and again twice more they were stampeded by rhinos that happened to get in our path. At last the buffaloes evidently became tired of being chased from place to place, and came to rest on a sloping hillside which we could approach only by crawling on our hands and knees in the grass for a considerable distance. In this maneuvering it happened that Mrs. Akeley was able to stalk the best bull, and a few minutes later he was finished off and we were busy photographing, measuring, and preparing the skin.

About twenty-five miles to the northwest from the Tana, across the plain on the Theba River, is a marsh where a herd of nearly a hundred buffaloes was known to live, but the Provincial Commissioner had definitely said that we were not to shoot these. We decided finally to ask for the privilege, which was granted, but with a warning in the form of an explanation: that he had told us not to shoot there because of the danger involved.

We found a reed marsh about one by two miles in extent with, at that time, a foot or two of water in the buffalo trails that criss-crossed it in all directions. On arriving, and while making camp at one end of the marsh just at dusk, we saw the herd come out on dry land a half mile away—but they returned to cover before we could approach them. In fact, during nearly two weeks that we spent there we saw them come outside the swamp only twice, each time to return immediately.

We made several attempts to approach them in the marsh, but found that while it was quite possible to get up to them it was out of the question to choose our specimens. Also it would have been impossible to beat a retreat in case of a charge or stampede; so we adopted a campaign of watchful waiting. From the camp at daybreak we would scan the marsh for the snowy cow herons that were always with the buffaloes during the daytime. These would fly about above the reeds from one part of the herd to another, and at times, where the reeds were low, they could be seen riding along perched on the backs of the animals. Having thus located the herd and determined the general direction of its movements, we would go to a point at the edge of the marsh where it seemed likely that the animals would come out, or at least come near enough to be visible in the shorter reeds. It was in this way that we secured the specimen that makes the young bull of the group—and two weeks spent there resulted in securing no other specimen. On this one occasion the buffaloes, accompanied by the white herons, had come to within about a hundred yards of our position on the shores of the swamp. They were in reeds that practically concealed them, but the young buffalo in question, in the act of throwing up his head to dislodge a bird that had irritated him, disclosed a pair of horns that indicated a young bull of the type I wanted. A heron standing on his withers gave me his position, and aiming about two feet below the bird, I succeeded in killing the bull with a heart shot.

SOURCES

"Tracks to Remember," by Tom Hennessey is from the Tom Hennessey book *Feathers 'n Fins*, Amwell Press, 1989, reprinted by permission of Nancy Hennessey.

"More Tsavo Man-Eaters," is from *The Hunt for the Man-Eaters of Tsavo*, by Lt. Col. J. H. Patterson, D.S.O., 1907.

"Whitetail Hunting," by Theodore Roosevelt, is from the *Wilderness Hunter*, 1893.

"That Twenty-Five-Pound Gobbler," by Archibald Rutledge is from *Outing*, 1919.

"Red Letter Days in British Columbia," by Lt. Townsend Whelen is from *Outdoor Life*, 1906.

"The Road to Tinkhamtown," by Corey Ford is from *Field & Stream*, November 1970. Reprinted with the permission of Dartmouth College Library.

"Hunting the Grisly," by Theodore Roosevelt. This text was prepared from a 1902 edition, published by G. P. Putnam's Sons, New York and London. It was originally published in 1893. It is part II of "The Wilderness Hunter.

"The White Goat and His Country," by Owen Wister is from *American Big Game Hunting*, 1893.

"The Forest and the Steppe," by Ivan Turgenev is from *A Hunter's Album*, 1917.

"In Buffalo Days," by George Bird Grinnell is from *American Big Game Hunting*, 1893.

The Carl Akeley stories "Hunting in Brightest Africa," "Leopards and Rhinos," and "Hunting the African Buffalo," are excerpted from Akeley's book, *In Brightest Africa*, Doubleday, 1920.

"The Heart of the Hunter," and "A Dangerous Moose," by Theodore Roosevelt are excerpted from his book *A Book-Lovers Holidays in the Open*, Scribners, 1916. The moose story was originally called "A Curious Experience."